Items should be returned to the library from which they were
borrowed on or before the date stamped above, unless a
renewal has been granted.

Swindon
BOROUGH COUNCIL

LNER

Soon after rebuilding on the lines of the 'A4s', Class W1 No 10000 dashes down Stoke bank towards Essendine with a Leeds to London express. Over two years elapsed between its withdrawal in its original 'Hush-hush' form and its reappearance, still as a 4-6-4. Note the permanent way gang, inconspicuous in the distance.

T. G. Hepburn, Rail Archive Stephenson

LNER

Geoffrey Hughes

LONDON

IAN ALLAN LTD

Contents

By the same author
The Gresley Influence

First published 1986

ISBN 0 7110 1428 0

Published by Ian Allan Ltd, Shepperton, Surrey; and printed by Ian Allan Printing Ltd at their works at Coombelands in Runnymede, England

Previous page:
The complex steelwork of the Forth Bridge is apparent in this picture of the 12.45pm train from Aberdeen to Edinburgh, in August 1937. The locomotive is Class A4 No 4486 *Merlin*, a Haymarket engine for almost all its career, running easily at the 40mph limit imposed on trains crossing the Forth Bridge. *E. R. Wethersett*

Acknowledgements

The material for this book has been obtained mainly from examination of original records, and interviews and correspondence with a number of personalities, most of whom served the LNER in various capacities. I am most grateful to all those who have allowed me access to their files, and who have given so generously of their time. Source material has been found mainly at the Public Record Office, the libraries of the Chartered Institute of Transport, the Institution of Mechanical Engineers, and the London School of Economics & Political Science, and the Central Libraries of Darlington, Hull and Newcastle-upon-Tyne.

I am particularly indebted to the Rt Hon the Lord Whitelaw CH, MC for contributing the Foreword; to Sir John Wedgwood Bart., and Dame Veronica Wedgwood OM, for information concerning their father; to Miles Beevor, Sir Henry Johnson CBE, T. C. B. Miller MBE and C. E. Whitworth for guidance on matters about the LNER in general; and to W. B. Yeadon, the doyen of LNER enthusiasts, for his wide ranging information and comment. Others who have kindly provided me with information on specialist subjects include W. H. Bradford, A. H. Emerson, D. F. Gowen, Professor Leslie Hannah, J. L. Harrington, A. A. Harrison, J. F. Harrison OBE, A. Henshaw, H. Kinsey OBE, F. G. Margetts CBE, J. P. Mead, H. M. Mitton ERD, N. Newsome, H. Ormiston, E. A. Rogers MBE and T. Henry Turner, as well as Eric Neve and Geoff Goslin, like myself, LNER enthusiasts since school days of long ago. Finally, I must express my gratitude to my wife, Mary, for reading the text and making many pertinent suggestions, and for her assistance in typing draft and final versions. I hope that I have heeded the advice given to me, but if any errors have crept in, then I apologise for these.

Geoffrey Hughes

Foreword

by
The Rt Hon Lord Whitelaw CH, MC

My grandfather was a boy during the period when steam was in its supremacy, before it had been challenged by other forms of power. Like so many of his generation, he was fascinated by the sight and sound of the passenger and freight trains which served the Scottish towns and countryside, and a youthful ambition was to take an active part in the running of a railway. Consequently, he was immensely proud when, soon after his 30th birthday, he was invited to become a Director of the Highland Railway. Later, he became its Chairman, and also of the North British Railway, and at the formation of the London & North Eastern Railway in 1923 he was elected Chairman of the new Company, remaining at the centre of affairs until his retirement in 1938.

He had many business interests, but his railway duties took priority. He was a true railwayman, and liked nothing better than a day out on an inspection tour in an 'Officers Special', talking to the staff and looking for himself into traffic and other matters. He was delighted when the first Pacific to be allocated to Scotland was named after him, saying that up till then he had had to make do with an NBR engine named *Wandering Willie*.

From my younger days I recall my grandfather's enthusiasm for 'his' railway, fighting to keep its head above water during a period when the going was never easy. But under his guidance the LNER came to lead the world in setting new standards of speed and comfort, and the organisation he built up was to give the nation invaluable service during the years of war.

I welcome this new study of the LNER, and trust that it will provide knowledge and pleasure to the many who look back with nostalgia to the days of the big four main line companies, particularly those in whose eyes there was nothing to touch Nigel Gresley's big Pacific engines, and those world-beating streamline trains.

William Whitelaw

Introduction

The London & North Eastern Railway has been the subject of two earlier major studies. The first of these, *The London and North Eastern Railway*, by Cecil J. Allen, was published in 1966 by Ian Allan Ltd, and the second, Michael Bonavia's *A History of the LNER*, in 1982/83 by George Allen & Unwin. Allen's book is particularly interesting in its description of events leading up to the formation of the LNER, and of locomotive performance, whilst Bonavia looks closest at the period late in the life of the company when he was personally at the centre of events. Both works deal with the unfolding scene from the point of view of the man on the inside; their sense of loyalty and their affection for their employer comes through strongly.

However, it has seemed to me that there is room also for a study of the LNER from the point of view of one who was not an employee, believing that to approach the subject as an outsider permits a greater degree of objectivity to be exercised. In this, however, I cannot claim to be entirely dispassionate as I have been an LNER 'enthusiast' since I first saw a Gresley Pacific in 1927!

There was, of course, a great deal more to running a railway 60 years ago than is appreciated by many observers today, however knowledgeable they may be about locomotives and train services; the aspect which has struck me most in researching for this book is the sheer complexity of the total railway operation as it was then. This called for a high degree of personal responsibility by all railwaymen, and was not made any easier by the continuing adverse financial situation in which the Company found itself, and which led to severe pressure on supervisors and staff to cut out 'waste' and make the railway run more efficiently.

Perhaps it was adversity which engendered an *esprit de corps* which, originating in the constituent companies, came to be a feature of the LNER, and which gained in strength as the group became more closely knit. This willingness to work together for the good of the railway also came through to me in my discussions with LNER employees of all grades, exemplified too in the spirit of friendliness which seems to have characterised the Company and its staff.

Right:
'First in the World', the LNER poster displayed at the Railway Centenary of 1925. *Railway Gazette*

A railway has responsibility to its owners for the efficient running of its operations, so that a reasonable return may be earned on their investment; to its customers for providing the services they are willing to pay for; and to its staff for rewarding them adequately for their often unstinting efforts. Outside influences — depressing economic conditions and government constraints — were influential in preventing the LNER from achieving financial success, as for much of its lifetime a third or more of the shareholders received no return at all on their investments. But at the same time it is a tribute to the Directors, management and staff of the company that the LNER led the country, and indeed the world, in the quality of its best

George Stephenson

Started us 100 years ago

L·N·E·R

First in the World

Above:
One each of the two LNER Scottish constituent companies' 4-4-0s have been saved from the scrapyard and restored to their pre-Grouping liveries. Here Great North of Scotland Class D40 No 49 (LNER No 6849) *Gordon Highlander* is in the green of its original owner, and is seen at Dumfries shed on 14 June 1959, far from its original haunts. *K. R. Pirt*

Left:
A lady worker cleaning an engine during World War 2. It is possibly a posed photograph to show a woman carrying out work normally done by a man. The engine is a Great Central Atlantic, Class C4 No 5261. *IAL*

express services. Given the circumstances of the period they could not have done much better, and lacking the initiative shown throughout the Company's existence, could easily have done a great deal worse.

It is appreciated that from the enthusiast's point of view, greatest interest is generated by rolling stock matters, train operation and the infrastructure; I have dealt with these, I hope, as adequately as space permits. But to preserve a balance, and to offer a reasonably complete and descriptive survey of the LNER, appropriate space has also been given to the railway's management, its commercial performance, and its labour relations, matters which are of particular interest to the many specialists in these fields, and about which so little has been written.

Geoffrey Hughes
Chorley Wood
1986

ONE

The East Coast Group of Railways

The first railway in the world to transport passengers and goods by steam power was the Stockton & Darlington, engineered by George Stephenson and opened on 27 September 1825. In 1863 the S&D merged with the North Eastern Railway, which on 1 January 1923 was amalgamated with six other railways to form the London & North Eastern Railway. So, the LNER could with justification claim to be 'The First in the World', with antecedents which could be traced back a hundred years.

Following the impetus gained by the success of the Stockton & Darlington, railways spread throughout the country, so that a good deal of the eventual national network had been built by the time King's Cross station, the London terminus of the East Coast route to Scotland, was opened in 1852. Subsequently, the railway systems which were to constitute the LNER became firmly established in their own corners of the country, creating their own traffic patterns, and each in its own way endeavouring to provide profitable services where these were needed by the public. Thus, the LNER effectively took over a going concern which it, as a corporation, had done nothing to establish, but which it maintained and developed for a period of a quarter of a century of almost continuous adversity before succumbing to nationalisation on 1 January 1948. This relatively short existence was in contrast to that of its constituents, which had enjoyed a lifespan of two and three times this period, often in conditions of comparative prosperity.

In particular, the constituent companies had experienced many monopolistic years of freedom from road competition, but the rapid development of the internal combustion engine in the early years of the 20th century, coupled with the proliferation of macadamised road surfaces, pointed to the future vulnerability of much of the traffic formerly regarded as entirely within the province of the railways.

The prospect of falling traffics was however only one factor bearing on railway organisation as the 20th century progressed. Another was the desire, gaining ground in many quarters, to coalesce the railways into fewer and larger units, to eradicate what was perceived to be the inefficiency of many of the smaller companies, some now barely profitable, and so obtain the advantages of large scale operation. And, in the aftermath of World War 1, organised labour strengthened its efforts to achieve a greater share of the revenues of major industries such as the railways.

Amalgamation of railway companies of course was nothing new; many of the railways as they existed at the turn of the century originated from the merging of smaller systems. Nevertheless, Government thinking around this period was strongly in favour of maintaining railways in competition, where such existed, to allow the traveller a choice. In spite of this, the South Eastern, and the London Chatham & Dover, had managed to establish a form of collaborative working, short of full amalgamation, in 1899, but somewhat similar proposals in 1909 by the Great Central, Great Eastern and Great Northern Railways did not come to fruition, due to Government opposition, even though they had few overlapping or competing services. World War 1 changed many attitudes and not only reorganisation but out-and-out nationalisation was mooted. In his Liberal period, even Winston Churchill, in a speech at Dundee before the General Election of 1919, appeared to advocate a state subsidy for the railways, perhaps to be run on the lines of the Post Office, which had been reorganised as a state-owned corporation 10 years before. However, the Prime Minister, Lloyd George, clarified the position in a policy statement which contained plans for the improvement of the country's transportation system, but in general terms only.

Firm proposals were published the following year in a White Paper which advocated that the railways in Great Britain should be reorganised in seven groups. These were on a regional basis, in the East, North East, North West, South and West of England and Wales, in Scotland, and the local lines in London. It was further proposed that each group should have a Board of Directors limited to 21 members, and whilst the shareholders would elect a majority of the Board, other members should represent the employees, two-thirds of whom would be elected by the manual workers and the remainder by the administrative staff. Later consideration of this revolutionary proposal, led to its rejection by the Trade Unions, which considered that they could not fully represent the interests of their members in an arena in which commercial considerations were paramount. The inclusion of the North Eastern as an independent group is interesting, as this would have meant that the North Eastern Railway (including the Hull and Barnsley) would have retained its pre-Grouping form, and end-to-end management of the East Coast main line by a single body would have been frustrated. The extent of the influence of NER officers on the proposals for Grouping can be seen not only in the presence of Sir Eric Geddes as Minister of Transport, but also in R. F. Dunnell, the NER Solicitor, who had been seconded to the Ministry specifically to take charge of the drafting of the Bill, and J. G. Beharrell, later to become Sir George, and Chairman of the Dunlop Rubber Co. The other General Managers, under the umbrella of the Railway Companies Association, led by Sir Herbert Walker, of the London & South Western Railway, strongly opposed this continued independence for the North Eastern, and the proposal was dropped, although the proposals for the enlargement of the Great Western Railway went through without overt dissent.

Whilst there was general — although by no means unanimous — agreement in principle that some form of grouping should take place, parts of the White Paper received a hostile response, particularly from Scotland, where segregation of the Scottish lines from those in England and Wales was opposed on the grounds of their weaker financial position, and the consequent probability that rates for conveying traffic would have to be higher in Scotland than elsewhere. An alternative system of grouping was put forward by the Railway Companies Association (a forum for discussion by the companies of matters of common interest, dating from 1867), very much on the lines of that finally adopted. However, when the Railways Bill was finally published, although the Eastern and North Eastern groups were merged, and the London lines omitted, *two* groups were proposed for Scotland — Eastern and Western. This idea did not persist for long, and during the committee stage of the Bill the two Scottish groups were added longitudinally to the corresponding English groups, so resulting in the Big Four railways as they became to be known, to administer the main line systems in Great Britain until World War 2 once again caused attention to be focused on the nation's rail communications.

Despite general support given to the Bill — the Government majority in the Commons was 175, the Labour Party regarding it as a step towards eventual nationalisation — it was not received favourably in all railway quarters, one Director declaring it to be an example of bureaucratic legislation, divorcing power from financial responsibility. This seems to have been the view of Sir Frederick Banbury, the Conservative Member for the City of London, and Chairman of the Great Northern Railway. During the debates in the Commons Banbury frequently interrupted Sir Eric Geddes (the Minister of Transport, who had introduced the Bill), for which Geddes reprimanded him in the House. (Banbury also quarrelled with Lady Astor on the subject.) Other opponents of the Grouping, whilst accepting the burden of the proposals, sought in vain to have the period before the amalgamations took effect extended. Another Member, Lt-Col the Hon A. C. Murray, Liberal MP for Kincardine, who was to become a Director of the LNER, strongly argued the Scottish point of view. Whilst the debates were in progress,

the railways were still under Government control. This, introduced as a wartime measure, was not ended until 15 August 1921, but the Bill received the King's signature four days later, to become the Railways Act, 1921, the 'appointed day' on which it was to come into force being 1 January 1923.

The 1921 Act probably provided the best solution to railway reorganisation in the light of conditions and opinions ruling at the time, given the desire for substantial amalgamation of the smaller companies but not for one single national system. Indeed, one may discern some lingering intention on the part of the planners to maintain a modicum of competition, as a number of parallel routes remained — notably from London to Scotland, and to Manchester and several cities in the Midlands and Yorkshire, as well as to Exeter and Plymouth. The two largest companies were based respectively on the West Coast and the East Coast routes to Scotland, merging companies which previously had enjoyed end-on collaboraation, whilst the two others resulted from an enlargement of the territory of the Great Western, and the grouping of the three railways serving the southern counties of England.

So, what was described in the Act as the Eastern, North Eastern and East Scottish Group of railways — but generally referred to as the East Coast Group — came into being, consisting of the Great Central, the Great Eastern, the Great Northern, the North Eastern, the Hull & Barnsley, the North British and Great North of Scotland, together with 26 smaller concerns, amongst the largest of which were the East and West Yorkshire Union Railways and the Mid-Suffolk Light Railway. In addition the group assumed a part interest in certain jointly-owned railways, notably the Midland & Great Northern, and the Cheshire Lines Committee, in which partnership arrangements continued with the West Coast group, which was to become the London Midland & Scottish Railway. The major constituents were regarded as being amalgamated, the smaller ones being absorbed by the group as subsidiary companies, to make their own terms with their new masters, although the Act contained some protection for minority interests. The Act made no provision for rearranging the systems, by transferring what were later to be known as 'penetrating' lines from one group to another. Had this been the case, perhaps the North British route from Glasgow to Fort William and Mallaig, the West Highland line, might have become part of the West Coast Group, and the Great Central enclave around Wrexham taken into the enlarged Great Western.

The backbone of the new system was the 392.7 miles of the East Coast main line from King's Cross to Edinburgh Waverley. Of this, the Great Northern ran from London to Shaftholme Junction, just north of Doncaster; no trains stopped there as it merely formed an end-on junction with the North Eastern, which took the line on to York, Newcastle-upon-Tyne and Berwick, at which point the North British took over for the remaining 57 miles to Edinburgh. But there were of course several other important routes, and the Great Northern for example gave prominence to its services from King's Cross to the West Riding, notably Leeds and Bradford, which were run in straightforward competition with the Midland Railway from St Pancras station, adjoining King's Cross.

The Great Northern also provided suburban services in a well-defined sector of North London, as well as possessing local networks in the West Riding, Lincolnshire and Nottingham areas, often competing with the Midland or other railways, and gaining access to other towns by means of joint ownership or running powers. Also, in the complex network of railways in the North Midlands and South Yorkshire, the Great Northern served many of the collieries in the locality.

Although the North Eastern's main line ran north and south, important traffic flows took place laterally, such as passenger services from Leeds through York or Selby to Hull, and a considerable number of colliery lines which ran from pits in the Northumberland and Durham coalfields to the staiths at ports on the northeast coast. In the year before the grouping the North Eastern had carried out its own amalgamation with the small, but locally important, Hull & Barnsley Railway, so adding to its system a further line primarily devoted to the export of coal. The H&B had originally been built with the strong support of Hull Corporation and other local interests to break the NER monopoly in the East Riding, and the 1922 merger was not readily accepted, unsuccessful attempts being made to unscramble this and to include the H&B in the West Coast Group, so maintaining a competitive route to Hull. There does not appear to have been similar pressure elsewhere, the North Eastern having managed to achieve the confidence of its customers without giving rise to

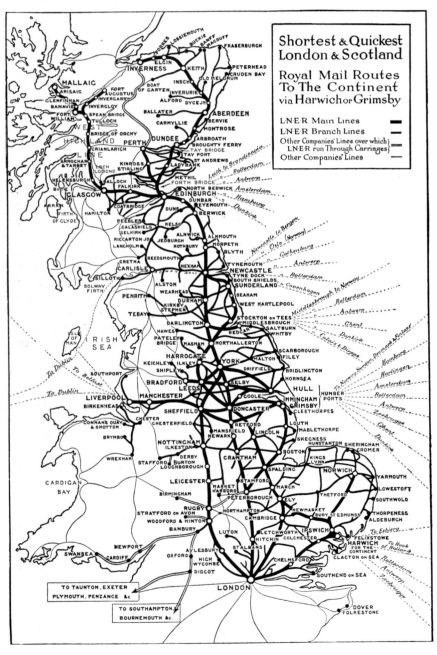

Left:
Map of LNER system from a 1926 advertisement.

complaints of exploitation. Other cross country lines owned by the NER included those from Newcastle to Carlisle, and over the Pennines to meet the West Coast main line at Penrith and Tebay, whilst there were also important suburban systems on Tyneside and Teesside, and lines to the Yorkshire coast resorts.

Flanking the Great Northern, the Great Eastern and Great Central possessed very different systems. The Great Eastern reached Norwich from Liverpool Street, in London, by two routes, one via Cambridge, and the other, used by the faster services, via Ipswich. It served East Anglia and its coastal resorts by a network of secondary lines, with an important branch to Parkeston Quay, Harwich, for Continental traffic. It possessed an intensively operated suburban system in northeast and east London, reaching as far as Southend-on-Sea, to which the Midland Railway provided a competing service from the LNER-owned station at Fenchurch Street, not far from Liverpool Street in the City of London. The GER reached York by virtue of the GN&GE joint line from March to Doncaster, and permitted the Great Northern access to Cambridge by providing running powers from Shepreth on the GNR branch from Hitchin. The Great Eastern was penetrated at its northern extremes by the Midland & Great Northern Joint Railway, which enabled these two railways to provide through trains from the Midlands to Yarmouth and from King's Cross to Cromer.

In contrast to the Great Eastern, enjoying a near monopoly of its limited traffic, the Great Central was in competition along practically all its system. Moreover, whilst the GER naturally fell in with the East Coast Group, alternative considerations might have put the GCR in with the West Coast, so permitting that organisation to close down services on which the GCR and the Midland overlapped; however, no one in official circles in 1921 was thinking about closing railways. In any case, the Great Central had working arrangements with the Great Northern which provided that railway with running powers to reach Sheffield and Manchester, and its detached lines in Staffordshire. The most important GCR trains ran from Marylebone to Leicester, Rugby, Nottingham, Sheffield and Manchester, with two exit routes from London, meeting at Grendon Underwood Junction, north of Aylesbury. Both were mainly joint lines, with the Great Western via High Wycombe, and with the Metropolitan via Amersham. The London Extension, as it was known, had been completed between Annesley, north of Nottingham, to Quainton Road Junction, near Aylesbury, as recently as 1899, the remainder of the system — on which much of its traffic originated — being mainly associated with the cross country line between Manchester and Grimsby. Also, together with the Great Northern and the Midland, the GCR was a partner in the Cheshire Lines Committee, whose system linked Manchester with Liverpool and other towns in Lancashire and Cheshire.

North of the Border, the North British main lines radiated from Edinburgh to Berwick and the East Coast route to London, along the Waverley route to Carlisle, to Glasgow Queen Street, to Fort William and Mallaig, and continuing the East Coast route northwards, across the Forth Bridge to Perth, Dundee, and over 38 miles of Caledonian metals to Aberdeen. The NBR also operated extensive colliery lines, notably in the Fife coalfield. The Great North of Scotland Railway based on Aberdeen, and physically separated from the rest of the LNER system, possessed a network of mainly single lines in northeast Scotland, including the Deeside line, which ran westwards from Aberdeen in the direction of Balmoral and Braemar, but terminating at Ballater, eight miles short of the royal residence. No mineral traffic of any consequence originated on the Great North of Scotland, but its fish traffic from Moray Firth ports was of significance.

In addition to its main purpose in achieving the grouping of the railways, the Railways Act contained other important provisions. One was to provide £60 million as compensation for outstanding claims arising from the enforced Government wartime takeover, this sum to be shared between all the companies as they mutually agreed. Also, a new charging body, known as the Railway Rates Tribunal, was to be set up to classify merchandise and decide the rates to be charged. (It is important to distinguish between 'rates' in this context, meaning charges made for a transport service, and 'rates' levied by a local authority.) The overall objective was to enable the railways to earn a 'standard' net revenue related to their position in 1913, net revenue being the balance remaining after deducting working expenses from the gross revenue received from traffic. (An expression known as the 'operating ratio', ie the percentage relation between expenditure and gross revenue, was used by railway management as a comparative measure of operating efficiency.) If more than the 'standard' revenue was earned, the surplus would accrue to the Government, ostensibly for the development of light railways, although, especially in the face of growing road competition, it was not clear where these were needed. Moreover, as a shareholders' association was to complain, the Government indicated its intentions to share in surplus revenues, but not in any losses. A substantial loophole was left in the Act: it was assumed that management would be efficient and economical, but it was not explained what criteria would be used to determine this in the event of a dispute between railway management and Government. In any case, the railways were never in sight of earning their standard revenue, but the Tribunal made no serious effort to assist them in achieving this, recognising the impossibility of the task in the the face of trade depression and increasing road competition.

The Railways Act left the groups pretty well on their own to organise their affairs, but the Government had sanction to act if they were tardy in carrying out their amalgamations. So, conscious of the obligations laid on them, as 1921 drew into 1922 the railways set up discussion groups and committees to decide on procedures which would lay the foundations for the new companies, how the new systems would be organised, and who would be appointed to run them.

TWO

The Board of Directors: Whitelaw and Matthews

Preparations by the Directors of the constituent companies in the East Coast Group took two forms. First there were discussions within Board Rooms, and private conversations between Chairmen and individual Directors, in endeavours to establish the best position for their own companies in the allocation of seats on the new Board, and for their proprietors in the terms under which new stock would be issued in exchange for existing holdings. These discussions were formalised in a committee on which each company was represented, Lord Faringdon of the Great Central being elected Chairman. At the same time consideration was given to the organisational shape of the new railway, and the appointment of its top managers; this led to the establishment of a further committee, which was to continue after the Grouping as a forum for consideration of significant matters concerning procedure and personnel, and was known as the Organisation Committee.

The amalgamation had been imposed by the will of Parliament, and as none of the constituent companies had shown any initiative in shaping the new group, the North Eastern, as the largest and most profitable, played the leading part in pre-Grouping discussions. Its Chairman was Lord Knaresborough, who had occupied the position for almost 10 years, whilst Earl Grey of Falloden, who had been Foreign Secretary in Asquith's government at the outbreak of war in 1914, was also on the Board, having been Chairman for a brief period before he joined the Government. The NER General Manager was Sir Alexander Butterworth, who had been in the saddle since 1906.

Amongst other leading personalities of the period was the Great Northern Chairman, Sir Frederick Banbury, a strong opponent of the Grouping, and who — unless it was to be on his own terms — wished to play no part in the new company. Other GNR Directors included Oliver Bury, who had been General Manager of that railway between 1902 and 1913, and B. A. Firth, who was connected with the steel industry in Sheffield. The leading Great Central figure was its Chairman, Lord Faringdon, whilst the Great Eastern Board was led by Lord Claud Hamilton, and included Col W. J. Galloway, who was patron and conductor of the Great Eastern Railway Musical Society. The North British Chairman was William Whitelaw, and other prominent NBR figures included Andrew K. McCosh, and Lt-Col the Hon A. C. Murray, who had led the Scottish contribution to

the Parliamentary debates during consideration of the Railways Bill.

An early decision had to be made on who was to act as Chairman of the new Board, but competition for the office was diminished by the fact that three of the leading contenders, Lord Knaresborough, Sir Frederick Banbury and Lord Claud Hamilton, were approaching the age of 80. Even had one of them been elected he could not have done more than act as a figurehead for a short period, whereas the position clearly called for an active personality prepared to devote a considerable amount of time to the job, particularly in the formative years. Despite his age (72) Faringdon appeared to be a strong contender, a respected Chairman of the Great Central and occupying a leading position in financial circles, but possibly for personal reasons he does not appear to have pressed his claim to the position. A name from outside the group, that of Sir Guy Granet, the Chairman of the Midland Railway, was mentioned at one time, although what certainty of

Below:
William Whitelaw. *Railway Gazette*

acceptance is not known. As it was, he went on to become Chairman of the LMS in 1924. Another candidate, the formidable Sir Eric Geddes, would have relished the appointment and it is well known that he actively canvassed his chances. Geddes had joined the NER in 1904, rising swiftly to become Deputy General Manager, with the expectation of succeeding Butterworth on the latter's retirement. However, with the intervention of the war, Geddes was seconded to the Government and such were his talents and drive that he rose to become First Lord of the Admiralty in 1917. Remaining in Government service he became Minister of Transport in Lloyd George's postwar coalition and virtually fathered the Railways Bill, although it is believed that his own private desires would have led to a single national structure for all British railways, with himself at its head. The North Eastern meanwhile had bought itself out of any contract of service Geddes had with it by payment to him of a sum of £50,000, and during the Commons debates on the Railways Bill, Geddes was not allowed to forget his past service with the NER, nor the amount of this payment, which would nowadays be regarded as a golden handshake of substantial proportions. Acrimonious questions were asked as to whether the NER had paid this sum out of taxed revenue, or from Government compensation funds. But, whatever were Geddes' abilities and personal ambitions, he was no longer persona grata with the North Eastern Board, nor, judging from the Parliamentary exchanges, with Sir Frederick Banbury. Cecil J. Allen has indicated however that Geddes might have had Lord Faringdon's support, and this is not unlikely. Evidence to this effect emerged in March 1922, when, during the inter-company discussions, Banbury asked if it were true, as he had read in the press, that Geddes was to be offered the chairmanship of the East Coast Group. This could only have come from one of the other Chairmen, and who, Banbury wanted to know, was this? He was not prepared to have Geddes in any circumstances, and was supported by W. K. Whigham, for the NER, as well as by William Whitelaw. However, Lord Claud Hamilton and Lord Faringdon merely said that they knew nothing of the press report. Consequently, although Faringdon had chaired this preliminary committee with distinction, if he had been seen to try to pave the way for Geddes he would have lost the support of the majority of his colleagues.

Even though Lord Knaresborough was not a serious contender, it was widely believed that due to its leading position the North Eastern would provide the Chairman of the new group, and the names of Earl Grey and Sir Alexander Butterworth were mooted. However, Grey, still only 59 in 1921, somewhat modestly expressed himself as being unsuited for the position, although certain NER circles saw Butterworth, 65, as the potential General Manager of the group, under Grey as Chairman. But Butterworth, although he had at one time visualised a position in which he occupied the chair, seems to have offended Banbury and Faringdon by the firm line he pursued on behalf of the NER in discussions concerning

Above:
A portrait of Andrew K. McCosh. *Kaye McCosh*

financial arrangements, and as a result felt that he was unlikely to command general support. Instead, he set in motion a train of events which was to lead to unanimous acceptance, at the same time ensuring that his beloved NER would remain at the centre of influence in the new company. This commenced when, in the late autumn of 1921, Butterworth determined to step down as NER General Manager at the end of that year in favour of his Deputy, R. L. Wedgwood, who had joined the North Eastern straight from obtaining a First at Cambridge, and who had become Secretary of the company when he was only 30. He had succeeded Geddes as Chief Goods Manager when the latter was appointed Deputy General Manager in 1911, and had served in the Army during the war, rising to become Director of Docks. On demobilisation, and following the confirmation of Geddes' severance of his NER connection, Wedgwood in turn had become Deputy General Manager. So when, consequent on Butterworth's action, Wedgwood became NER General Manager on 1 January 1922, the North Eastern was in the position, if not of having a nominee for the chairmanship, at least a front runner for the position of General Manager of the new group. Butterworth remained as special adviser to the NER Board, and worked quietly behind the scenes throughout 1922 in furtherance of its interests; he was very highly regarded by his Directors, and on his final retirement was voted a special payment of £20,000 as a personal testimonial.

Meanwhile, William Whitelaw was engaged in his own exchanges with Geddes, as Minister of Transport, over delays in settling the compensation to be granted to the railways — and the Scottish railways in particular — in return for Government assumption of control during the war; in this he earned the respect of the other Chairmen. Geddes privately regarded Whitelaw as 'impossible to deal with', but his Board acknowledged him as a 'bonny fechter'. He had been Chairman of the North British since 1912, and indeed had joined the Board of the Highland Railway as far back as 1898, becoming its Chairman in 1902, so he had had plenty of experience at the centre of affairs in not too profitable circumstances. Whitelaw had steel interests, was a Director of the Bank of Scotland, and an active member of the Church of Scotland. A landowner, inclined perhaps to a paternalistic rather than a 'democratic' way of life, he was highly regarded for his unfailing courtesy, his wisdom in dealing with difficult problems, his insistence on strict financial rectitude, and a benevolent, though firm, attitude towards his staff. When it became apparent in 1922 that the North Eastern had no willing claimant of adequate stature for the position of Chairman of the new group, but in Wedgwood had an outstanding candidate as General Manager, Whitelaw was unanimously elected Chairman. He was to hold the office for 15 years, directing the group's operations through a period of almost unremitting financial adversity until he retired in 1938, handing over to his successor a system which by then was in the forefront of railway practice throughout the world. Lord Faringdon was elected Deputy Chairman, with special interest in financial matters, and he and Whitelaw worked closely together until Faringdon's death in 1934.

Agreement on the constitution of the new Board was not reached without some dissent, mainly due to North Eastern insistence on taking a substantial majority of seats over each of the other companies. The Act allowed a maximum of 28 Directors, but this total was not taken up; in the event, the North Eastern got its way by having a total of nine seats — including one for the Hull & Barnsley — the GCR, GER, GNR and NBR taking four each and the Great North of Scotland one (being represented by its Chairman, Alexander Duffus, an Aberdeen lawyer). Whitelaw in the meantime had exercised his statesmanship by producing a series of comparative analyses, based on size, capital expenditure, revenue and so on, showing that the NER should have no more than eight Directors; evidently some sleight of hand took place over the H&B representation, as this was finally agreed as additional to, not included in, the NER quota.

The Directors formed themselves into a number of committees to oversee particular aspects of the railway. Amongst the more important of these were the Organisation Committee, which continued in being to consider relevant topics of importance, and committees dealing with Traffic, Locomotives, Works, Finance and Stores. These committees, attended by the appropriate officers, made recommendations to the Board for final approval, and formed a closely knit policy making organisation for the guidance of the management as well as approving major items of expenditure and staff changes. Generally the Board met on the last Friday in each month, and the committees on the two previous days. To preserve regional contacts three Local Boards were established consisting of Directors residing in the area or having regional interests. In addition to considering matters of local importance, these Boards possessed delegated authority to sanction limited amounts of expenditure. Although their powers were not great, the Local Boards had an important influence and their presence gave encouragement to the staff. During World War 2, the committees were suspended, and all business was conducted at 'Emergency Board' meetings. The Board as a whole was voted annual fees of £25,000 (of which the Chairman received £4,600) compared with an aggregate of £36,400 for all the Directors of the pre-Grouping companies. In later years, as the number of Directors declined, so did the total of fees paid to the Board; during the depression, the Directors took the same percentage pay cuts as were suffered by the staff.

An important preliminary decision was to agree on the title of the new company. The 'Great North Railway' received support at one time but the final solution, achieved by prefixing 'London and' to the name of the largest constituent, probably described the territory of the new company reasonably well, assuming that 'North Eastern' applied to Great Britain as a whole, and not just to England. So, the group became known as the London & North Eastern Railway, abbreviated to LNER after a very brief period of use of L&NER. Also, the grant of a coat-of-arms was obtained, a splendid device bearing the motto of the Great Central, 'Forward'.

William Whitelaw remained in office until his retirement at the end of September 1938. He maintained his LNER interests by joining the Scottish Local Board, remaining a member until his death in 1946. He was succeeded as Chairman by Sir Ronald Matthews, who had joined the main Board in 1929 and who had steel interests in Sheffield, having been Master Cutler. He stayed with the LNER until the end, maintaining a coherence of direction which continued to act to the benefit of the railway, despite the fact that most of his period in office was in wartime and the immediate postwar prelude to nationalisation. Matthews was a more extrovert personality than Whitelaw; those close to him recalled the poker schools which followed meetings of the Directors. But he took a keen interest in all around him, and continued to purvey the atmosphere of friendliness which characterised the LNER hierarchy.

Lord Faringdon, the first Deputy Chairman, died in 1934, to be succeeded by Sir Murrough Wilson, originally a Director of the North Eastern. Wilson was followed in 1946 by Walter K. Whigham, who too had been on the North Eastern Board and who was also a Director of the Bank of England. Membership of the LNER Board changed from time to time as Directors retired and were replaced, but the numbers remained at 26 for several years, long after any pre-Grouping influence could have retained any value. New members were invited on a personal basis, for the benefits they could bring to the Board and to the railway. The balance of the Board was generally maintained according to region, so that it was represented in each of the principal LNER centres, with representatives of banking, industry and the land-owning community — the last said to have been important in dealing with complaints that sparks from locomotives had caused lineside fires. Amongst well known figures to join the Board were Sir Harold Bibby, of the Bibby Steamship Line, and the Marquis of Exeter, who in his day had represented his country at the Olympic Games, and who was irreverently alluded to as 'that hurdler feller who is always asking questions'. The number of Directors was later reduced, and at the end of 1947 stood at 19. Of the original 26, Walter K. Whigham, Andrew K. McCosh, and three other Directors, served throughout the LNER's lifetime, together with Sir Charles Newton, who after being appointed Assistant Chief Accountant in 1923 rose to become Chief General Manager and finally to a seat on the Board on his retirement in June 1947. McCosh played an important part in rolling stock matters, becoming Chairman of the Locomotive Committee in 1929 in succession to B. A. Firth.

Below:
Sir Ronald Matthews, Arthur Peppercorn, Miles Beevor and family at the renaming of Class A4 No 26 at Marylebone in November 1947. *Miles Beevor*

THREE

Organisation and Management: Wedgwood and Newton

Whilst negotiations were being concluded on the re-disposition of stock and on the composition of the Board, consideration was being given to the central question of the organisation and top management of the new group. The North Eastern clearly expected its candidate, R. L. Wedgwood, to be nominated as chief executive, but initially he did not have the field entirely to himself. Of the General Managers of the constituent companies, Charles Dent of the Great Northern was 60 and Sir Sam Fay of the Great Central 66. Fay, in particular, was a forceful character, and both appeared to have plenty of running left in them, but Wedgwood had the advantage of being much younger. James Calder of the North British was 52, but exhibited no desire to leave Scotland, and in any case, with his Chairman taking similar office in the LNER, the other constituents would not have agreed to Calder becoming General Manager. An important figure was Sir Henry Thornton. He had left the Long Island Railroad in the USA to take charge of the Great Eastern, following the premature departure of W. H. Hyde, when, under the nose of the GER, the Midland Railway had become owners of the rival line along the Thames Estuary, the London Tilbury & Southend. It is not known to what extent Thornton's attributes were recognised by the Directors of the other LNER constituent companies, but despite his obvious capability he does not seem to have received support as a serious contender for the post of General Manager. Perhaps he was cast too much in the mould of Geddes; certainly he was extremely ambitious, having been seconded to the Army during World War 1 to become Inspector General of Transportation, in France. At one time he had been engaged in discussions intended to lead to the formation of an electrified East London suburban system (it is not clear how he might have achieved this, in view of the certain opposition of the owning railways), but in the event when he realised that his future did not lie with the LNER he returned across the Atlantic to become President of the Canadian National Railways. He was succeeded as Great Eastern General Manager by his assistant, S. A. Parnwell, only six weeks before Grouping.

Thornton's prior departure from the scene left Wedgwood as the outstanding candidate, and, with no overt opposition, or desire to bring in an outsider — even if anyone with his talent and qualifications could be found — Wedgwood's appointment to the post of Chief General Manager was recommended by the Organisation Committee, and confirmed at the first meeting of the LNER Board itself, on 2 January 1923, at an annual salary of £10,000.

As to organisation, large scale business had by now evolved a practice in which broad direction of policy was clearly distinguished from the conduct of day-to-day affairs, and in which dual lines of general and functional management were established. The topmost executive position would be held by the general manager (or, if he was on the board, the managing director) or, in the USA, the president. Under the general manager, specialist managers would be appointed according to the activities of the organisation — in a railway company, to operate the railway, to be in charge of civil and mechanical engineering, and to provide legal, accounting and secretarial services. Also, depending upon the size and complexity of the business, multi-functional units would be established under the day-to-day charge of regional or local general managers, supported by specialists reflective of the the functional chief officers at the headquarters. These would be required to run their units with delegated authority, the extent of which would depend upon the philosophy of the company in question. Without precise terms of reference conflict could occur in subordinate units between local managers intent on having their own way and functional officers under instructions from their head office seniors. On the other hand, delegated powers could allow much greater freedom of action locally, and quicker decision making. The future LNER had to decide to what extent authority should be retained centrally, and what could be delegated downstream. The LMS, in somewhat cavalier fashion, but having regard to the existence of strong pre-Grouping rivalries likely to continue after the amalgamation, decided at the outset on a firm policy of centralisation. Would this also be the best way forward for the LNER? Several voices were raised against such a plan, but evidently Wedgwood, at least initially, favoured centralisation. (The North Eastern had operated a partial divisional structure, but the number of divisional appointments had diminished by 1920. Perhaps Wedgwood's experience with this arrangement had not been too satisfactory.)

In the knowledge that he was to occupy the topmost management position, Wedgwood composed a paper setting out the merits of a strong head office management team, with 'all-line' chief officers in charge of the main functions, plus a not very powerful divisional structure based on the areas of the constituent systems. This, however, did not attract the support of a majority of Directors, and, basing their opinions on their experience, Sir Hugh Bell of the North Eastern, Lord Faringdon and in particular William Whitelaw, believed that over-centralisation at the outset would have an adverse effect on the operations and morale of those constituents which would not wish to be tied too closely to the heels of North Eastern practices. It was possibly anxiety on the part of Whitelaw which was crucial to the final decision, which was to decentralise: he supported the claims of Wedgwood to become General Manager, but did not want him to impose NER methods on the remainder of the group.

In the light of these considerations, it is of interest to look at the evolution of the management structure of the LNER as it emerged from the meetings of the Organisation Committee, which met at frequent intervals with Whitelaw in the chair. Each of the constituents contributed one member to the Committee, except that the North Eastern was able to exert its influence by sending two. In an unambiguous statement it was declared that no chief officers should be appointed except for 'solicitors, secretaries and accountants', but that the heads of each department in the existing companies should form departmental conferences, each electing a chairman, who would 'stand in the relation of the head of his department towards the Chief General Manager'. This inferred that there would be no chief officers other than the three mentioned, ie there would be no all-line Chief Mechanical Engineer.

So, a system was devised which, in general, served the LNER well. The Chief General Manager (the importance of the 'chief' is emphasised, since there were to be other general managers) was to act as chief executive, under the direction of the Board. He would be assisted by a small number of specialist officers, but for day-to-day operation the railway would be divided into three Areas, each under the control of a Divisional General Manager, who, with his own functional officers, would be responsible to the Chief General Manager for the performance of his Area. The areas were to be the Southern Area, consisting of the Great Central, Great Eastern and Great Northern; the North Eastern Area, comprising the NER plus the Hull & Barnsley, already becoming integrated into its larger neighbour; and the Scottish Area, for certain functions to be divided into the Southern Scottish Area (North British) and the Northern Scottish Area (Great North of Scotland). The practical advantage of the Area system was the limitation of physical size, so tending to overcome the otherwise remoteness of the Head Office, which although regarded as a stern father by the more timorous members of Area offices, by no means exerted the omnipotence which Euston was said to have held over the LMS. The Chief General Manager's unofficial dictum was 'we decide the policy and deal with the Board. You get on with operating the railway'. In fact, little firm guidance was given

Above:
Sir Ralph Wedgwood. *Railway Gazette*

to the Divisional General Managers, whose powers were wider in practice than on paper.

However, these organisational decisions, under which much authority was delegated away from Head Office, meant that there was no central LNER policy on many aspects of railway working, because the chairman, for the time being, of a functional officers' conference could hardly be in the position of a strong chief of department, able to determine long term strategy for instance; at best he would be bound by a consensus of opinion, which, on contentious issues, might not be capable of achievement. So, when the LNER sent delegates to meetings of all four main line railways, to discuss matters of common interest, it was sometimes impossible to present a corporate LNER view; there might be three ways of tackling a particular problem, one for each Area.

The administrators which the Organisation Committee had recommended were appointed towards the end of 1922. The Chief Legal Adviser, Sir Francis Dunnell, came from the North Eastern, whilst at first two Joint Secretaries were appointed, James McLaren from the North British (to keep an eye on Scottish affairs for the Chairman) and G. F. Thurston, from the Great Eastern; this cannot have proved wholly satisfactory, and after Thurston was promoted in 1925, McLaren continued alone. The first Chief Accountant was C. L. Edwards, from the Great Northern.

Whether a lack of strong functional management from the Head Office would have lessened overall efficiency is a moot point; anyway, there was considerable internal pressure to establish additional chief officers. This was aired at the first Board meeting under LNER auspices, when, referring to authority to pass invoices, mention was made of a Chief Buying Agent and a Chief Mechanical Engineer. In fact, the first additional all-line officer to be appointed was W. M. Teasdale, the NER Advertising Manager, who was appointed to a similar position with the LNER, although this was not regarded as of chief officer status. It was soon accepted nevertheless, that the purchasing and distribution of supplies for the whole system should be placed under a Chief Stores Superintendent, and W. T. Weeks from the Great Northern was appointed to the post. (This would be the Chief Buying Agent already mentioned. In later years the position was to be re-designated Chief Purchasing Agent.) But undoubtedly the post which excited the most interest was that of Chief Mechanical Engineer (CME), no announcement of which was made during the first seven weeks of the LNER's existence. (It is an intriguing thought that had the original intentions of the Organisation Committee been adhered to, there might have been a CME in each Area.) In all probability the delay was due to two reasons: first, the case for an all-line CME had to be accepted, and secondly a decision had to be taken on who was to occupy the position.

The CME of the North Eastern was Sir Vincent Raven, who had been in the post since 1910, except that he had been seconded to the Government during World War 1, becoming Chief Superintendent of the Royal Ordnance Factory, Woolwich; at the end of 1922 he was 63. The Great Central incumbent was J. G. Robinson, aged 66, whilst the GER post was held by A. J. Hill, with W. Chalmers on the North British and T. E. Heywood on the Great North of Scotland. The Locomotive Engineer of the Great Northern (not all the constituents favoured their senior mechanical engineer with the title of CME) was H. N. Gresley, aged 46. Gresley had already made a name for himself by introducing a series of designs which were in the forefront of locomotive development of the period, notably a powerful but elegant Pacific type express engine, the first of which was completed in April 1922. Raven had continued his predecessors' policy of solidly-built loco-motives adequate for the tasks required of them, and Robinson too had a number of successful designs to his credit, but neither exhibited the flair and originality of Gresley, whilst Hill, Chalmers and Heywood hardly possessed the stature or experience called for by the job. In view of the age of Raven and Robinson, Gresley looked like the front runner and Raven, perhaps sensing that events were not moving in his favour, intimated his desire to retire at the end of 1922. He was elected to the Board of Metropolitan Vickers, the electrical engineers, and was also appointed Technical Adviser to the LNER Board, so he was well occupied during his first year of retirement. During his period as technical adviser he chaired a committee to look into the possibilities of electrifying the Great Northern suburban lines, and also produced three major reports for the Board, all of which had an important bearing on the organisation of the mechanical engineering department. The first of these dealt with the control of locomotive running, in which he recommended that — contrary to the practice of most of the constituents — this should not be part of the CME's responsibility, but it should be delegated to a Locomotive Running Superintendent in each Area,

answering to the Divisional General Manager. Another report dealt with the organisation of workshops.

Although their style of design was different, there was considerable mutual respect, and indeed friendship, between Raven and Gresley; Marjorie, Gresley's younger daughter, told a delightful story of an occasion when the Ravens visited her parents for Sunday tea at their house in Avenue Road, Doncaster. As was customary in those days, Raven wore his top hat, and the young Marjorie, later to become an actress, put it on. Gresley, who possessed a sense of fun not always apparent to his junior staff, laughed at this, but the more serious Raven was said to have been 'Not Amused'. Probably Gresley had a hand in affairs in 1925, when at the Stockton & Darlington centenary celebrations and Raven was President of the Institution of Mechanical Engineers, it was a Raven, not a Gresley Pacific, which hauled the 'Flying Scotsman' train in the procession.

Raven may have been instrumental in getting the Board members not only to change their mind and appoint a single CME, but also to give the post to Gresley, whilst Robinson, according to his own account, was offered the CME's position, but declined it, recommending Gresley instead. Gresley was eventually appointed, at a salary of £4,500, not by the Organisation Committee, which up to now had the responsibility for making recommendations to the Board, but by the Locomotive Committee at its meeting on 22 February 1923, this being confirmed by the Board the following day. The two Scottish engineers remained in their offices for the time being, Chalmers being appointed Mechanical Engineer (Southern Scottish Area) until his retirement in 1927, when he was succeeded by Heywood; Hill took the opportunity to retire early, in March 1923.

In the meantime, before 1922 was out, other positions at top level were being filled. As his Assistant, and deputy in all but title, Wedgwood brought Robert Bell from York, and Kenelm Kerr as AGM in charge of general staff matters. Two other Assistant General Managers were also appointed, one to take charge of parliamentary matters and new works, and the other to look after rates and statistics, but the personalities occupying these posts, and their duties, changed from time to time. It was decided to locate the Head Office in London, although the NER offices in York were given serious consideration, but despite the policy of decentralisation none of the pre-Grouping premises was adequate to house the entire head office staff, which was divided between King's Cross and Marylebone, two miles apart, the only rail link being an indirect one by Underground. The Chief General Manager, Chief Mechanical Engineer and Chief Accountant were located at King's Cross, whilst the Joint Secretaries and the Board room were at Marylebone. The NER possessed an office in Cowley Street, Westminster, and this was retained for meetings concerned with parliamentary matters. (In 1939 the London offices were evacuated, the Chief General Manager and his staff moving to a country house known as 'The Hoo', near Knebworth, whilst other departments were widely scattered, the Secretary being as far away as York.)

Above:
Robert Bell. *Railway Gazette*

The next positions to be filled were those of the Divisional General Managers, and of these the one presenting the most difficulty was that in the Southern Area, in which the incumbent would be faced with the problems of integrating the operations and staffs of three constituent companies. Sir Sam Fay of the Great Central and Charles Dent of the Great Northern had been unsuccessful as candidates for the post of Chief General Manager, and neither seems to have been seriously considered for the Southern Area post. The Organisation Committee requested Wedgwood to 'see Sir Sam Fay, Mr Dent and Mr Parnwell to discuss the working of the three railways in order to secure single Area management'. No record exists of these discussions, but it was later reported that Fay and Dent would be relieved of their executive duties but remain at the disposal of the Chief General Manager at their existing salaries until the end of 1923. Unlike Raven, there is no record of their being asked to carry out any specific duties, but Fay continued his railway career by becoming Chairman of the locomotive manufacturer Beyer Peacock. So, S. A. Parnwell was appointed to the position of Divisional General Manager, Southern Area, at a salary increased by £1,000 to £4,500 a year, his second promotion within a couple of months. The post of Divisional General Manager, North Eastern Area went to Alex Wilson, who had been Wedgwood's assistant at York, also getting a £1,000 a year rise to £3,500, whilst the North British General Manager, James Calder, became General Manager (Scotland) at a salary of £4,000, it being made clear that he would have to pay his own income tax. Even so, this was a substantial improvement on his previous £2,500 tax paid, as had been the usual case for senior posts in Scotland.

Reporting to the Divisional General Managers were the superintendents, responsible for operating the railway; the Locomotive Running Superintendents, to provide the locomotives to work the trains and to maintain them in good order; Passenger Managers and Goods Managers, to get and retain business in their respective market sectors; the (Civil) Engineers, to be responsible for buildings and the permanent way, including signalling and communications; and the necessary administrative and accountancy officers. Other important posts were connected with hotels, docks, steamships, security and medical services, as appropriate to the particular Area. Below the Area level were District organisations, with the occupants of functional posts reporting to their respective seniors at the Area office. In many localities the grass roots organisation was left undisturbed at Grouping, but there were several promotions or retirements as the Area organisations took shape. This was particularly the case in the Southern Area because with three railways being grouped into one there was room for only one Superintendent, for instance, where formerly there had been three. The pattern of District organisation depended upon the local functional needs, these not always being conterminous. An operating District would be based on an important traffic centre, with a District Superintendent in charge, but District Locomotive Superintendents would have offices at the main sheds. Local Passenger and Goods Managers — sometimes the post would be combined — were based at the main stations or depots, where traffic originated. As opportunity offered there was a gradual coalescence of these posts, particularly the smaller ones, as there was sometimes an overlap between pre - Grouping companies serving the same town.

Once the appointments resulting from the amalgamation had been settled, there were few changes in the staffing of the higher echelons of the LNER within its first few years, the managers having been selected so that they could expect to serve for a number of years before retirement, so providing for the continuity which would be so desirable after the upheaval caused by the Grouping. However, as might have been expected, all did not run smoothly in the tripartite Southern Area, and it became evident that Parnwell was not a strong enough character to be successful as Divisional General Manager; pressure was placed on him to resign, and this he did. In a message to his staff he said that he had 'severed his connection with the company by arrangement with the Directors' whilst a somewhat curt minute by the Organisation Committee records that he was 'to retire not later than 31 July 1924'. His colleagues must have felt sympathy for him, as they presented him with a set of cut glass, at a dinner which was not attended by any of the Directors or chief officers. By profession a chartered surveyor, he returned to the City firm with whom he had been associated before joining the Great Eastern. It is perhaps interesting to speculate on his lost career with the railway; only 39 at the Grouping he could have stayed on until the end. No fewer than six more occupants of the Divisional General Manager's chair

rolling stock. The Great Northern's main problem was the number of sections of track which did not have relief lines and which gave rise to a great deal of delay as a result. Division of the Area enabled the Superintendents to give their undivided attention to the major problems in their respective Sections.'

Sir Ralph Wedgwood — he had been knighted in 1923 — remained as Chief General Manager until he retired in March 1939. He had attracted universal admiration for the way in which he had conducted affairs on behalf of all the railways, not only the LNER, in parliamentary and other committees, especially before the Railway Rates Tribunal, and, later, when the railways were striving to obtain a greater degree of freedom in the 'Square Deal' campaign which commenced in 1938. When the railways were once again brought under Government control during World War 2, Wedgwood became Chairman of the Railway Executive Committee, effectively in control of all the railways in Britain. He was succeeded by C. H. Newton, who earlier in his railway career had served with the Great Western, and who had been Chief Accountant and Divisional General Manager (Southern Area) with the LNER: he too, received a knighthood, in 1943. Robert Bell continued in office until May 1943, over three years after his normal retirement date. He had filled the position of Assistant General Manager with distinction, twice taking charge when Wedgwood was away for lengthy spells. These were in 1933 when after developing appendicitis, complications set in, and in 1936/37 when he was abroad in connection with the Committee of Enquiry into Indian Railways.

followed Parnwell in succession, and had he remained in office many later promotions would have been stifled.

Parnwell was succeeded by Alex Wilson, who was brought from York and replaced there by George Davidson, the Scottish Area Solicitor. The erstwhile Great Northern staff must have wondered at that time what had hit them, as they were managed first by a Great Eastern man, and then by one from the North East, the Area office moreover not being at King's Cross, where the GNR offices had been taken over by the Chief General Manager and his staff, but at Liverpool Street. Further, both the Superintendent, William Clow, and the Locomotive Running Superintendent, Percy Maclure, were from the Great Central.

Traffic congestion on parts of the Great Northern main line, and increasing difficulties arising on the Great Eastern, notably the growth of holiday traffic and criticism of the shortcomings of the Liverpool Street suburban service, brought problems which the organisation appeared to be incapable of solving. This led to a formal proposal being put to the Board in 1927 that the Southern Area should be divided into two, each with a Divisional General Manager at its head; the matter was dealt with at less expense by retaining the one Area, but, on Clow's retirement, appointing two Superintendents to operate the railway, H. H. Mauldin on the Eastern section (Great Eastern) and V. M. Barrington-Ward on the Western section (Great Central and Great Northern). A railwayman who was there at the time summed up the problem succinctly as:

'The Great Central was no trouble, but the Great Eastern suffered from increasing traffic on a system which was not designed for it, with lightweight track and lightweight

Newton retired in June 1947, when he became one of the very few railway officers to be elected a member of the Board of his company; he was succeeded by Miles Beevor, who took the post on an acting basis until nationalisation. Beevor had been a solicitor in private practice until 1943, when he joined the LNER as Chief Legal Adviser in succession to I. Buchanan Pritchard, who had occupied this position since Sir Francis Dunnell died in 1927. Pritchard had taken his duties on a somewhat insular basis, neither the Chief General Manager nor the Board being able to get him to submit detailed reports of his activities, and Beevor's initial instructions required him to rectify this practice. The benefits of a fresh mind are illustrated when, after having been in the post a month, he was called to Scotland to discuss the LNER's liability for local authority rates for the Forth Bridge; such was his advocacy that a reduction of 10% was obtained, so his first report was undoubtedly regarded as satisfactory. On Newton's retirement it was thought that the new Chief General Manager would be C. M. Jenkin Jones, then Divisional General Manager, North Eastern Area, but he too was approaching retirement and was reluctant to leave York. 'J-J' had been at the heart of North Eastern Area affairs for the whole of the LNER period, first as Superintendent, and from 1936 as Divisional General Manager. With the legal implications of approaching nationalisation, the appointment of a lawyer as Chief General Manager was clearly in the company's interest, but as it happened Beevor was appointed as Chief Secretary and Legal Adviser of the British Transport Commission in October 1947, and was forced to divide his time between managing the LNER and setting up the BTC.

After the new Chairman and Chief General Manager had taken up their offices, in 1938 and 1939 respectively, it may be thought that some internal review of the management structure would have been initiated; after all, the company had been in existence for 15 years and the stresses of amalgamation would have worked themselves out, so leading to the opportunity to explore the possibilities of tighter central control and greater standardisation of procedures. Indeed, two new all-line appointments, stimulated however by wartime pressures, indicated the way matters might have gone. In 1942 a Chief Engineer was appointed, J. C. L. Train, at that time Engineer (Southern Area), whilst later in the same year Barrington-Ward, by now Superintendent of the entire Southern Area (the two Sections having been rejoined when Mauldin succeeded Newton as Divisional General Manager in 1939) was given the position of Assistant General Manager (Operating), on a temporary basis. He was already the Chairman of the Operating Committee of the Railway Executive Committee, and hence in effect concerned with operations on all the railways, so that in his new-found authority over all three Areas of the LNER, a situation was corrected which previously he must have found anomolous from the countrywide point of view. Shortly after the end of the war, in September 1945, Barrington-Ward became Divisional General Manager, Southern Area, and the post of Assistant General Manager (Operating) was allowed to lapse. That this post was abolished, and the important fact that at no time was the establishment of further all-line positions such that of Chief Commercial Officer seriously considered, indicates the continual emphasis on the Area-based organisation, with the Divisional General Managers firmly responsible for marketing and, except for the later war years, operations within their Areas. The intention in 1923 to delegate authority down the line in the interests of customer relations had evidently been proved preferable to a policy of centralisation, and if the LNER had continued in private ownership there is no reason to suppose that any substantial change would have been made in the management structure.

At nationalisation, members and officers of the British Transport Commission, and of the functionally organised Railway Executive, were mostly railwaymen, and the LNER — probably because of its training, since most had been traffic apprentices — obtained more than its proportionate share of top appointments. Because of their opposition to nationalisation, none of the members of the Board were contenders for positions at the top of the new organisation, but Miles Beevor became Chief Secretary and Legal Adviser of the BTC, and Edward Marsden, who had been with the LNER, was appointed Secretary of the Railway Executive. Michael Barrington-Ward became member of the Railway Executive for Operations, and J. C. L. Train the member for Civil Engineering; both were to be knighted. W. P. Allen, who had started life as an engineman on the Great Northern, and risen to become General Secretary of ASLEF, was appointed member for Staff and Administration; and another trade union officer, John Benstead (later Sir John), who originated on the North Eastern, and had been General Secretary of the NUR, became BTC Deputy Chairman.

C. K. Bird was appointed Chief Regional Officer of the Eastern Region, C. P. Hopkins went to the similar position on the North Eastern Region, and T. F. Cameron, from being the LNER's Divisional General Manager, Scottish Area, took the ex-Caledonian, Glasgow & South Western and Highland lines of the LMS under his wing as well, as CRO for Scotland. The list of successful LNER traffic apprentices did not end there, as later Sir Henry Johnson and Sir Robert Reid made their way to the very top as Chairmen, and F. C. Margetts as Member of the British Railways Board. All acknowledged the benefits they had gained from the company's comprehensive scheme of operational and management training.

FOUR

The Railwaymen

The staff taken over by the LNER in 1923 totalled some 202,000; by the end of 1939 the number had fallen to 177,000. Of these, 15% were in management or some form of supervisory or clerical function, a quarter were in the workshops, and the remainder were traffic staff. For the information of management, a staff census was held annually to establish precisely how many employees the company had, and their grades, as there was no formal establishment of staff. To the travelling public, those mostly met with were the booking clerks, platform staff and stationmasters; enginemen and train staff; and those employed in the refreshment rooms, hotels and ships. Signalmen, platelayers and shunters would be seen at the lineside, but there were many others who were largely unseen by the passenger, such as those working in the offices, the workshops and sheds, and the marshalling yards.

As payments to staff amounted to some two-thirds of the LNER's total expenditure, it was natural that the wages bill was constantly under scrutiny, pressure not only being exerted to lessen the number of employees, but also to reduce their pay. At the formation of the LNER, the general level of railwaymen's wages, although appearing pitifully low by today's standards, was above that which applied to most of the country's workforce. Further, the basic wage was often supplemented by payment for overtime (although this was strictly controlled) and shift, bonus or other payments. In certain instances, such as for staff in contact with the travelling public, uniform clothing was issued — a fringe benefit which did not extend to the general provision of overalls, nor, to the chagrin of foremen, to the bowler hat, the symbol of their authority. The 1923 'standard' wage of a labourer was £2 a week, whilst a senior engine driver might expect a basic £4 10s (£4.50). Clerical and administrative staff, including such grades as junior stationmaster and canvasser, were divided into five classes, up to a maximum of £350 a year, above which they were known as 'special class'; at a point of £500, 'officer' status was achieved. Within the classes, annual increments of £10 were paid up to the maximum of the class; above this, increases were only granted on merit. Junior clerks started at £35 a year at age 15, having to pass an examination — which included shorthand — before entering the scheduled classes. London weighting amounted to £10, for those stationed within 10 miles of Charing Cross. At the other end of the scale, the Chief General

Manager's salary seems excessive, but this was one of the most important executive positions in industry at the time, and was not out of line with that paid in comparable posts elsewhere in the private sector; the actions of the Chief General Manager could of course affect the fortunes of the company one way or another to a far greater extent than the amount of his salary. (Wedgwood was said to be a brilliant man, who 'towered above everybody'.) The Divisional General Managers and Chief Officers were paid £3,500 to £4,500 a year (except that the first Chief Legal Adviser, Sir Francis Dunnell, received £7,000; his successors were paid materially less). Works managers and senior Area officers were generally in the £1,000 to £2,500 bracket, whilst stationmasters might be thought to be under-rewarded for their unstinting efforts, a typical salary for the man in charge of a medium sized station being around £400 a year. Even at the most prestigious stations such as King's Cross and Liverpool Street, where not just a bowler but a silk hat was obligatory, the salary was no more than £650. It was a common cause of complaint amongst LNER staff that they were paid less than their opposite number on the LMS. This was sometimes, but not always, the case; the LNER tended to give a lower classification to otherwise equivalent posts. There were discrepancies, too, between the rates of pay of the constituent companies, which caused difficulties when, due to transfer, men at the same workplace were paid under different arrangements; the Great Eastern, for instance, paid certain grades time and a third for overtime working, whilst the Great Northern paid only time and a quarter.

Staff matters were regarded as one of the most important functions of District and Departmental officers, who were under constant pressure to reduce staff costs. Nevertheless, except at the foot of the ladder, where labour was virtually engaged on a casual basis depending on the level of business, there was little enforced redundancy, despite the ease with which a man could be discharged in those days; staff numbers were mainly reduced by natural wastage, generally on retirement.

As an important aspect of cost control a form of revenue budgeting was introduced in 1930, under which departmental expenditure was 'rationed', a limit being set for each Department and District, the 'ration' being adjusted, usually downwards, from time to time. Staff costs were an important ingredient of the 'ration', and to assist local management efficiency units were set up, unofficially

known as 'razor gangs', to investigate procedures and point
to cost savings, particularly in staffing levels. Local
managers were kept on their toes by perceptive questions
being asked from the top: why, for example, in a year when
traffic had fallen by 6%, had staff costs fallen by only 1%?
And, after a report by outside consultants had demonstrated that clerks in Scotland worked harder for longer
hours than their colleagues in the North East, how could
this be turned to advantage?

In 1924 the Chairman told shareholders at the Annual
General Meeting that not only must claims for higher wages
be resisted, but they must be reduced to bring them into
line with those paid in other industries, and in a later plea
before the National Wages Board, the Chief General
Manager based his case for wages reduction on a *fall*
having taken place in the cost of living. Reductions were in
fact negotiated, as much as 5% in 1931, although
minimum rates were preserved, the cuts later being
restored. However, a shareholder pointed out that holders
of preferred ordinary stock had suffered much worse, to the
extent of a 95% reduction in dividends.

In contrast to the management's efforts to reduce the
wages bill, the men's representatives tried hard to increase
the remuneration of their members, and a strong dissenting
body known as the 'minority movement' sought to have
the cuts set aside. It was not until July 1939 that wage rates
were increased, the minimum rate then being raised to
£2 5s (£2.25) a week. By the end of 1947, wartime inflation
had led to a senior driver's wages being increased to £6 14s
(£6.70), the working week consisting of 44 hours. Two
weeks' paid holiday was then granted, as well as enhanced
rates for overtime.

Many grades of railwaymen managed to obtain additions
to their remuneration in other ways than directly from the
company. Porters and dining car attendants earned tips, as
sometimes did drivers and guards, but such perquisites did
not come the way of signalmen and platelayers who
however in rural areas might supplement their larder by
catching rabbits and even game birds. Stationmasters in
some mining districts were allowed to be agents for the
local colliery, the combined income often being sufficient
to deter a stationmaster from accepting promotion to a
larger station without an agency.

Privilege ticket facilities were extended widely to the staff
and to their immediate family. The top echelons received
'gold passes', whilst 'silver passes' were issued to

management and equivalent staff broadly down to District Officer level, each providing first class travel throughout the system. Lesser grades received a number of free passes, or tickets at quarter fare, first class travel being granted to those in 'special class' and above.

As is usual in large businesses, a staff suggestion scheme was in operation, the usual reward for a successful suggestion being a guinea. One of the largest awards was for Driver Woodall's conception of a 'pocket pilot' summary to assist drivers to learn a particular road. He received £100, but no advantage seems to have been taken of the idea.

A firm policy was laid down at the outset on the question of the age of retirement, at least so far as officers were concerned; they could retire at 60, but must retire at 65. In the years of depression, and again in 1938, when staff numbers were in excess of those justified by the level of business, accelerated retirement at the age of 60 was encouraged. During the war, shortage of staff led to this restriction being lifted, and those who so wished were persuaded to stay on. However, retirement did not always lead to happiness, but often to even greater anxiety over making ends meet, in days when the old age pension was 10 shillings (50p) a week, and no index linked superannuation fund was in existence to provide for a relaxed retirement for the wages grades.

Pressure on the management for the introduction of an adequate pension scheme for all staff was renewed from time to time, but whilst the question received consideration it was rejected on the grounds of expense. This however was not untypical of the period, as few employers then offered pensions to manual workers. To a small extent hardship was sometimes alleviated by the award of a gratuity to an employee retiring early, or on health grounds. A Bill was introduced in Parliament on behalf of the company as early as 1923 with the objective of establishing a pension scheme for salaried staff, but this failed due to opposition by shareholders and certain staff who were members of existing funds. Opinions changed over the years and a scheme was eventually adopted in 1939 to replace the modest arrangements in force for the salaried staffs of the pre-Grouping companies. The LNER scheme offered a lump sum on retirement equal to one year's salary, plus a one-third pension, in return for a contribution of 4% of salary, to which the company added a like amount.

The railwaymen up to salaried staff level were organised in trade unions, these being the Associated Society of Locomotive Engineers & Firemen (ASLEF) representing most of the footplate staff; the National Union of Railwaymen (NUR) representing the majority of the manual staff including a small number of drivers and firemen; and the Railway Clerks Association, in later years to become the Transport Salaried Staffs Association (TSSA), covering clerical grades. In addition national unions were also involved in specialist cases, such as for the seamen, whilst skilled workmen such as boilermakers and electricians tended to belong to the appropriate craft union. From the

Above:

A lookout man at St Forth Junction, Fife. His duties are to look out for approaching trains and to blow his whistle to enable his mates to get clear. He will use the appropriate flag to signal to the driver if the line is clear, or if he is to stop. There is no distinctive clothing to date the photograph, which was taken in 1948. *Gavin L. Wilson*

railwaymen's point of view, their position could have been stronger had they been of one mind and established one union to represent all staffs, but the locomen were adamant in maintaining an elite position in relation to their colleagues, whilst the white collar workers also wished to preserve an arm's length relationship with other railwaymen.

The Railways Act provided for a Central Wages Board to consider questions of national application of pay and conditions, together with local committees, and a National Wages Board as an appellate body. At the national level, negotiations were conducted for the bulk of the traffic staff as a whole, these being known as the 'conciliation' grades. Another main category comprised the railway shopmen, whilst smaller categories covered workshop supervisors, staff in electricity generation and distribution, professional and technical staff, and classified salaried staff. Sir Ralph Wedgwood personally took a leading part in the most important national negotiations, acting as spokesman for the companies' side; he was respected for his capable handling of affairs, but from the employees' point of view he gave little away. Administratively he was assisted by Kenelm Kerr as Assistant General Manager (Staff) who remained in charge of matters concerning wages grades, including representing the company on the Wages Boards until his retirement in 1946, when he was succeeded by H. H. Halliday. For those better off members of the staff who earned more than £350 a year, all salary changes were subject to Board approval, through the Organisation Committee in the case of new appointments and promotions, and the Salaries Committee for increases.

Widespread trade union organised disruption to services took place on only two occasions, each resulting from nationally sponsored initiatives. In January 1924 ASLEF believed that locomen's conditions would be adversely affected and differentials eroded by proposals put forward by the railway companies, and called its members out on strike for a period of nine days. This, reflecting inter-union rivalry, was not supported by the NUR. However, in 1926, as part of the National Strike, members of all unions affiliated to the Trades Union Congress ceased work. This strike was called in support of the mineworkers, who were faced with an enforced reduction in wages without negotiations having taken place with their Union. Before long a formula was worked out which was acceptable to the TUC but not to the miners, who remained out for several months; railwaymen returned to work in 10 days. Serious consideration was given to industrial action by the rail unions in 1939 in furtherance of a pay claim, but this was overtaken by the war. The LNER, as employer, took a grave view of what was termed disloyalty by the staff on strike, as in 1926 services virtually ceased until partial restoration became possible as railwaymen drifted back to work, and volunteers from outside lent a hand. Strikers were informed that they would only be taken back as work became available for them, and undoubtedly many men suffered enforced idleness as a result of the later loss of business caused by the interruption to services. Volunteers often put in long hours under exceptional circumstances, and, if railwaymen, were given a bonus of up to a week's extra pay, whilst outside volunteers qualified for pay according to the grade in which they worked. However, appropriate work was not always available for volunteers unused to manual toil, although brief training courses were hurriedly organised, whilst it was said that Turkish Baths enjoyed additional business from the 'society blades' whose muscles found unaccustomed exercise. Despite the enthusiasm of the volunteers, and the efforts of the management, only a shadow of the normal service was provided — by the end of the strike, only one passenger

train in eight and one freight train in 40 was running, with little adherence to the published timetables, although of course the traffic offering was greatly reduced. One indirect effect of the coal strike was a shortage of steel, such that the CME had to report the following year that this prevented him carrying out full maintenance on the rolling stock in his charge.

Many sad and tragic events took place during the 1926 strikes. The worst was a collision at St Margaret's, Edinburgh, when a passenger train overran signals and collided with goods wagons; three passengers were killed. Potentially the most serious was the deliberate derailment by non-railwaymen of the 'Flying Scotsman' at Cramlington, for which those responsible were imprisoned.

Along with its staff, the LNER inherited a considerable investment in their housing, entire estates having been built in years gone by to house workers in places which had been transformed from green fields to major railway centres, as well as smaller groups of houses or even single cottages, sometimes at the lineside for a platelayer or crossing keeper. In all, in 1923 the LNER owned over 18,000 domestic premises of one kind or another, let to the employees living in them. Rents were low, even nominal if there was a requirement to live on the job. For those, generally in junior management, whose duties on promotion involved removal, assistance might be given in the purchase of housing, but provision of a container might be all that was done to facilitate the removal itself. There was also a considerable welfare effort, supported by the management but mostly the result of staff initiative, such as ambulance classes, athletic clubs and debating societies, as well as Old Comrades Associations, and the LNER Temperance Union. Railwaymen's services were held at York Minster and St Nicholas' cathedral in Newcastle. And the Musical Society, originally conducted by Col Galloway, gained fame outside the confines of the railway, but was believed to have been subsidised personally by Galloway and William Whitelaw.

Staff magazines had been produced by the constituent companies, and these were incorporated into an all-line publication, the *LNER Magazine* which became a widely read journal of inside and outside news of interest, with a readership extending beyond the staff of the railway. Despite the ever present financial strictures, on appropriate occasions the company recognised its wider social obligations. For example, all staff were given a day off with pay to mark the Silver Jubilee of King George V and Queen Mary, whilst in 1937 a gift of £200 was made towards the cost of a stained glass window in St Mark's Church, Longmoor, to commemorate the Railway Troops, Royal Engineers, who served in the Great War.

The LNER was probably in advance of its time in the degree of formal training offered to its staff, and a Training Committee was in existence in each of the three Areas. After the appointment of Sir Charles Newton as Chief General Manager, specialist training was expanded, residential schools being established — an example was the Commercial School at Faverdale Hall, Darlington, opened in 1946. Those who took craft apprenticeships went through the usual rigours of the workshops, to pass out of their time with a job in their trade, if one was available. One strange weakness was in the training of footplate staff, where drivers and firemen were not always given instruction on the niceties of a new type of locomotive, although for the understanding of the more general subject of the theory and practice of steam locomotive operation, Mutual Improvement Classes were organised by the men themselves, with the support of the technical staff. A well known example of lack of understanding of new design techniques was seen in the first posting of Gresley Pacifics to Tyneside sheds: drivers accustomed to Worsdell and Raven locomotives found these new giants, with different footplate arrangements and firing methods, difficult to manage. Gresley himself had to attend a meeting of the enginemen, to hear their complaints and attempt to put them at ease.

A small number of technical apprenticeships were provided in the Chief Mechanical Engineer's Department, and in the Civil Engineers' offices in the Areas, whilst Nigel Gresley was permitted to take on pupils, a form of trainee who was not paid for his attendance and who could select his own programme of training. Also, a few engineering

Below:
Footplatemen look at the road ahead as their Class O2 2-8-0 leaves Boston North goods yard soon after Nationalisation. This is one of the earlier examples of the class, with the GNR pattern of cutaway cabsides, and Gresley's older type of pull-out regulator. Note the mixture of coal in the tender.
Les Perrin

scholarships to Queen Mary College were granted in the 1930s. More technical apprentices were taken on than could be absorbed after they had completed their training, but this was acknowledged, as the quality of training was such that many apprentices found work outside the LNER, often on overseas railways. Professional training was not confined to engineering, and accountancy apprentices and 'improvers' in the Estate and Rating Surveyor's Department were examples of other professions in which trainees were accepted.

However, it was in the field of management training that the LNER held a leading position amongst large firms of the day. This had been originated by the North Eastern Railway, in the concept of the 'traffic apprentice', under which young men from outside the company — generally graduates — and the brightest from the clerical staffs, were given a three-year period of training in all branches of railway operation. Sir George Gibb, then General Manager of the NER, had been behind the idea in the first place: 'feeling handicapped by the absence of senior men who could give me an unbiased opinion of the working of the railway, I decided to train a few young men of better education and wider outlook than those who had risen to high office from the ranks'. The scheme was continued by the LNER under the guidance of Robert Bell, who maintained a personal file on the careers of those who had started as traffic apprentices — or 'TAs' as they were popularly known. The opportunities to become a senior manager on the operating or commercial sides were of course limited, but these posts were generally filled by men who had been trained as TAs. Bell earmarked the files of those who were considered for high rank, for which imagination and enterprise were needed, in contrast

perhaps to mere organising ability and a cool head needed by say a stationmaster. Indeed, a note in Bell's file that an individual 'would make a good stationmaster' was held to mark the end of the road for many who aspired to higher office. To aid the selection of TAs from the clerical staff, an examination was held from time to time, in which questions were posed on railway procedures, such as the system for accounting for tickets issued from a booking office, together with a carefully constructed general paper. (An example of this is accompanies the chapter.) The Area system of management, with its high degree of decentralisation, of course aided the development of the aspiring traffic apprentice.

Because the railway operated 24 hours a day, seven days a week, many railwaymen necessarily worked shifts, or extended hours, in conditions which ranged from the merely uncomfortable, as in the cab of a locomotive, to the hardship of one of the many outdoor tasks, or from the noise of the workshops to the silent loneliness of many an isolated signalman or crossing keeper. Yet there was never any difficulty in recruiting staff to work on the railway. Frequently there was a family tradition, and fathers and grandfathers, uncles and brothers, were railwaymen — indeed it was often the case that family influence was necessary to obtain a job, however humble, on the railway. Despite what seems to us today as low wages — and those on the lowest grades had a hard job to keep a family on their meagre earnings — any job was better than the poverty of the unemployed, and the railway held out better hopes of security than many other industries in the years of depression. Moreover there was the fraternity of the railway — not necessarily defined as one of service to the community so much as being a part of this great

organisation, epitomised by the sheer size, and noise, of the railway itself, and its trains. Yet the feeling was not one of being just a number, one of 200,000 working for an amorphous body known as the LNER, stationed anywhere between London and the North of Scotland, but of an individual playing a part in making the railway run. Despite the autocracy of the day, when there was a wide social gap between master and man, the management created the quality of leadership which is essential to create good morale. Whilst undoubtedly there were many petty tyrants and jacks-in-office, there was an overriding camaraderie of spirit and pride in the job, which although broken during the occasional periods of externally generated stress transcended the normal bounds of supervision and grading. It was this self-accepted discipline which was to enable the railway to function in wartime, when circumstances often leading to violence and personal tragedy were to present such appalling difficulties.

Of course, this is not to say that everything was always cosy and benevolent. Imposed discipline was often harsh: a driver guilty of carelessness, such that his engine became derailed in a yard, could expect two or three days' suspension, whilst reduction in grade was a frequent punishment for minor infractions of the rules. Dismissal without notice was the rule in cases of dishonesty (although a reported case at Alloa, when a shunter was dismissed for

Below:
Reballasting in the late 1930s, using purpose-built hopper ballast wagons. The trackmen are aiding the release of the ballast to prevent the discharge shutes from becoming blocked. *Real Photos*

abstracting whisky by drilling into a cask, was represented as being unfair, as the whisky was only partly matured).

The contribution by members of the LNER staff to the war effort from 1939 to 1945 is impressive. Not only did 102,000 join the Forces (including a number who formed specialist Royal Engineer units), but those who remained in railway service performed wonders in dealing with the increased pressure of traffic in the blackout and in the dangerous conditions posed by air raids. Large numbers of temporary staff, many of them women, were recruited to fill the gaps left by those who had left for the services, and played their part alongside the regular railwaymen. A total of 303 civilian staff were killed as a result of enemy action, and of those in the Forces, 1,092 lost their lives and a further 500 were taken prisoner or reported as missing. In 1941 the Board instituted the 'LNER Silver Medal', to recognise conspicuous acts of bravery in dealing with dangerous situations in wartime; it was awarded to 22 members of staff.

Of the many 'incidents' during the war, the 'Flying Scotsman' was bombed and machine gunned from the air, fortunately without serious casualties. But one which involved great heroism took place at Soham, near Ely, when an ammunition train exploded despite the efforts of the crew to isolate the burning wagon which initiated the explosion. This happened just before 'D' day in June 1944, information being withheld by the censor for several months. The George Cross was awarded to the driver, who was seriously injured, and posthumously to the fireman.

Many railwaymen took part in local politics, members of ASLEF and the NUR generally following middle-of-the-road Labour policies, whilst stationmasters and similar grades tended to be Conservative. It was quite often the case that the chairman of a council, or the mayor, was a railwayman. Nationalisation was greeted with general enthusiasm by the majority of the wages grades, not because of any built-in antipathy towards the company, its Directors or its managers, but because, in the political wisdom of the Government of the day, it was preferable for the railway industry to be owned by the State rather than by private investors. The immediate transition to British Railways was fairly uneventful at local level, three Regions being established to take the place of the LNER Areas. But, before long, the stresses of the nationalised organisation began to make themselves felt, and a new spirit, and new loyalties, had to be forged.

Examination for Candidates for Traffic Apprenticeship
5th July 1925   2-4pm

1. Write down from memory a sentence dictated to you.

2. Name in order of size the ten most populous towns and cities served by the LNER.

3. What is the difference between   laziness and idleness
    a delegate and a representative
    poverty and misery
    character and reputation
    insulation and isolation

4. What are   cumulative preference shares
    excise duty
    the budget
    minutes of a meeting
    gilt edged securities

5. A wooden box must contain 108 cu. ft. It must have an open top and a square base, the side of which must not be less than 3ft nor more than 8ft and must be a whole number of feet. What must be the dimensions so that the amount of wood is a minimum?

6. Suppose that a circular disc of paper about 6 inches in diameter is folded along a diameter and pressed flat. Suppose this semi-circular disc is again folded to form a quarter-circle and again to form an eighth-circle. There will now be eight layers of paper. Suppose that with a pair of scissors a small triangular notch is cut from the middle of that side of the folded paper which presents but one edge. Draw a circle of about 6 inches diameter and show how the disc of paper would look if unfolded and laid flat, drawing lines to indicate the creases in the paper and the position and shape of the notches. (To be solved by imagination unaided by any sketches.)

FIVE

Business Record

The 1921 Railways Act created four corporations which were huge by contemporary standards, the largest being the London Midland & Scottish Railway, with an issued capital (including borrowings) of some £400 million at 1923 prices, and an employer of 250,000 people. Next was the LNER, similarly capitalised at £348 million and employing 202,000. In those days, before the growth of conglomerate and multinational firms, no other British commercial organisation even approached the size of the railways, the largest, such as Lever Brothers, Imperial Tobacco and J&P Coats (the textile group), all being capitalised at below £50 million. Imperial Chemicals had yet to enter the scene, being formed by amalgamation in 1926, whilst Dorman Long, the steel maker, as an example of a contemporary industrial company, was relatively small at £8 million. In fact in the United Kingdom there were only three organisations which were comparable in size with the railways: the Armed Forces (with which no useful parallel may be drawn), the Civil Service and the Post Office. The Civil Service in 1923 employed 425,000 staff, and was organised almost wholly on a departmental basis to administer Government affairs, but the Post Office, with a staff of some 150,000 and a 'capital liability' of £70 million, was a commercial organisation, although without real competition in its mainstream activities. The volume of business of the Post Office was influenced by economic activity generally, but in the longer term was on an upward trend, reflecting the expansion of modern communications methods. In contrast, private organisations — including the railways — were in a competitive arena, and their volume of business and profitablity could rise or fall dramatically in a small space of time. Perhaps it was the predictability of future performance which was the important factor in deciding the salaries of the top men in the Civil Service and the Post Office, in contrast to those received by the men who ran the LNER. The Head of the Permanent Civil Service received no more than £3,500; the political head of the Post Office, the Postmaster General (at that time Neville Chamberlain) had a Parliamentary salary of £2,500 and the chief executive officer of the Post Office earned £3,000.

The main line railway groups in fact fell somewhere between the public sector and the unregulated private sector, possessing a statutory monopoly of rail transportation in their defined areas, except for those overlapping services which still remained after the Grouping. But overall they were subjected to growing competition from private road hauliers, bus companies and motorists. The railways' volume of business was also related to the general economy, but to a limited extent they could generate more business in their own sphere — or they could lose it to their competitors. Unlike other industrial or commercial companies there was little scope for further rationalisation, whilst the Railways Act did not provide for expansion into other areas of business, except in directly related activities such as shipping and hotels.

An essential preliminary to the establishment of the LNER as a corporation was the formation of its capital stock, to replace that of the constituents; this was done by transferring the stock of the pre-Grouping companies into LNER stock, at its market value. Some keen bargaining took place at Director level to preserve the worth of the pre-Grouping stock, and the result of this was that the nominal value of the LNER stock was rather more than that of the stock which it replaced. The following table set out the stock issued on 1 January 1923; graded in descending order of priority, it forms a list necessarily made more complex by the variety of stocks it was to replace, but in hindsight unnecessarily so, almost as if it was prepared to cope with a situation of falling profits.

Capital Formation of LNER at 1 January 1923

Stock	Nominal Value	Opening Price of £100 stock
3% debenture | ranking	£66,352,793	£62
4% debenture | 'parri passu'	£33,617,629	£82
4% first guaranteed	£29,838,251	£88
4% second guaranteed	£27,329,739	£79
4% first preference	£48,145,988	£78
4% second preference	£65,683,531	£74
5% preferred ordinary	£41,873,116	£77
Deferred ordinary	£35,514,228	£33½
	£348,355,275	

The opening prices give an interesting commentary on the views of investors of the time about the Company's likely ability to pay dividends, having regard to the then gilt-edged rate of 5%; clearly there was no expectation of bumper payments for the deferred stockholders.

Only small additions took place in its issued capital during the lifetime of the LNER, primarily because its financial position deteriorated to the extent that in its later years up to half its 200,000 shareholders received no dividend at all, and it would have been impracticable to think about raising money through the issue of further stock. Consequently, the main source of new funding was the Government, firstly in 1929 when, as part of the Budget for the year, Winston Churchill removed the last vestige of Passenger Duty — a tax on railway operations dating back to the earliest days — on the condition that 90% of its capitalised value would be spent on improvements which would benefit heavy industry. This was worth about £1.5 million to the LNER, and all the money was earmarked for track improvements. In the same year, under the Development (Loan Guarantees & Grants) Act, the railways became eligible for Government guarantees on loans to meet expenditure on approved capital schemes, but there were evidently difficulties as little advantage seems to have been taken of this. More substantial Government loan aid became available under the 1935 'New Works' programme, the LNER share of this amounting to £6 million. William Whitelaw believed that the chief attraction of the loan was that it was acquired under debenture conditions which might otherwise never be obtained. Nevertheless one angry shareholder wrote protesting that this was a 'sop to the electorate to help the Government', and enquiring if the interest on the loan would rank before payment of dividend on the preference shares. Nearly half of the money was reserved for electrification between Sheffield and Manchester (but not in the event to be completed until 1954), whilst other sums were allocated towards new works such as station improvements and schemes for better movement of traffic, as well as new rolling stock, track circuiting and experiments with automatic train control. In 1937 a second tranche of funding was made available, enabling the LNER to increase the total from this source to some £10 million.

A curious entry in the LNER books was a loan of £250,000 from the LMS which had its origins in money lent by the Midland Railway to the Hull & Barnsley in 1910. The terms must have been satisfactory to both the LNER and LMS, as there seems to have been no move to have the loan repaid.

Internally generated funds plus Government help enabled the LNER to report that it had spent over £8 million by the mid-1930s on new projects. Today's accounting conventions would regard this figure as low, as much expenditure which nowadays would be regarded as on capital account was charged to 'renewals', the effect being that the value on paper of assets such as rolling stock was maintained, and only additions charged to capital. The reason for this lay in history: mid-Victorian railways had been known to enhance the amounts available for dividends by debiting revenue expenditure against capital. In fact, railway accounting was regulated by rules laid down in 1911, and C. H. Newton, when LNER Chief Accountant, had written the standard work on the subject, *Railway Accounts*, in 1930.

In the LNER Balance Sheet, the railway system was by far the most valuable asset, at some £250 million; rolling stock was worth some £50 million and docks £25 million, the balance being mainly the workshops, ships and hotels. In contrast to its original capitalisation of £348 million, at the end of its existence the market value of LNER stock had fallen to some £220 million; it would however have been almost impossible to place a break-up value on its assets. The debentures and guaranteed stock, on which payments had been maintained, had improved their worth, reflecting the lower cost of money in the immediate postwar years, but the more junior stock had fallen in value, the ordinary stocks (on which dividends had not been paid for years) becoming almost worthless; deferred ordinaries were quoted at 3½. The transfer into fixed interest British Transport stock at market value did however result in a very small income for holders of ordinary shares, who previously had had to live on hopes that the Company might eventually improve its position.

In shaping the Railways Act, the Government of the day appeared to be blinkered against the growing competitive facts of life by adhering to the Victorian belief that the public needed protection against the railways' freedom to set their own rates — that is, the charges made for conveying passengers and freight — evidently fearing extortion if these were left unregulated. The rating theory expounded by the Act was a fine piece of reasoning which completely ignored the market place; in effect, rates were to be 'adjusted' to enable the railways to earn a 'standard revenue' related to conditions in 1913, but due to the complexity of the subject, discussions on the details of the rates schedules dragged on until 1928. By then, the LNER was nowhere in sight of achieving its standard revenue, and would have welcomed any adjustment as promised by the Act, where this could have been borne by the traffic without having it driven away; but no such adjustment took place.

To a small extent the delay in implementing standard rates reacted in the railways' favour, since in the absence of a published rate this could be determined locally. Such, however, was the railways' bureaucracy — the local agent having been brought up to abide by the Rate Book — it is unlikely that any real advantage was gained by this. It is said that the Great Northern was very good at making the most of an opportunity, but once having made a rate stuck to it, whilst the Great Eastern adopted a more flexible attitude, local staff being encouraged to strike a bargain in the Company's interest.

From his long experience of managing the Great Central, Sir Sam Fay, in his Presidential Address to the Institute of Transport in 1922, put his finger on the nub of the problem: the fixing of rates by statute was a restriction on the right of a business to vary its charges at will. The point of course was that the Railway Rates Tribunal set maximum rates on the assumption that an ordinary person or trader did not have the bargaining power of a railway company; but the Tribunal gave no protection to a railway company if it saw its profitable traffic being creamed off by a competitor and was left with high-cost/low-revenue traffic for which it was obliged to charge no more than was permitted by the rates schedule. William Whitelaw in his first Annual Report to the LNER shareholders, underlined another aspect: since 1913, coal and engineering products had almost doubled in cost, while labour costs were up by 148%. On the other hand, rates charged by the railways had increased by no more than 50-60%.

So, from the commercial point of view, the LNER commenced its trading operations in the worst of two worlds: it was increasingly assaulted by competition, often at lower cost (although, it must be said, sometimes at greater convenience to the customer), yet it was bound by a rate system based in theory on the cost of providing the service, but without the benefit of ability to adjust particular rates to be more in tune with the needs and pressures of the market place. In this situation the railways were virtually on their own; not only was the Government adhering to its own belief that the railways' commercial position could still be related to prewar conditions, but pressure groups such as industrialists and trade associations were intent on extracting the best from the situation through restraint on railway rates, plus the right to divert from the railways such traffic as could be conveniently carried by roads. In 1923 the Federation of British Industries considered that rates should be no more than one-third above prewar. Sir Eric Geddes was now President of the FBI and was active in attacking his erstwhile industry, making extravagant claims about the savings which he said were brought about by the Grouping.

Looking back to the time of the Grouping, 1922 had not been a bad year for trade generally, and in its last year of independent operation the North Eastern had paid no less than 7½% on its ordinary shares, after having put £430,000 into reserve. However, the Great Eastern could only manage 2¾% on its lowest class of shares, and the Great Central nothing at all: North Eastern fears that its profits would be used to bolster the fortunes of the financially weaker constituents were to be proved correct. Nonetheless, 1923 opened with hopes high, and in May a financial commentator considered that the dividend on the LNER preferred ordinary stock was well covered, and that the deferred ordinaries were worth buying at their then current price of 34¾. (Indeed, they had risen briefly to 39¼ in the previous month.) But an enforced downward revision of rates from 75% to 50% of those applying in 1919, 'with the view of stimulating the trade of the country', cut nearly £3 million from the Group's forecast receipts, and the year ended with a net income of £14 million, arising from a gross income from all sources of £68.8 million, less working expenses of £54.8 million, of which two-thirds went to pay the staff. Since £14.5 million was needed to pay interest and dividends (including a modest 2½% on the deferred ordinaries), after some heart searching a sum of £550,000 was appropriated from the Compensation Fund paid by the Government under the Act. This enabled the accounts to be given a more respectable appearance, including the payment of a

LNER Net Revenue

Source: *LNER Annual Accounts*

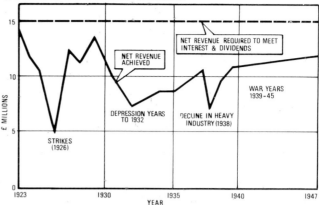

——— — ——— Net revenue required to meet interest and dividend payments.
——————— Net revenue achieved.

Notes:
1. The first year was the best.
2. Severe falls in 1926 (strikes) and 1938 (fall in heavy industry).
3. Rapid fall in depression years to 1932.
4. Gradual recovery after 1932, except for 1938 (helped by rearmament).
5. Wartime traffic justified a higher net revenue than that allowed by the Government.

dividend on the deferred shares, plus a modest amount to be carried forward.

The volume of business in 1923 in fact turned out to be better than in the previous year — with 361 million passenger journeys compared with 357 million, and goods tonnage up from 114 to 130 million — but insufficient to counteract the reduction in rates. The next year, 1924, started badly with a strike of enginemen, and passenger journeys fell as a result. The rates reduction provided a small boost to goods traffic, but again not nearly enough to make up the shortfall. The year ended with net revenue down by £2.3 million, and a further appropriation from the Compensation Fund, this time a hefty £2¾ million, was necessary to enable dividends to be held at the previous year's level. These first two years represented the Company's best returns to its shareholders, but even so only after substantial transfers from the Compensation Fund; it is doubtful whether the Government had intended this to be used to bolster dividends.

1925 turned out to be very disappointing, and despite a further £4 million being taken from the Compensation Fund, the dividend on the deferred shares fell to 1%; the picture from then on was one of gloom for holders of junior stocks, many of whom were to find their investment to be of little more than paper worth. 1926 was the year of the General Strike, and the much longer miners' strike, leading to the need to import coal at an additional cost of £1½ million. The year had actually commenced on a bright note, net receipts in the first four months being up by £1 million, but the out-turn was one of net revenue barely covering payment of interest on loans and debentures, despite substantial reductions in working expenses. A major saving of course was the loss of wages suffered by staff on strike. A massive transfer took place from the Compensation Fund, as well as from the Contingency and General Reserves, totalling £6.9 million in all, compared with only £4.6 million net revenue earned, a third of which came from sources only indirectly concerned with the railway. Even so, no dividend was paid on the deferred, and only a token ⅛% on the preferred ordinaries.

In 1927 overall receipts returned to the level of 1925, and this, coupled with the benefits accruing from a determined attack on costs, resulted in the previous year's result being achieved without transfers from reserves; ⅜% was paid on the preferred ordinaries. In the following year, pressure on the Government bore fruit in that a concession was obtained by the railways over payment of local authority rates. Initially these cost the Company over £2 million a year, but from 1928, under a somewhat complicated formula, a 75% reduction in rates paid was allowed in exchange for a corresponding reduction in the value of freight rates charged by the Company. This still left the LNER with a rates bill of some £½ million a year, and it was the job of the Estate and Rating Surveyors, with the backing of the Legal Department, to negotiate reductions in assessments whenever possible, especially at the quinquennial revaluation. On the other hand, very little was paid to the Government by way of tax.

1929 began relatively well, trade picking up and further significant cost reductions being made; over £1 million was saved for example on locomotive running, partly due to 'careful driving and firing' and, as William Whitelaw said, 'to the more economical types of engine now being used'. In fact, 1929 was, after 1923, the Company's best year, but hopes for a general revival of trade were dashed by the worldwide slump which was to follow. Traffic receipts fell alarmingly in the next two years, and although expenses were still further pared, savings could not match the loss of revenue. By now, the Compensation Fund was exhausted and prudent consideration weighed against more than token transfers from other reserves, which meant that the Board had to consider the position of the prior stocks which enjoyed Trustee Status. The criterion for these, by special dispensation of the Court of Chancery, was that a dividend, however small, had to be paid on the ordinary stock for a period of 10 consecutive years. The position had been held in the Company's earlier years, but despite the better operational results, crisis point was reached in 1929, when a token dividend was paid out of cash realised from the sale of investments; however, the situation could not be repeated two years later, when the Chairman was forced to report that a dividend could not possibly be paid on the preferred ordinary stock, and hence the position of Trustee Status for the prior stocks had to lapse, a grave psychological blow for the Board, to say nothing of the feelings of the unfortunate stockholders.

1932 represented another low point for the Company's finances, net revenue being no more than £7.2 million, half that needed to pay dividends in full, despite a 5% cut in salaries and wages estimated to save over £1 million. The following year was little better, but then began a four-year period of modest recovery. Total receipts reached £56.4 million in 1937, when, helped by a 5% increase in rates, a net income of £10.1 million was achieved, and £200,000 was transferred *to* reserve, even though the second preference shareholders were not paid a full dividend. The 5% wages cut had by now been restored in stages. An important contribution to cash flow was generated during this period when the Tyne Dock was sold for £808,000.

After the enouragement of the mid-1930s, 1938 was a year of severe setback, with revenue down and expenditure up, so that net income slumped to £6.7 million and the dividend was again passed on the second preference stock. Such was the alarm generated in all four railway companies that through their representative body, the Railway Companies Association, a national 'Square Deal' campaign was launched to alert public opinion and to persuade the Government to free the railways from regulatory restrictions on rate setting. A recovery was staged in 1939, but it represented the transition from peace to war; Government control was introduced through the Railway Executive Committee and the railways had to submit to imposed figures of net revenue, agreed annual sums being based on the average of the three years 1935 to 1937, hard bargaining on the part of the companies getting the Government to omit consideration of the bad year, 1938. The need for secrecy precluded statistics being published during the war, but the rise in traffic and enforced lessening of expenditure on maintenance, coupled with burgeoning inflation, led to a gradual increase in the agreed payments representing net revenue, these rising from £9.5 million in 1940 to £11.1 million in 1945, controls not being lifted before the LNER ceased to exist. The great increase in traffic arising from the war should have resulted in much higher revenue for the Company than was allowed under the formula; instead, the Government established an 'Arrears of Maintenance' Trust Fund, accumulated out of traffic earnings in excess of the agreed net revenues. This was made available at the end of the war, and amounted to some £40 million, which was spent on the permanent way and on new rolling stock. In addition to this work of immediate necessity, a two-stage postwar plan was prepared to cover a variety of new works, to a total of £50 million, but it was not made clear how this was to be funded.

In the last year, a minimal dividend was once more paid on the preferred ordinary shares. This was originally to have been 0.81%, it being proposed that the Directors should receive £63,000 as compensation for loss of office. This proposition was rejected at the final meeting of the Company, so the dividend was increased to 0.96%, taking almost all the cash in the revenue account and leaving just £228 to be carried forward to the British Transport Commission.

SIX

Civil Engineering

The major asset of a railway company is its permanent way, the trackbed and track to carry the trains which earn the company's revenue. Of the LNER's assets, almost two-thirds were made up of the permanent way and its infrastructure and buildings, extending to 6,714 route miles, or 17,271 track miles, of railway, including lines jointly owned. There were some 2,600 stations and depots, as well as tunnels, viaducts and bridges.

The constituent companies' contributions to these totals varied in amount and quality according to the original intentions of the promoters at the time the lines were planned, and to the money spent on renewals subsequently. The East Coast main line was generally well engineered and capable of carrying the heaviest locomotives in service, with only relatively few speed restrictions imposed by curves, mostly at stations (such as Peterborough North, which required through trains to keep to a speed not exceeding 20mph). Sharp curves, like steep gradients, resulted from decisions taken at the time the lines were originally planned, when compromises were sought in face of the competing factors — space required for traffic purposes, the cost of land and construction work, and the availability of finance. The Great Northern main line was built to a ruling gradient of 1 in 200, apart from such stretches as the 1 in 107 through Gas Works and Copenhagen tunnels against locomotives starting from King's Cross, and three miles at 1 in 178 in favour of southbound trains at the beginning of the long incline from Stoke Box, on which many high speed recordings were made. The NER, north of Darlington, and the NBR, passing through country more hilly than that traversed by the Great

Northern, had steeper banks, certain of which were notorious for the obstacles they presented to locomotive crews. The Cockburnspath bank, 4½ miles at 1 in 96 against southbound trains, is a well known example, whilst much of the road between Edinburgh and Aberdeen is both hilly and curved, stations often being sited in the valleys, and starts difficult, facing uphill curves.

The Great Central cross-Pennine main line and the London extension were also soundly engineered, with a generous load gauge, although the former, with its long climbs averaging 1 in 120 to the summit at Woodhead, and the latter, built to a ruling 1 in 178 but with steeper gradients in the Chilterns, made for difficult locomotive working. In contrast, the Great Eastern suffered a considerable weakness in that its trackbed was lightly constructed by 20th century standards and many main line underbridges were incapable of carrying an axle load of more than 18 tons, so inhibiting the use of the heaviest locomotives. An early LNER report on the costs of bridge renewal indicated that 120 bridges on the Great Eastern section would need attention at a cost of £1.3 million, compared with only £118,000 on the Great Northern.

The Great North of Scotland's original investment limitations were also to be seen in its track, its routes to Ballater and northeast Scotland being subject to severe weight limitations. The North British main lines, however, although subject to load gauge restrictions, were generally capable of carrying the heaviest locomotives then in service.

As part of the LNER's heritage, many noble structures passed to the Company. Foremost amongst these were the

Left:
The main line departure platforms at King's Cross, looking towards Gas Works Tunnel in March 1933. The locomotive yard is at the left and York Road platform, serving up trains descending into the 'widened lines' leading to Farringdon Street and Moorgate, is at the right. The gantries carrying cables for the newly installed electric signalling system suffered serious damage following a derailment in February 1945. *IAL*

this was built the route was over the High Level Bridge, which also carries a roadway.) Scotland was entered shortly after passing over the Royal Border Bridge at Berwick-upon-Tweed, and beyond Edinburgh were the Forth and Tay Bridges. Also of note elsewhere on the system was one of Bouch's more successful achievements, the delicate lattice girder bridge at Belah, on the line from Darlington to Penrith, now demolished.

The stations passing into LNER ownership represented good functional design of their periods, but many, particularly the larger ones, had suffered piecemeal modifications and additions to meet the demands of increasing traffic, often becoming cramped because there was no more room in which to expand. The North Eastern had evolved a standardised approach to the design of its largest — and certain of its smaller — stations, each featuring a vaulted roof of pleasing proportions; because later additions were generally contained within the original precincts, these retained their architectural attributes. Newcastle Central and, in particular, York, are attractive because of the curving formation of the stations, which does not seem to inhibit pedestrian movement, although imposing a speed limit on the few trains running through — a circumstance no doubt unforeseen when the stations were planned. Measured on acreage, the three largest stations on the LNER were Edinburgh Waverley, Liverpool

Forth Bridge, owned in fact by a consortium, in which the LMS, as successor to the Midland Railway, was a minority shareholder. Completed in 1890, its designer clearly built into it a considerable factor of safety, having regard to the fate of Bouch's Tay Bridge, which collapsed in a gale in December 1879 whilst a train was crossing. Fifty years after its construction the Forth Bridge proved to be capable of carrying the heaviest locomotives of the LNER, subject only to a speed limit of 40mph. At one time the East Coast route was known as the 'Bridges Route' as the traveller to Aberdeen passed over the Welwyn Viaduct, the swing bridges at Selby and Naburn, Durham Viaduct, and the King Edward Bridge over the Tyne at Newcastle. (Before

Left:
York station from the south, showing clearly the sharp curvature of the track through the station. The East Coast main line veers away to the top left and the Scarborough line to the upper right. *Real Photos*

Below:
Holbeck High Level station looking towards Leeds Central, the GNR station also used by Lancashire & Yorkshire trains to Manchester. The Midland Railway line from Leeds to Settle and Carlisle runs below the High Level station, through Holbeck Low Level. *Kenneth Field*

Left:
Hertford North station, the outer terminus of Great Northern suburban services via Gordon Hill and Cuffley. This view is looking north, with the line to Hertford East curving away to the right, and, soon after the War, the station is still in a 'green field' situation. *J. Spencer Gilks*

35

Right:
At the far end of the Great Northern system, an afternoon train from Bradford to Halifax pauses at Queensbury hauled by an Ivatt Class N1 0-6-2T. Queensbury station was on the three sides of a triangular junction to Keighley. *J. E. Oxley*

Below:
Otterington station, on the East Coast main line between Thirsk and Northallerton, as reconstructed in 1933 after track widening. The station has a pleasing frontage of contemporary design. *IAL*

Street and Newcastle Central, whilst Cambridge was unique for its size in that all through and much terminal traffic was handled at one platform, 1,254ft long. Liverpool Street was the busiest station, with over 1,200 trains a day. Some stations, even in important locations, left a lot to be desired, especially Queen Street, Glasgow, at the foot of the 1 in 42 Cowlairs incline, up which outgoing trains required banking assistance (runaways were an ever present hazard) and which was reputed to be one of the most grimy stations on the system.

The LNER also came into possession of a number of lengthy tunnels, which were bored to penetrate high ground or to ease the passage of trains through hilly country as an alternative to circuitous routes and deep cuttings. The Woodhead Tunnel through the Pennines was the longest at 3 miles 13 chains; its lack of ventilation made it difficult to work and maintain, and when the line was electrified after nationalisation the original single bores were replaced by one double track tunnel. Others included the Ponsbourne Tunnel, near Cuffley, opened in 1924, on the Great Northern loop line from Wood Green to Stevenage; and bores at Bramhope, near Harrogate, Catesby, on the Great Central, and Drewton, at the summit of the Hull & Barnsley.

This brief survey of the LNER way and works indicates the extent of the problems facing the Board and the civil engineering staff of the Company in 1923; little had been done for 10 years to cope with changed traffic conditions, apart from essential maintenance and repair work. In addition to the continuing requirement to provide sufficient minimum maintenance to keep the system in order, there was an urgent need to upgrade a good deal of it by strengthening bridges, re-laying track with heavier rails, providing relief lines to remove bottlenecks and remodelling station buildings and layouts. Clearly this was not a task which could be tackled comprehensively at the outset, even when hopes were high for a reasonable financial future for the railway. Amongst the first priorities was the renewal in 1924 of 171 miles of the North Eastern permanent way, three times as much as on any of the other sections; this must have been unexpected, having regard for the high reputation of the North Eastern generally. In the pre-Grouping discussions between Directors, and in the House of Commons, Sir Frederick Banbury had made much of the excellence of the Great Northern permanent way, and this is underlined by the lesser amount spent on that section of the railway. A nice compliment to the GNR was paid in 1927, when, following a disastrous derailment at Sevenoaks on the Southern Railway, the locomotive type concerned, the 'River' class 2-6-4T, was tried on the Great Northern main line between St Neots and Huntingdon to compare is riding there with its performance on the Southern. In fact, the locomotive was reported to have run very steadily at speeds of up to 80mph, and the Ministry of

Lossiemouth station, on the Great North of Scotland, the terminus of a branch from Elgin. The bell was rung to announce departures, in this case of an afternoon branch train headed by a Class D40 4-4-0 working back to Elgin tender first. The bell was recovered from a ship named *Lady Gordon* which was wrecked nearby in the middle of the last century, and gave five minutes warning to passengers, including fishwives hurrying to the station with their creels strapped to their backs, full of fish which they sold in Elgin. It was also rung to welcome home Lossiemouth's most famous son, the Labour politician Ramsay MacDonald. *IAL*

Pelham Street Junction and the Durham Ox level crossing outside Lincoln Central station; of the many level crossings for which Lincoln was notorious, this was one of the worst. At the platform is the down Colchester to Newcastle train. *IAL*

Architectural detail of the hammerbeam roof at Thornaby station. Designed by the NER architect, William Bell, this has been described as 'probably the best example of its kind, for grace and restrained artistry' (Gordon Biddle, *Victorian Stations*). *Rodney Wildsmith*

Transport Inspector commented on the superiority of the LNER permanent way.

In 1935 the introduction of streamlined trains on the East Coast main line, running at much higher speeds than before, came about without any preliminary upgrading of the track, but experience showed that improvements were necessary at certain points, calling for studies of the transitional entry to curves, and their superelevation, as well as of junctions and crossings. The main problems were not associated with the downhill stretches, where speeds rose from 90mph to 100mph, but with rising gradients, where speeds went up from 60mph to 90mph.

Over half of the LNER system was double track; many minor lines, and some stretches of main line in Scotland, were single. Four tracks were provided on certain sections, including the most heavily congested routes, such as King's Cross to Peterborough, York to Northallerton and Liverpool Street to Romford. Four-tracking also existed in industrial areas in which there was a considerable freight traffic, such as from Staddlethorpe to Hull. Nevertheless, even the two sections of the East Coast route mentioned were not wholly four-tracked, some intermediate lengths possessing only two or three, tracks. The Great Northern had given a great deal of thought to augmenting the line from Wood Green to Stevenage, and concluded that as an alternative to costly widening, an extension of the Cuffley branch via Hertford to Langley, near Stevenage, would

serve as a loop line and break new ground for potential traffic. This was not completed until 1924, and was the last addition to the route mileage of the LNER, apart from short colliery extensions, wartime links to other lines and to stores depots and airfields, and the Watford branch, built jointly with the Metropolitan Railway and opened in 1925. However, four-tracking was extended at certain localities, between Huntingdon and Offord on the Great Northern, and at Beningborough and between Alne and Northallerton on the North Eastern. An expensive doubling of the Arbroath to Montrose section of the Aberdeen road, originally built as single line, was completed in 1932, whilst four-tracking was extended to Gidea Park on the Great

Eastern, and later to Shenfield, with a burrowing junction to allow Southend trains to avoid conflicting with London bound trains on the main line. At Grouping, 337 route miles were four track, 133 of these being on the East main line; a further 41 route miles were converted by 1940.

However, these stretches of four track main line were insufficient to eradicate delays, particularly on the Great Northern main line, where the confliction between loose coupled mineral trains and fast passenger services on the double track bottlenecks brought inevitable delays. A committee of the Board commented on 'the great waste due to delays in the Southern Area' in 1926, making several recommendations. Probably the most desirable improvement, notwithstanding the loop line, would have been to convert to four track the section between Greenwood Box, Hadley Wood and Potters Bar, involving widening (or cutting out) the short tunnels and rebuilding two stations. The necessary land was acquired and the work estimated at £650,000, but other projects were given priority and the work was not to be carried out until after nationalisation. However, some relief was afforded farther north by the insertion of passing loops and the diversion of some coal traffic to the March to Temple Mills line, on the Great Eastern, but the stretch over Welwyn Viaduct, together with the adjacent tunnels, was never seriously considered for widening, and remains two track to this day.

From time to time during the lifetime of the LNER, as a result of advances in technology, improvements were

Above:
Stratford Market was established by the Great Eastern Railway in 1879, and by Grouping had extended to over 100,000sq ft, with warehouses, and tracks flanked by cartage roads. Early morning trains brought produce to the market from East Anglia, another important commodity being bananas, delivered from Manchester. This view probably dates from about 1928 — note the many horse-drawn carts.
BBC Hulton Picture Library

Left:
The 40-arched Welwyn Viaduct over the River Mimram in Hertfordshire is one of the many notable engineering structures on the East Coast main line. Built for the opening of the Great Northern Railway in 1850, its condition is still such that nowadays it is crossed by 100mph trains. Here we see a Class V2 2-6-2 heading the 'Aberdonian' sleeping car express. *C. R. L. Coles*

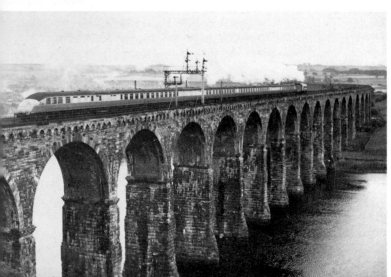

Below left:
The Royal Border Bridge, carrying the East Coast main line over the River Tweed, near Berwick. Built in 1850 to the designs of Robert Stephenson, this is a fine example of the continuing strength of well-built masonry bridges. The 'Coronation' express, complete with observation car, is seen heading south. *Locomotive Publishing Co (LPC)*

Top right:
In its day one of the engineering wonders of the world, the Forth Bridge was opened in 1890, having taken eight years to build; including approaches, the bridge is 1½ miles long. A Gresley Pacific is here seen heading an Aberdeen train.
E. R. Wethersett, LPC

made to the standards of the permanent way. Rail weights and lengths were increased, becoming standardised at 95lb/yd and 60ft, whilst experimental lengths of 90ft rail were laid at Thirsk and over Welwyn Viaduct, and 100lb/yd, 120ft lengths at Holme near Peterborough in 1937. Trials of continuous welded rail up to a quarter of a mile in length were initiated in 1934, and, in 1939, flat bottomed rail was tried as a less costly alternative to the traditional bullhead type keyed into chairs. The use of cast manganese steel rail at selected crossing points, pioneered at Newcastle Central by the NER, meant that the life of the crossings could be measured in years rather than months. The first reinforced concrete sleepers used in lieu of imported softwood were not very satisfactory because flexing under load initiated cracks, which resulted in deterioration due to ingress of water and frost, but later, pre-stressed concrete sleepers were successful. Track, both plain line and junctions, was increasingly pre-assembled and laid in place by cranes; in 1932 a Morris tracklaying machine was purchased, this having the advantage that possession was only needed of the track being renewed. The extent of the task involved in maintaining the permanent way is illustrated by the amount of materials needed. In a typical year, 60,000 tons of rail would be used, 1¼ million sleepers, and over half a million cubic yards of ballast.

Routine track maintenance was carried out to a systematic plan under which specific tasks were allotted to certain times of the year. Inspection was carried out at specified intervals and was assessed twice a year by independent observers, awards being made to the gangs responsible for the best-kept sections. Mechanical aids to maintenance were introduced, such as the Hallade system of recording track conditions, first used in Britain by the Great Northern in 1922, whilst trials took place in 1947 of a Swiss self-propelled ballast tamping machine.

An important influence in the design of bridges was the report in 1928 of a Government Committee chaired by Sir Alfred Ewing on practice in the design of girders for railway bridges, and known as the Bridge Stress Committee. This led to the publication of a revised British Standard for girder bridges. A key factor in the Committee's report was its conclusion that the hammer blow exerted by a two-cylinder locomotive was far worse in its dynamic effect than the concentration of engine weight on the coupled wheels. The report of the Committee was contributory to the introduction of new forms of bridge construction, increasingly prefabricated and rolled into position, so speeding construction and reducing the period of service slacks during which passing trains were required to submit to speed restrictions.

Some reconstruction of stations took place during LNER days, at Berwick-on-Tweed and Clacton-on-Sea, for example, whilst a small number of new stations were built, mainly to serve commuters, such as Welwyn Garden City and Brookmans Park, and Seaburn, near Sunderland; Filey Holiday Camp station was opened in 1947 to serve the adjacent Butlin's. Soon after the Grouping, King's Cross

station was provided with additional platforms, but the area between the station frontage and Euston Road became cluttered with shops, stalls and, at one period, a brick-built show house, comprising what was known as the 'African Village', to the detriment of railway amenities.

Having regard to the importance of freight traffic, the Board gave high priority to the provision of new marshalling yards, where the case for these was proved by savings resulting from speeding-up traffic flows. The most important new projects of this type were the yards at March, in Cambridgeshire, to provide for better handling of the increased goods and mineral traffic in and out of East Anglia. Here, the hump shunting principle was employed, the wagons being propelled to the summit of the hump and then allowed to run downhill into the road selected for them. Hydraulically operated retarders were employed at the up yard, steel beams squeezing the wheels of the wagons as they passed, so slowing them down under the control of the shunting operator. These German-made devices were not entirely successful because the Mansell type of wheel, with protruding bolts, was damaged by the beams. This did not result in any modification of the system itself, although when the down yard was constructed an eddy current type of retarder was employed which was able to brake Mansell wheels without damage. (Appointment as Assistant Yardmaster at March was much sought after by traffic apprentices, this post being said to lead to higher office.) A further yard was opened at Mottram, near Manchester, in 1935, and another at Priory Yard, Hull, where retarders were also installed.

Three important classes of building, whilst the operational responsibility of other departments, were designed and built by civil engineering staff. These were the rolling stock workshops, goods depots and the locomotive sheds.

Above:
The control tower and sidings at Whitemoor up concentration yard, near March in Lincolnshire, just after opening in June 1929. All train movements were controlled from the tower, and one of the mechanical retarders designed to slow down the wagons after they had passed over the hump can be seen in the foreground. *IAL*

Left:
Goodman's Yard warehouse, a seven storey building 360ft long, was opened by the London & Blackwall Railway in 1861, and destroyed in the bombing of London in 1940. The depot had been modernised in the early 1930s and a 30-ton wagon hoist installed. The contents of the depot included perishable goods, and wines and spirits in bond. The depot was later partially reopened and was not closed finally until 1951. *IAL*

Little was done structurally to the workshops, except to reconstruct the carriage shops at Doncaster and York, which were largely destroyed by fire during the war, but new goods depots were built, as at Ardwick East, Manchester, to take advantage of mechanised operating, and new locomotive sheds at Sheffield Darnall and Frodingham. Mechanical coaling plant was installed at the most important locomotive depots, designed and constructed by contractors, whilst an important factor in reducing the costs of boiler maintenance was the introduction of water softening installations in the 1930s, under the guidance of T. Henry Turner, Gresley's Chief Chemist and Metallurgist; £600,000 was allocated in 1932 for 18 plants on the Great Northern section. The renewal of turntables was an ever present problem, new 70ft installations being needed for the Pacifics as their numbers increased and their sphere of operation widened; the smaller tables replaced were relocated. Carriage washing plants were another example of labour-saving investment, these being installed in the vicinity of the major terminals. Finally, to provide ready-made concrete components for buildings, trackside equipment and bridges, concrete manufacturing yards at a number of locations were enlarged and refurbished.

The war brought severe damage to LNER installations, particularly in the 1940/41 blitz, when King's Cross station was hit by two 1,000lb bombs chained together, and in 1944, caused by flying bombs and rockets. No less than £5.2 million was spent on air raid precautions alone, but considerable additional resources, and the working of long hours in adverse and often dangerous conditions, was called for by members of the engineering staff, alongside those of other departments, to get traffic moving again and to effect longer term repairs.

Maintenance difficulties arising from wartime shortages led to the continuation of a 60mph speed limit being retained for a time after the war, although this had been originally introduced as an air raid precaution; the renewal of 579 miles of track and the repair and repainting of 300 stations were items identified as first priority on which to spend money accruing from the Arrears of Maintenance Trust Fund.

The two-stage postwar development plans took in the quadrupling of the Greenwood to Potters Bar bottleneck, the estimate by now having increased to over £1 million, the tunnels being assumed to be opened out. Also included was major reconstruction of the layout and stations at Peterborough, Edinburgh Waverley and Glasgow Queen Street, as well as new marshalling yards at York and Peterborough. £10 million was to be spent in aggregate on improvements to passenger stations, goods depots, workshops and engine sheds, plus a further £3.86 million on marshalling yards. The second, less detailed, set of proposals, included remodelling schemes for York and Scarborough, and a new station to be called 'Long Sands' on the North Tyneside electrified line between Cullercoats and Tynemouth. Modernisation of company owned houses, to an amount of £1¼ million, was another feature of the programme.

Until 1942, when J. C. L. Train, then the Engineer (Southern Area), was appointed Chief Engineer, no equivalent all-line position existed. Instead, Engineers were appointed for each of the three Areas, reporting to the Divisional General Managers. As in other functions, the three met to discuss mutual problems, but there was no overall LNER policy on civil engineering matters other than what might be agreed between the Areas. This was in sharp contrast to mechanical engineering, in which, where it was appropriate, a firm central policy was laid down by the CME. Incidentally, it is interesting to note that the title was simply 'engineer', not 'civil engineer', continuing the tradition of a 'civil' (as distinct from a 'military') engineer, having responsibility for all aspects of engineering; the man in charge of rolling stock in the past had often been the 'locomotive superintendent'. However, as other branches of engineering grew in importance, the title of 'engineer' became qualified by a particular branch of the profession, and the LNER appointed a Chief Mechanical Engineer and later a Chief Electrical Engineer. Nonetheless, the Engineer continued to be described as such, although his function excluded engineering matters not directly concerned with structures, the permanent way, and signalling and telecommunications. A Signal and Telegraph Engineer was an appointment on the staff of each of the Engineers in the Areas, and later, when Train had been appointed Chief Engineer, the post of Assistant Chief Engineer (Signals) was established. The Southern and North Eastern Areas had separate Chief Engineers for Docks, whilst responsibility for road motor engineering lay with the CME. As an important adjunct to the engineering function, each Area had an Estate and Rating Surveyor to adminster the Company's estates and properties, and to acquire new ones or dispose of any declared redundant.

A number of eminent engineers served the LNER; J. C. L. Train became Civil Engineering Member of the Railway Executive, and later, as Sir Landale Train, Member of the British Transport Commission responsible for all engineering functions. Others included Charles Brown, who left the North British Railway to join the Great Northern, and who served as Engineer in the Southern Area for 14 years; John Miller, of the Great Eastern, who was transferred to the North Eastern Area soon after Grouping, and who claimed he could carry out the job of any workman on his staff; and F. E. Harrison (who followed Miller) who was a descendant of earlier Harrisons who had been responsible for the major bridges of the NER.

A railway system is by its nature a product of heavy engineering, and is necessarily long lived. Rolling stock can achieve a life of 40 years or more before being scrapped, whilst structures could last twice that period or more. Each would become obsolete well before life expiry. It is a tribute to successive generations of railway engineers that so many examples of construction work are still in existence more than a hundred years after their completion, coping with traffic demands well beyond the comprehension of their designers, and facing their present owners less with problems of maintenance than of modernisation. The LNER, during its 25 years of stewardship, did not fail to maintain its engineering heritage, indeed in many cases handing on structures in better condition to cope with modern needs than when it took them over.

Below:
Wartime damage due to daylight bombing at Middlesbrough station in August 1942; the train was empty at the time. The locomotive was not seriously damaged, despite appearances — it is Class V1 No 416, built at Doncaster in 1935, the first of the class to be fitted with a hopper type bunker. *IAL*

SEVEN

Passenger Services

By the Grouping, many of the passenger services in Britain had recovered from the decelerations and cancellations of the war years, except that the longer distance services were heavier and somewhat slower than before, generally because little nor no increase in locomotive power had been provided. The LNER led the way in start-to-stop timings, trains running the 44.1 miles between Darlington and York and the 22.6 miles between Leicester and Arkwright Street Nottingham, each at an average speed of 61.5mph. This lead was lost to the Great Western in the summer services of 1923, when the 2.30pm from Cheltenham was timed at 61.8mph between Swindon and Paddington, fractionally faster than the two LNER runs. No effort was made to restore the LNER position by clipping a minute from the Darlington to York schedule, and the Great Western continued to claim the lead until the introduction of the 'Coronation' express in 1937. The best 1923 run on the Great Northern, which had established a

reputation for fast running over long distances, was 56.1mph, over the 50.5 miles between Grantham and Doncaster.

In marked contrast to the block services of today, many longer distance LNER trains, on the East Coast main line and the Great Eastern section in particular, were made up of groups of coaches for more than one destination; carriages were detached at intermediate stations, running onwards as independent trains, or part of another. In the reverse direction, coming up to London, the separate portions joined the main line train at junctions on the way. For example, trains from King's Cross to Scotland might include through coaches for Glasgow, Perth and Aberdeen, and in the summer one of the overnight sleeping car trains would include a through coach for Fort William. West Riding trains, of which the major part would go through to Leeds Central, would have portions for Bradford and possibly Halifax, and perhaps detach a Hull portion at Doncaster. This concept of through coaches was widely publicised, and carriages were clearly labelled with their destinations, generally by roof boards.

Because of the restrictions on traffic operations imposed by the double track bottlenecks, the tendency was to run important passenger services out of King's Cross in groups, as in the morning (around the 10am departure time of the 'Flying Scotsman'), at lunchtime, in the late afternoon, and in the evening. For example, in the 1939 summer timetable there were departures for Newcastle at 1.05pm, Edinburgh at 1.20, the West Riding at 1.30, and Harrogate at 1.40, but

Above left:
One of Doncaster shed's duties during the summer of 1939 was to provide the engine for the 'Yorkshire Pullman' to King's Cross and the return working later in the day. Class V2 2-6-2s were frequently used on this turn in place of Pacifics, and No 4817 is seen accelerating down the grade past Bell Bar, between Brookmans Park and Hatfield, with a nine-coach train weighing some 380 tons full.
Colling Turner, Eric Neve collection

Left:
Much of the finest work performed by the Ivatt Atlantics was on the King's Cross Pullman services, shared by engines stationed at King's Cross and Copley Hill, Leeds. Here, Class C1 No 4444 of King's Cross, built at Doncaster in 1908, is seen near Stoke summit with the down 'Queen of Scots' in 1935. *Real Photos*

Right:
Class A4 No 2511 *Silver King,* **south of Chaloner's Whin Junction near York, with the up 'Silver Jubilee' on 26 August 1936. The 'Jubilee' was normally a King's Cross working in both directions, and of the original four 'A4s', three were kept at Top Shed for this duty.** *Silver King* **was stationed at Gateshead to take over the up express if the incoming engine was stopped for any reason. This was not often the case, and consequently No 2511 was seldom seen in London.**
Gresley Society collection

Below right:
Class A4 No 4498 *Sir Nigel Gresley* **approaching Grantham with the up 'Flying Scotsman' c1937. The 100th Pacific built to Sir Nigel Gresley's designs, No 4498 was given the name of this illustrious engineer, and has been preserved. It is now owned by the A4 Locomotive Society, and is based at Steamtown, Carnforth.** *IAL*

no more fast long distance trains left until the next group began at 4pm. Frequent regular-interval departures could not be arranged — again, a contrast with the present day — as slower moving trains were channelled into the intervals between the groups of expresses.

The most prestigious trains on the LNER were the two main daytime Anglo-Scottish services, the 'Flying Scotsman', 10am in each direction between King's Cross and Edinburgh Waverley, and the corresponding early afternoon trains, together with the Hook of Holland boat trains from Liverpool Street to Parkeston Quay. These were given priority for new stock, the 'Flying Scotsman' being provided with new coaches in 1924, 1928, 1938 and 1946.

As well as the trunk Anglo-Scottish route and the main lines between London and other provincial centres, there were also important cross country services, notably the cross-Pennine links between Hull and Manchester and Liverpool, as well as joint through services between Newcastle and Bournemouth, Newcastle and Swansea, and (although usually only a single carriage throughout), Aberdeen and Penzance, the country's longest through working. Farther afield, the 'Hook Continental' connected with the Company's sailings to the Hook of Holland and European trains such as the 'Rheingold' express. A through train also ran to Parkeston Quay from Liverpool, known unofficially as the 'North Country Continental', and through coaches from Glasgow also carried passengers for the Continent. Rail connections were provided to link up with sailings from the Tyne Commission Quay at Wallsend; the principal service from King's Cross became well known in later years as the 'Norseman'. Boat trains were also run from Marylebone to Immingham in connection with Orient Line cruises from that port. Advantage was taken of the opportunity for rationalisation afforded by the Grouping, such as the concentration of services from London to Sheffield and Manchester into Marylebone, and the diversion of Grimsby traffic from Marylebone to King's Cross.

The Company's timetables were under continuous scrutiny, and major revisions took place from time to time, as in the general accelerations of 1932 and the introduction

of interval operation of certain short distance services. There were considerable differences between the main line summer and winter timetables, to cater for additional summer traffic, whilst Sunday services were less frequent and slower than those on weekdays. With the 5½-day working week in vogue, Saturday morning was regarded as a peak period, with additional suburban workings at midday. The timetable was revised and published twice and sometimes three times a year; the summer schedules would operate from July to mid-September, and the winter timetable would then apply until May, when modifications and additions would be made for the short period until the full summer service came into operation.

The introduction of more powerful locomotives of the Pacific type enabled certain East Coast trains to be accelerated substantially in the summer of 1923. Edinburgh was brought within 7¾ hours of London by a night express, for example, half an hour faster than the 'Flying Scotsman', which due to a restrictive agreement with the LMS imposing minimum timings for Anglo-Scottish day trains following the 1895 Race to Aberdeen, was compelled to maintain an 8¼-hour schedule until the agreement was abandoned in 1932. With some paring of minutes from the timings, the fastest services from London to the major provincial cities and towns were gradually restored to prewar level, and generally where services were in competition, the best LNER trains were faster than those of the LMS.

For many years the Great Western had operated the longest non-stop run working in the country, the 10.30am down 'Cornish Riviera Express' running the 225.7 miles from Paddington to Plymouth at the respectable rate of

Right:
One of the highlights of the career of No 10000 in its original form was the working of the down non-stop 'Flying Scotsman' on 1 August 1932. Here it is seen leaving Platform 10 at King's Cross, with Class A1 No 2582 *Sir Hugo* of Gateshead shed waiting with the 10.05am 'Junior Scotsman'. *IAL*

Below:
The concept of headboards for titled trains originated at Haymarket shed. The first was made for the up non-stop 'Flying Scotsman' in 1928, and the idea was soon adopted generally. This turn is not the complete 'Flying Scotsman', but only the Perth portion, approaching Haymarket c1929 headed by one of the Class C11 Atlantics, No 9906 *Teribus*.
T. G. Hepburn, Rail Archive Stephenson

Above:
Class A3 No 2544 *Lemberg* climbs from Grantham with the up 'Scarborough Flier' on 3 September 1932. It being a Saturday, the train is loaded to 14 coaches, weighing altogether over 450 tons and providing the engine with a difficult task on its non-stop run from York to King's Cross. *Lemberg* was one of the first Pacifics to be given a boiler pressure of 220lb/sq in, and reclassified 'A3' in consequence.
T. G. Hepburn, Rail Archive Stephenson

54.8mph. The longest on the LNER in 1932 was over the 188.2 miles between King's Cross and York, in each direction, at 53.8mph. However, in 1928 Nigel Gresley introduced the corridor tender, which enabled two crews to share the locomotive working and led to the 'Flying Scotsman' being booked to run non-stop between King's Cross and Waverley in each direction. Nevertheless, maintaining the 8¼-hour schedule over the distance of 392.8 miles meant that the end-to-end speed was no more than 47.6mph, the same as that of the following train with four stops. 1932 began a period of general acceleration, the 'Flying Scotsman' leading the way by coming down to 7 hours 50 minutes, or 7½ hours when working non-stop, later to be reduced to seven hours. As well as the 'Flying Scotsman', further speeding up took place in 1932, and each year up to the outbreak of war saw an improvement in some services. The Great Central section, in competition with the LMS for traffic between London and Leicester, Nottingham and Sheffield, maintained its share of a growing market, despite the adoption by the LMS of mile-a-minute timings between principal centres. Not only were the Great Central section trains accelerated, but additional coaches were added, calling for more powerful locomotives. Also, the Great Eastern, generally free from railway competition but increasingly assaulted by road transport, saw the acceleration of selected services, despite being limited to the use of medium power locomotives because of permanent way weaknesses. The boat trains, with their substantial Continental patronage, retained their importance, but with the increasing industrialisation of East Anglia more attention was paid to the Ipswich and Norwich services, notably in 1937 when a new train, titled the 'East

Anglian', was put on between Liverpool Street and Norwich. In northern England and Scotland, times were pared on such services as Newcastle to Carlisle, and Edinburgh to Glasgow.

The outstanding event in the entire LNER history of passenger services took place in 1935, when following a small number of trials, a train was introduced which brought a completely new dimension to long distance travel. Contemporary with the Jubilee of King George V and Queen Mary, this was a fully streamlined train which ran between King's Cross and Newcastle in no more than four hours in each direction, with one stop. Titled the 'Silver Jubilee', the train formed an addition to the timetable, and generally ran to capacity, providing businessmen in the northeast with their first ever opportunity to travel to London and back in a day, with sufficient time to conduct business in the capital. The streamline vogue was extended to the 'Coronation' in 1937, taking six hours between King's Cross and Edinburgh with two stops, and the 'West Riding Limited', non-stop to Leeds in 2 hours 42 minutes. These new trains broke all records for speed in normal service, and brought

the LNER to the head of the table of fastest trains. The Great Western had accelerated its Swindon to Paddington express, now known as the 'Cheltenham Flyer', to 71.4mph, but this was over 77.3 miles of gently falling line; the down 'Coronation' was booked to reach York, 188.2 miles, with long banks at 1 in 200 or steeper, at 71.9mph. A cost/benefit examination of the 'Silver Jubilee's' first year of operation underlined the stimulus the train had given to the total volume of traffic between London and the northeast, and, with an 86% load factor, concluded that the gross revenue (including supplementary fares) was as much as six times the operating cost. Some anxiety had been expressed in advance that the 'Coronation' would draw traffic from the sleeping car services, but this does not appear to have been the case. Not mentioned anywhere in any comparison was the cost of delays to lesser trains, held up to allow the streamliners priority of passage, but such considerations were swept aside by the sheer pride in the railway's ability to run these superb trains to time, in such fast schedules. The streamline services gave the LNER world leadership in passenger speed and comfort, and whilst more recent developments

46

Right:
One of Edward Thompson's final class of 6ft 2in Pacifics, No 518 *Tehran*, was built at Doncaster in 1946 and stationed at Heaton shed, Newcastle, for most of its life until withdrawal 16 years later. No 518 is seen leaving Newcastle Central with an Edinburgh train in August 1947. *Tehran* the racehorse was owned by the Aga Khan and won the 1944 St Leger.
E. R. Wethersett

Above:
Class D49 No 298 *The Pytchley*, one of the 'Hunt' series with Lentz poppet valves operated by rotating cams. It is seen leaving York (where it was stationed) on 22 August 1937, with an up train whose composition does not appear to warrant the 'express' headcode. Note the elaborate North Eastern signalling arrangements. *H. C. Doyle, G. Goslin collection*

Left:
Amongst the Great Central locomotives working temporarily on the Great Northern section soon after the Grouping was Class D10 No 437c, which spent a week or so at King's Cross in July 1924. It is seen at Greenwood box, Hadley Wood, on the 6.15pm stopping train to Huntingdon, with an assortment of coaching stock. A goods train is on the down slow line awaiting a path through the two track bottleneck to Potters Bar. *F. R. Hebron, Rail Archive Stephenson*

have brought increases in speed, the luxury provided by the streamline coaches ceased when the trains were withdrawn.

Another particularly interesting aspect of LNER passenger services was the provision of Pullman car trains. Of the constituent companies, only the Great Eastern had made any use of the high standard of comfort and service provided by these coaches. A contract between the GER and the Pullman Car Co, initiated by Sir Henry Thornton as a result of his experience of the Company's services in the USA, had not turned out successfully, but had several years to run. Consequently, as the LNER had inherited the obligations of the contract, alternative uses for the cars were investigated, and a suggestion was put forward by the Pullman Co that the spa town of Harrogate would justify a daily service, notwithstanding the supplements charged, and would also attract Leeds and Bradford traffic. Although not at first welcomed by the LNER Passenger Managers, the proposal was supported by the Chief General Manager, and it proved to be the commencement of a long and profitable collaborative service. Inaugurated on 9 July 1923, the down train ran through to Harrogate in four hours, and on to Ripon and Newcastle. The success of this venture led to the introduction of a further train the following year, to Sheffield, extended in 1925 to Manchester, but this turned out to be poorly patronised and was withdrawn. The Yorkshire service was modified, with Leeds and Bradford being served by the 'West Riding Pullman', and the Harrogate train, routed direct via Knottingley and Church Fenton, was extended to

The lightweight Garden Cities and Cambridge buffet expresses (popularly dubbed the 'Beer Trains') were introduced in May 1932, usually being hauled by Ivatt Atlantics. Allocation of new 'B17s' to the Great Central section in 1936 led to a number of Robinson Atlantics being transferred away, amongst them being No 6083. This engine found its way to Cambridge, in turn replacing a withdrawn Class C2 Atlantic, and for a period of two years worked services to King's Cross, including the buffet trains when a 'C1' was not available. It is seen here outside Cambridge with the empty stock of a buffet train, waiting to enter the platform. *Real Photos*

Edinburgh and later to Glasgow, to become known as the 'Queen of Scots'. The distance between King's Cross and Harrogate was 198.7 miles and was the longest non-stop run on the LNER until the 'Flying Scotsman' commenced its non-stop working to Edinburgh; despite the roundabout route and the stops on the way, Edinburgh was reached by the 'Queen of Scots' in only five minutes more than the time taken by the 'Flying Scotsman'. Two new trains of eight all-steel cars were provided for the 'Queen of Scots' in 1928, and in 1935 a Hull portion was added to the 'West Riding Pullman', this being renamed the 'Yorkshire Pullman' and booked to Doncaster from King's Cross on a 60mph schedule.

Pullman cars continued to be used after the Grouping on the Great Eastern, the 'Hook Continental' including a first class Pullman car in addition to LNER restaurant cars — an unusual arrangement, in which meal service was provided by two different caterers. Other boat trains included Pullman cars to provide restaurant facilities, whilst in the 1930s an all-Pullman train, the 'Eastern Belle', ran day excursions on summer weekdays to a different destination each day. Pullman race specials were also organised, sometimes by a travel company, for meetings at Newmarket for example, or to Aintree for the Grand National, and Doncaster for the St Leger. After 1928 single Pullman dining cars were employed on certain services radiating from Edinburgh to Glasgow, Perth and Carlisle.

Above:
All six of Robinson's Class B3 4-6-0s worked on the Great Northern section in the early post-Grouping years, notably on the Pullman services. In this photograph No 1169 (LNER 6169) *Lord Faringdon*, still in Great Central livery in 1924, is approaching Greenwood box with the 11.30am down stopping train to Doncaster. The Gresley coaches — not by any means new ones — are a considerable contrast to the antique six-wheelers. *F. R. Hebron, Rail Archive Stephenson*

The long stretch of coastline served by the LNER was well publicised as 'The Drier Side', and the many seaside resorts were well provided with regular services, supplemented by excursion trains at periods of popular demand. An important innovation in 1925 was the summer 'Scarborough Flier', running non-stop from King's Cross to York initially in 3½ hours, but later, following the accelerations of the 1930s, taking no more than three hours at 62.9mph, and reaching Scarborough in under four hours. In pre-Grouping days holiday traffic was generally concentrated into summer weekends and, in particular, the August Bank Holiday period, but with the spread of paid holidays more families took themselves to the seaside for a week or more, so that the summer Saturday timetable bore little resemblance to that of a weekday, trains to the East Coast resorts running in several parts. On such occasions,

Left:
In 1927 the 'B3s' were transferred back to the Great Central section and took their turn with other classes in working regular and other services. In 1936, No 6165 *Valour* was stationed at Neasden and is seen here at Willesden Green on a down excursion. *Valour* was named in memory of GCR staff killed in World War 1, and one of its nameplates is preserved in the National Railway Museum. *E. R. Wethersett*

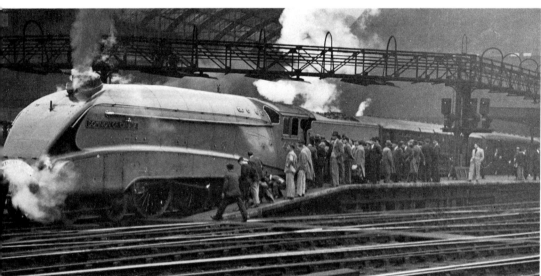

Below left:
Class A4 No 4489 *Dominion of Canada* is exciting interest as it leaves King's Cross with one of the 'Northern Belle' land cruises in 1937. The following year a Canadian type locomotive bell was fitted below the chimney, a gift from the Canadian Pacific Railway.
Locomotive Publishing Co

with trains running in close succession, the schedules had no reserve for out-of-course delays, so that whenever some failure or other untoward occurrence took place, punctual working became an impossibility until a new day commenced.

Summer holiday workings often took on through bookings not otherwise seen in the timetables, as for example from Glasgow and Paisley to Whitley Bay, to coincide with the holiday weeks in the Scottish towns. Inter-railway trains were also run, to Blackpool for example, over LMS metals, whilst trains of maroon stock could be seen at Scarborough and elsewhere. Special trains were arranged in connection with football matches, vandalism seeming not to be a problem; Cup Finals at Wembley in particular provided lucrative traffic. An early example of what could be achieved was demonstrated when the British Empire Exhibition opened at Wembley in 1924 and 1925, when not only were many long distance special trains organised, but a loop line was specially laid in to serve the exhibition, and an intensive service provided from Marylebone. The excellence of railway communications was held to be partly responsible for the excessive attendance at the 1923 Cup Final, when an estimated 120,000 overfilled Wembley Stadium; many others, unable to gain access, returned to the railway station to catch an early train home — but the operators had not envisaged the need for services at this time, and until return trains were

hastily laid on, a great deal of trespassing took place on the line, fortunately without serious casualty.

In addition to trains provided by the LNER, special excursions were often arranged by travel agents, who might charter complete trains; those organised by a Grimsby firm were well known as 'Eason's Specials'.

A tourist train of a kind unique in Britain was introduced in 1933, titled the 'Northern Belle' and offering customers a packaged week-long tour of beauty spots in northern England and Scotland. Described as a 'land cruise' (holiday cruises by sea were beginning to become popular) the luxurious carriages provided first class accommodation in sleeping and restaurant cars, 60 passengers being looked after by 27 staff, the train being made up to as many as 15 coaches. The innovation was a decided success, three or four cruises taking place in June of each year until 1939, the itinerary changing each week.

In 1923, catering whilst on the move was mainly a preserve of the long distance traveller, but over 200 restaurant cars were handed over to the LNER, the practice being to serve a table d'hote meal at a reasonable price — six shillings (30p) for a five course meal. In addition to the Pullman services, the number of restaurant cars of all types had increased to 306 by 1939, but the introduction of the buffet car in 1932 brought a new and more popular form of railway catering. Originally providing little more than drinks and sandwiches, the buffet concept was later extended to a

The weight of the 'Northern Belle' — generally it loaded up to 15 coaches — required it to be double headed or even divided over certain sections of its 'cruise'. Class J39 No 2736 is piloting a Class K2 2-6-0 on the Waverley Route near Hawick, both being stationed at St Margarets shed, Edinburgh. Note the white roofs of the coaches, indicating that they had not long been out of the workshops. *R. B. Haddon*

Above:
A total of 185 Class B1 4-6-0s were delivered in 1947. Built by Darlington Works, the North British Locomotive Co and the Vulcan Foundry, they found their way to all parts of the LNER system. No 1135 was allocated to the Great Eastern section, and, clean and green, is seen at Wrabness on the Harwich branch with a train of British Army of the Rhine personnel returning from leave on 16 July 1947. *C. C. B. Herbert*

range of hot dishes, served on demand. The first buffet cars were incorporated in fast, lightweight trains running between King's Cross and Cambridge, also serving intermediate towns such as Welwyn and Letchworth Garden Cities, and were later introduced to many other short and long distance services, even supplementing the conventional restaurant cars on the 'Flying Scotsman'. As for sleeping cars, the long established first class service to Newcastle, Edinburgh and Aberdeen and other destinations in Scotland was complemented by the introduction of third class sleeping coaches between King's Cross and Aberdeen in 1928. This new service was not introduced without serious consideration being given to its profitability, concern being expressed that business might be diverted from first class. However, after consultation with the LMS, the decision was taken to introduce this new four to a compartment 'lying down' service, for which a supplement

of seven shillings (35p) was charged, to include pillow and blankets.

A little known facility operated by the LNER, a relic of pre-Grouping practice, was the provision of slip coaches in lieu of stopping certain early evening residential trains. Two were provided on the Great Central, at Finmere and Woodford, and two on the Great Eastern, at Mark's Tey and Waltham Cross. The total was the same at Grouping (compared with 43 on the Great Western) as when they were withdrawn in 1936/37 following a rear end collision when a slip coach caught up with its parent train.

Each of the constituent companies provided suburban services of varying extent and intensity, particularly those with London terminals. The Great Eastern had long proclaimed that it ran the most intensive suburban service in the world on the Enfield and Chingford branches, known even in official circles as the 'Jazz Service', a term which originated from the practice of painting different colours on the cantrails to distinguish the three classes. This was operated at a headway of no more than two minutes at the busiest periods, and called for the smartest of operating procedures to ensure that no delays occurred. Great Northern services worked not only into King's Cross, but also through the Metropolitan 'Widened Lines' to Moorgate, providing through trains to the City, paralleled by LMS trains which exploited a long-standing agreement by operating to Broad Street from certain GNR suburban stations — and hauled for many years by small tank engines designed for shunting work. As a result of the urgent need to replace obsolete stock on both the GER and GNR sections, considerable LNER investment went into the provision of new suburban sets for both services, but as the years passed, complaints grew concerning overcrowding and delays. Electrification, considered on a number of previous occasions, was the only answer, but although schemes were prepared, funds were not made available until 1935 when, as discussed in Chapter Fifteen, Government decisions resulted in a radical alternative being imposed. This took the form of a new multi-purpose transport authority, the London Passenger Transport Board, which eventually assumed responsibility for the Epping and Ongar traffic on the Great Eastern, and the High Barnet and Edgware branches of the Great Northern, the LNER being partly compensated under a pooling arrangement.

Great Central services from Marylebone were less intensive, extending to Aylesbury via Amersham, jointly with the Metropolitan, which operated the inner suburban

trains, and via High Wycombe, partly over the joint line also used by Great Western expresses to Birmingham and Birkenhead.

However, the London season ticket holders (contract ticket holders in Scotland) were not by any means the only ones on the LNER, as several provincial cities had their own local networks of short distance services, depending on population density and the extent to which the railway had developed. Tyneside was particularly well provided, the North Tyneside (and later the South Tyneside) services being electrified, whilst Edinburgh Waverley, Glasgow Queen Street, Nottingham Victoria and Aberdeen Joint were examples of stations on which suburban services were centred. Competition from electric trams had already, in pre-Grouping days, eroded some of the railway traffic, but

Above left:

Two Great Northern engines, Class D3 No 4301 and Class J6 No 3538, heading a Skegness to Leicester return excursion at Nottingham Victoria in 1936. Although the 'J6' was built a year after H. N. Gresley had assumed office as Locomotive Superintendent of the GNR, both this and the 'D3' are of Ivatt design, and exhibit the plain but pleasing lines adopted by that engineer. *T. G. Hepburn, Rail Archive Stephenson*

Above right:

Class V2 No 4831 *Durham School* was built at Darlington in May 1939, and is here seen departing from Nottingham Victoria with a Sunday Cleethorpes to Leicester train on 27 August of that year. Early preparations for war are evident in the figure of a Territorial soldier on guard duty with rifle and fixed bayonet, but no uniform.
T. G. Hepburn, Rail Archive Stephenson

Right:
The sight of steam traction is exemplified by this view of a Class B1 4-6-0 leaving Peterborough North with a train for Grimsby. The cold clear air of a winter's afternoon makes the best of the engine's exhaust.
B. Richardson

Above:
A total of 110 2-4-0s with 7ft driving wheels were built for the Great Eastern Railway towards the end of the last century to the design of James Holden, and 60 were rebuilt with a leading bogie and larger boiler as 4-4-0s. No 8030 was one of these, classified 'D13' by the LNER. It is seen here in sparkling condition c1926 whilst stationed at Peterborough East, entering Peterborough North with the empty coaches of a train for March. Note the relatively new Gresley third brake, marshalled between ex-GER coaches.
T. G. Hepburn, Rail Archive Stephenson

other forms of transport grew in competitiveness, particularly within a few miles of the city centres. The Aberdeen suburban service was forced to close in 1937 because of loss of traffic to road competition.

Shorter distance main line services were often of considerable importance, notably from Newcastle to Middlesbrough, and York to Hull and other towns in Yorkshire, whilst main line branches serving as feeders into major junctions were a significant adjunct to longer distance traffic. However, the LNER, like the other railways, was concerned about the losses being made on many small branch lines. There was a great deal of reluctance to acknowledge this, as closures were damaging to the railway's image as a universal carrier, and rural communities often placed reliance on the branch line as their major communications link. But, although some value accrued from such traffic, especially on market days and in connections with main lines, few rural branches were able to show an operating profit. Consequently, experiments were conducted to see what could be done to reduce costs, by minimising staff and reducing services, and by the introduction of the steam rail car as an alternative to the push-and-pull auto-train, or other conventional service. It was found that the steam rail car, labour saving could halve the cost of providing a service on branch lines, but it had a

serious drawback in that it lacked the reserve to cope with additional coaches on market days. Moreover the vehicles exhibited mechanical deficiencies which led to unreliability and a short life; few lasted more than 10 years in service. In the event, several branches were closed over the years; for example, the line from Alnwick to Coldstream was closed in 1930, at an estimated saving of £3,965 per year. In a similar effort to save money, most of the intermediate stations between York and Scarborough were closed in the same year.

Second class having been abolished on most trains before Grouping, the LNER provided the usual first and third class accommodation, except that second class was retained on the Continental boat trains from Liverpool Street and until 1938 for the GER and GNR London inner

Below:
A familiar sight on the Great Northern suburban system throughout the LNER period, Class N2 No 4758 is near New Southgate, hauling a down New Barnet train consisting of two four-coach sets of articulated coaches. Note the somersault signals, off for both the slow and the main lines.
Photomatic, Gresley Society collection

Left:
A halfway stage to electrification: the articulated suburban sets are still in use, but with BR maroon paint peeling from the teak side panels. Brush Type 2 diesel-electric No D5651 hauls a commuter train northwards from Hadley Wood on 31 May 1963.
Brian Haresnape

suburban services, abolition of first class leaving these as third class only in 1941. Maximum fares were regulated by the Railway Rates Tribunal, first class fares being 50% greater than third class. Supplements were chargeable where justified, such as on the Pullmans (eg 12 shillings (60p) first class, King's Cross to Edinburgh) and on the streamline trains. It might have been thought that had the Rates Tribunal agreed, a still higher premium might have been warranted for first class and other special facilities, but such matters were not within the Company's freedom of decision. Tickets could of course be purchased not only at railway booking offices, but at travel agents, of which the firm of Dean & Dawson was owned by the LNER. A form of easy purchase was introduced in 1936 in the form of one-shilling (5p) 'save to travel' stamps, which could be encashed when buying a ticket. Discounted fares were offered for excursion travel; and day, half day and evening fares were available on selected occasions, such as a Sunday trip to Clacton, departing at 11.15am and costing 4s 6d (22½p), and an evening out to Southend to see the illuminations, for two shillings (10p). With the summer timetable of 1933, on the initiative of the LNER, the four main line companies introduced monthly return tickets at

Above:
The 1923 proposals for Great Northern suburban electrification would have led to a 650V dc third rail system. When eventually a 25kV 50Hz overhead system was adopted over 50 years later, the infrastructure was transformed. A Class 313 three-coach set is seen approaching Oakleigh Park with the 3.16pm Welwyn Garden City to Moorgate train on 24 March 1978. *Les Bertram*

Right:
Although the LNER introduced articulated stock for use on many of the Great Eastern suburban services, for several years trains on the Ilford line were made up of coaches which had been converted by mounting two four-wheel coach bodies on 54ft underframes. This up train, seen near Brentwood in 1926, is hauled by Class N7 0-6-2T No 987. *Real Photos*

Right:

Class V1 No 2909 was built at Doncaster in February 1931 and stationed at St Margarets shed, Edinburgh. It is seen at Corstorphine in 1931, about to leave with a train for Edinburgh Waverley. The first 34 engines of this class were all allocated to Scotland, some replacing 'N2' 0-6-2Ts which were sent south.
T. G. Hepburn,
Rail Archive Stephenson

Left:

A North Eastern Area branch train including both clerestory and high roofed coaches, headed by Class G5 0-4-4T No 1886. Over 100 of these capable engines were built to the design of Wilson Worsdell, No 1886 being one of a batch of 20 turned out from Darlington in 1896.
E. R. Wethersett

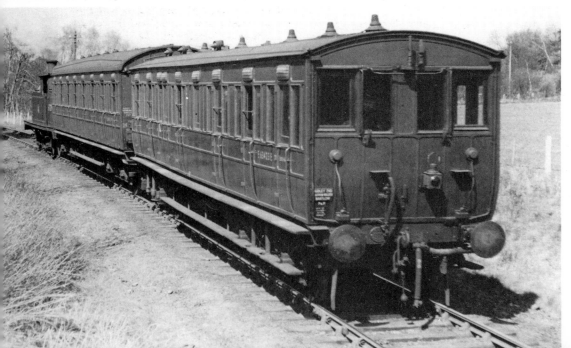

Left:

The push-and-pull auto train was a feature of country branch workings, particularly on Great Eastern and North Eastern services. Several, like this Bartlow to Audley End train, persisted after 1947. The locomotive is an ex-NER Class G5 0-4-4T, LNER No 1882, and was transferred to the Great Eastern section in 1939 for this type of working. The leading coach is believed to be of 1897 origin.
Dr Ian C. Allen

an (old) penny a mile, and this was regarded as so successful in the fine summer of that year that the experiment was made a permanent feature of the fare structure. But the ability to follow an unregulated and imaginative fare policy designed to exploit remunerative travel, whilst capturing more of the casual traffic, was not to be achieved in the lifetime of the LNER.

An important source of non-passenger revenue, although carried by passenger train, was the Post Office mail business. The value of this is illustrated by the signing of a five-year contract with the GPO in 1927, for the sum of £368,000. Provision was made on a number of services for travelling Post Office mail sorters, and for automatic collection and delivery of mail at the trackside.

The coming of war in September 1939 changed the character of LNER longer and middle distance services overnight, the streamline and Pullman trains being withdrawn, as were other high speed and non-stop trains. One of the first special tasks was the well-planned evacuation of children from London and other centres of population to reception areas in the country. The pattern became one of slow trains with frequent stops, sub-ordinated to the needs of the armed forces, for whom a great many special trains were run. By 1945, the 'Flying Scotsman' took around nine hours to reach Edinburgh, and restaurant cars had been taken out of service. Many trains were loaded in excess of 20 coaches, with which timekeeping, even to the decelerated schedules of the day, was impossible, although records exist of prodigious efforts by Gresley Pacifics hauling trains of 800 tons or even more. Restoration of normal services after the war was slow, and fuel shortages in 1947 led to further cuts in services, although of short duration. In the winter timetable of 1945/46 restaurant cars were re-introduced, and a beginning made to restore the prestige services by the reappearance of the 'Yorkshire Pullman' and the 'East Anglian', whilst in 1947 the first named train on the Great Central, the 'Master Cutler', commenced running between Marylebone and Sheffield.

In the summer of 1947 a high speed trial was conducted between King's Cross and Edinburgh in each direction, during which the streamline Pacific *Silver Fox* touched 102mph down Stoke bank; but there was too much yet to do on the permanent way before such speeds could become commonplace once more, and re-invigoration of the East Coast service had to await nationalisation. The non-stop Edinburgh run was re-introduced by the 'Flying Scotsman' in 1948, and later by the 'Capitals Limited' and the 'Elizabethan'. But the streamlined trains were never to be seen again in their original form, and the coaches, after being stored out of use in the war years, were repainted in BR livery and used piecemeal in ordinary express work; changing patterns of passenger needs and altered policies as nationalisation took effect led to the disappearance of the LNER style of passenger train.

Above left:

Cromer Beach station was used by LNER trains to the main station at Cromer High and along the main line to North Walsham, and by the Midland & Great Northern Joint Railway to Melton Constable and beyond, as well as to North Walsham via Mundesley. Three six-wheel coaches owing much to Great Northern design make up this M&GN train, which with only 10 compartments (including first class) was unlikely to carry enough passengers to make the service pay. The locomotive was built at the M&GN works at Melton Constable in 1909 and taken into LNER stock as No 020. Great Northern influence can also be seen in the somersault signals.
T. G. Hepburn, Rail Archive Stephenson

Left:

In 1893 James Holden introduced a 2-4-2T version of his 5ft 8in 2-4-0 tender engine (LNER Class E4) and these locomotives were used for many years on outer suburban work in the London area. Later in their life they were transferred to country districts, and a small number shedded at Cromer. This is No 8083 of Class F3 waiting to leave Cromer Beach with two coaches which although of pre-Grouping design appear to be more modern than those of the M&GN train in the accompanying photo.
T. G. Hepburn, Rail Archive Stephenson

EIGHT

Coaching Stock

The coaches of the constituent companies of the LNER had developed along quite different lines, both in construction and appearance, so that it was not difficult to identify the origin of many pre-Grouping coaches. In addition to the differences in the coaches themselves, at the Grouping the stock of all companies included a substantial proportion of obsolete vehicles, many four- and six-wheeled, with large numbers of gas-lit (and even oil-lit) coaches. Thus, the LNER not only had the need to develop and build new standard coaches for its more important services, but was faced with the task of replacing large numbers of time expired stock — work, which even by the end of its 25-year existence, it had been unable to complete. Altogether some 21,000 vehicles classified as coaching stock, including miscellaneous vehicles such as horse boxes and milk vans, passed into LNER ownership, fewer than 4,000 being fitted with electric lighting. By the end of 1947, some 11,772 new vehicles had been brought into service, of which a few were to pre-Grouping designs, but otherwise all were built to LNER standard diagrams; over 16,000 had been withdrawn, still leaving a quarter of pre-Grouping stock in service.

The Great Northern had followed a progressive and coherent policy in coach design, the Victorian fixed wheelbase coaches with flattish roof contour being supplanted at the end of the 19th century by bow-ended bogie coaches with teak panelling, a stylish clerestory roof and a rather florid interior decor, reflective of the fashions of the period. On the retirement of E. F. Howlden as Carriage and Wagon Superintendent in 1905, his successor was H. N. Gresley, who made his mark soon after his appointment by the introduction of a high pitched elliptical roof with rounded ends, which although by later standards was regarded as an unnecessarily expensive form of construction, became a symbol of Gresley's future corridor designs. The elliptical roof also found favour with the North Eastern for its final batches of both corridor and non-corridor stock; strangely for such a major railway, the NER did not build a great many corridor coaches for its own internal services, which were often covered by comfortable non-corridor stock, some provided with toilets.

The Great Central had built some impressive coaches for its principal services, matching the locomotive style of J. G. Robinson; with vertical matchboarding below the waist, and high, well-rounded roofs, they made the most of a generous load gauge. The last series of GCR coaches featured a corrugated anti-overriding device of cast iron construction fitted to the coach ends, which added materially to the weight of the coach, but which fortunately was never put to the test in a collision, apart from a minor incident at Marylebone in 1923. In contrast, load gauge restrictions and lower permanent way standards on the Great Eastern precluded that line from building other than relatively lightweight coaches of panelled construction, a number of the non-corridor coaches achieving some distinction with clerestory roofs. Of the Scottish companies, the North British was noted for its introduction in 1919 of six all-steel dining cars of great weight, but in general the North British coaching stock, as well as that of the Great North of Scotland Railway, was undistinguished, and by 1923 a large proportion was obsolete.

In operating the through King's Cross to Edinburgh services, over the systems of three railways, agreement had been reached that the carriages would be jointly owned and designated 'East Coast Joint Stock' (ECJS), and would follow Doncaster practice. Similar arrangements applied to the coaches owned by the Great Northern and North Eastern for through services between King's Cross and Newcastle. Thus the Howlden, and later the Gresley, outlines became familiar to travellers not only south, but also north of York. When Gresley was promoted to be Locomotive Engineer of the Great Northern in 1911 he appointed Edward Thompson of the North Eastern as his Carriage and Wagon Superintendent, but no alteration to Gresley lineaments ensued, Gresley continuing to be responsible for design, and maintaining as close an interest in his coaches as in his engines.

The Great Northern had introduced a number of innovations in coach design, and these were carried through into LNER practice. An example of Gresley's ingenuity was seen in his conversion of a number of Howlden's older fixed wheelbase carriages into bogie stock, by applying a system of articulation (first patented 60 years before) such that one bogie carried the ends of two adjoining coaches. This made possible considerable savings in weight and expense, especially when applied to multi-coach units, but a weakness of the system was that if one coach of an articulated set developed a defect the entire set had to be withdrawn from service. Whilst the system was to be applied fairly widely on the Great Northern and later on the LNER, particularly to non-corridor stock, it did not find great favour elsewhere,

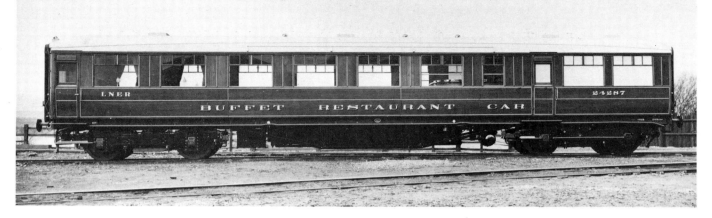

Above:

A Gresley elliptical-roofed coach, with teak panelling, beading and lining, No 24287 was one of two buffet restaurant cars built in 1939 at Dukinfield for working on the York to Swindon section of the through service between Penzance and Aberdeen. Offering snacks or a full meal service, No 24287 had an end kitchen with electric catering facilities, and two saloons seating 30 people. Renumbered 9195, it was refurbished by British Rail and continued to work in everyday service until the late 1960s. *Author's collection*

Below:

Sixty of the new green and cream coaches were built for the Southern Area in 1933. The buffet cars were constructed at York, the brake thirds at Doncaster, and the open thirds by contractors. The first two (shown here) were an articulated pair, Nos 45001 and 45002, from the Birmingham Carriage & Wagon Co. Further sets of tourist stock were subsequently built for work elsewhere on the LNER system. *IAL*

Bottom:

No 1905 was a steel-panelled four-compartment brake built at York at the end of 1947; finished in replica teak paint, without lining and lettering, it is here presumably awaiting a decision by the new owners. Note the curved corners to the windows — earlier steel stock had square corners which were prone to rusting. *IAL*

apart from a few examples on the Great Western and the LMS; possible anxieties about failures in service overrode demonstrated savings. Anyway, by revitalising old coaches in this way Gresley was able to create good riding stock at a minimum of expense. The first twin set was converted from a pair of six-wheelers in 1907, and others followed until there were well over 100 twin, triple and quadruple sets. New articulated carriages appeared in 1911, when an eight-coach train consisting of four twin sets was constructed for London suburban work. These, and others similar, were rebuilt after World War 1 into quadruple units, becoming the predecessors of the trains built for the King's Cross suburban services after the Grouping, and known in BR days as 'quad-arts', lasting until 1966.

Other important features of coach design introduced by the Great Northern and originating in America, were the Pullman type of vestibule connection of rectangular section, providing a more spacious passageway than the round top standard type, and the buckeye coupler, first employed in 1897. The buckeye coupler utilised the principle of two hands grasped together in a firm grip, and was of material assistance in keeping a train upright and preventing telescoping in the event of a derailment, in articulated stock the same effect was obtained by Gresley's twin coupler device.

The introduction of electric lighting, with the advantage not only of safety and convenience but also of through control, so that the lights in a train could be switched on or off by the guard, aroused Gresley's mind to the possibility of using electricity for cooking purposes in kitchen cars, so removing gas entirely and eradicating a potential fire hazard. He studied the development of electric catering appliances, even to the extent of taking part in discussions at the Institution of Electrical Engineers when papers on the subject were presented. His first practical application was in 1921, in a five-car articulated set — itself an innovation in that it constituted the first extensive application of that principle to contemporary express coaches, although a number of articulated corridor pairs had been built, the earliest in 1915. This quintuple set was built for the Leeds service, and being to the maximum of the GNR load gauge was unable to visit other parts of the system; it remained on this work until it was withdrawn in 1953, following damage sustained in a collision.

A feature of Gresley's later Great Northern coaches, contributing not only to their appearance but also to their riding qualities, was the double bolster bogie, invented by Alex Moulton and introduced by Gresley in 1908. With its distinctive pressed steel sides, this type of bogie featured an extra stage of cushioning against shock, although being heavier, more difficult to maintain and more expensive than conventional types; after some years a heavy duty variation was evolved for carrying the heaviest coaches and for articulation purposes, when each bogie was in effect carrying the weight of two half-coaches. Later thoughts intervened in the case of suburban sets, when it was realised that the extra cost of the double bolster was unwarranted for comparatively short journeys, and so a heavy duty single bolster bogie was developed for this purpose, and for use under luggage vans. A still heavier version, designed to carry 24 tons, was introduced for the articulated stock of the 'Coronation' train.

H. N. Gresley's appointment as Chief Mechanical Engineer of the LNER led to the appearance of his style of coaching stock in all parts of the system, but of course it was many years before a majority of trains were made up of standard pattern coaches. Nevertheless, an early decision was taken to continue the style of varnished teak panelling first introduced by the Great Northern in 1850, or, where teak had not been used before, to repaint coaches in 'teak paint'. The Great Central, Great Eastern and Hull & Barnsley had also adopted varnished teak, so no obvious changes took place to their coaches, but the North Eastern and North British had applied different shades of dark red, and the Great North of Scotland dark red with white upper panels, so coaches from these companies were turned out in teak colour as they passed through the shops. A subtle change in lining out took place on Great Northern coaches, primrose yellow edged with red taking the place of the original blue edging. The finish of a Gresley teak panelled coach was extremely complex, requiring no fewer than 18 stages of cleaning, varnishing and rubbing down, and taking at least three weeks to complete. Undoubtedly a work of art when turned out new from the paint shop, the varnished teak retained its appearance for a considerable period, until it became cracked through age, when it tended to darken. The raised beading covering the joints in the panelling attracted soot and no doubt for this reason suburban coaches did not receive the lining out accorded to corridor stock. Roofs were finished with white lead paint, but the smart effect of this was very soon lost through blackening by soot. When steel panelled coaches were introduced, every effort was made to paint these to resemble teak, and not only was the graining faithfully rendered, but facsimile beading, complete with lining, was added. When, in BR days, maroon and cream was adopted as the standard livery, it was discovered that varnished teak did not take kindly to modern spray painting methods, a mangy appearance resulting after repainted stock had been in service for a while. Teak however was not the only livery used by the LNER; special finishes were accorded the Tyneside electric trains, the steam railcars, special coaches for tourist trains, and in particular the streamline expresses.

As well as the adoption of a uniform livery, an early review of coaching standards led to a number of dimensional and other decisions being taken. Corridor stock was to be of a uniform underframe length of 60ft (61ft 6in over the buffers), with bow ended vestibules, Pullman corridor connections and buckeye couplers, and non-corridor coaches would be 51ft over the body, with screw couplings. There were some exceptions to these general rules; most articulated carriages were of a non-standard length, and early construction for the Great Eastern section included shorter corridor coaches because of sharp curves in certain Liverpool Street platform roads, and to accommodate more easily the assembling of trains with portions for more than one destination. Boat train sets were of standard 60ft length. As to the width of coaches, pending a decision on a standard load gauge for the group as a whole, corridor stock was to be 8ft 9in at the waist, with door handles projecting a further 1½in at each side, whilst articulated suburban stock — unlikely to move very far from its usual habitat — was allowed 9ft 3in in width. A committee to recommend a standard load gauge was set up as early as August 1922, but because of the complexity of the subject was unable to report until the end of 1925. Gresley then acted swiftly, pointing out that for only a small amount of money expended at half a dozen locations in Scotland and the North East, coaches could be built marginally wider. This would be useful in that additional space would be made available in restaurant and sleeping cars (where the width would be 9ft 3in, with recessed door handles) and in third class open carriages (enabling two persons to be seated abreast on each side of the central gangway). The maximum height of all coaching vehicles would be 12ft 10in.

One important feature could not be resolved at once: the question of brakes. A decision in principle was taken to standardise on the automatic vacuum brake, but there was no possibility of this becoming effective for many years, as the Westinghouse compressed air system had been adopted by the GER, the NER, the NBR and the Great North of Scotland. So, new stock allocated to these parts of the system would have to be fitted with the Westinghouse brake or, if there was the prospect of wider use, then the coaches would be dual fitted. As older Westinghouse stock was withdrawn, a gradual changeover to the vacuum system took place, the Westinghouse pumps on loco-motives being replaced by vacuum ejectors. The Great Eastern suburban services continued to be operated by Westinghouse fitted stock, it being contended that the slower application and release time of the vacuum brake would make the intensive service impossible to operate.

In the first year after the formation of the LNER, high hopes were entertained that rapid progress would be made in modernisation of the rolling stock of the new company, and the first carriage building programme, approved in 1923, identified three priorities: new stock for the main King's Cross to Edinburgh services; new sleeping cars; and new trains for the Great Eastern and Great Northern suburban services. (It was also said that where LNER trains alternated with those of another company, the LNER coaches must 'stand comparison with those of the other company'.) Four complete trains were built for the East Coast service, comprising 56 vehicles, and 140 other corridor coaches were included for other services, together with 124 non-corridor types. Triplet articulated restaurant car sets were introduced, five sets being included in the programme, comprising first and third class dining cars flanking a central kitchen car; eight other restaurant cars were also to be built. The current stock of sleeping cars was reported to be 48, most of which had clerestory roofs; complaints were being received about their lack of comfort, and the West Coast pattern was said to be superior to that of the East Coast. So, authority was given for the oldest to be withdrawn and 10 new cars to be built. Four of these would be articulated in twin units, so extending this system to sleeping cars. It was also realised that the LNER owned *two* royal trains; that of the General Eastern was converted for general use, and the East Coast train was renovated at a cost of £6,750.

As for the inner London suburban services, these were still largely operated by close coupled four-wheeled vehicles, no fewer than 1,311 being in use, all gas lit. An early decision was taken to withdraw half of these and replace them by new articulated sets, grouped in triple for the Great Northern and quintuple for the Great Eastern sections. The brake end coaches were to be convertible to electric working, as at that time it was thought likely that an early start would be made on suburban electrification. The choice of triple sets for the GNR seems curious in view of the fact that 20 trains of quadruple stock were already in service; in the event, although 21 sets were authorised, this part of the programme was later cancelled and quadruple sets were substituted the following year. All these coaches were constructed by contractors, but a final batch of quadruple sets, of different composition from those built for the Great Northern section, were turned out from York in 1929 for the Hertford East service.

The pace of construction slackened in the later 1920s, but numbers of coaches continued to be built, including complete new trains for service between Liverpool Street and Parkeston Quay, and for the Great Central section. Clerestory-roofed ECJS coaches replaced by new stock were re-allocated elsewhere, and lightweight Great Eastern coaches found a new home on the Great North of Scotland. The detail design of new carriages was frequently varied, and on occasion major alterations took place. Many types of accommodation were built on the standard underframes, depending upon the use to which each coach was to be put. The most common arrangement was the compartment third, but other third class coaches were built in an open format. All-first and first/third composite were turned out as needed, as were bogie brake vans, some fitted for the conveyance of racing pigeons. Since many long distance trains had through portions which were detached or added at intermediate stations, but which had to be self-contained with first, third, luggage and brake compartments, care had to be exercised to match the accommodation to the demand. Consequently, depending upon the amount of baggage to be conveyed — and hence the size of the luggage compartment — brake composites would have three, four, five or six third-class compartments, or in some cases both first and third, as well as accommodation for luggage and the guard. Non-corridor stock comprised fewer varieties, being entirely compartment stock, but one fairly common composite design provided lavatory facilities.

An important advance in coach design took place in 1930, when a new format for compartment stock began to appear, in which vestibules with doors were provided at each end of the coach, replacing individual outside doors

Above:
The interior of a first class coach for the 'Coronation' train, built at Doncaster in 1937. Note the individual swivelling armchairs and the cutaway tables, meals being served at every seat. The anodised aluminium door frames gave a vista along the two coaches of an articulated pair and fresh air and heating was provided by a pressure ventilated system. The windows were double glazed. *IAL*

to the compartments. This was not only a move towards greater safety, but also enabled the compartments to be fitted with large picture windows; this was at the price of one less compartment per coach. An interesting move at this time was a competition for the public, seeking designs for compartment interiors, a first prize of £25 being offered.

In the early days of railways a passenger was not expected to smoke, other than in compartments specially designated as 'Smoking', which were first seen in 1869. With the increase in cigarette smoking it became necessary to protect the position of the non-smoker, and from 1931 certain compartments bore the label 'Smoking Prohibited'. Another special category was 'Ladies Only', generally located next to the guard's compartment. In those London suburban trains in which the first class compartments were reclassified as third, this was appreciated by the experienced commuter of the time as the erstwhile first class compartments possessed spring interior cushioning, which was a great improvement on the hard seats of the original second and third classes.

New triplet restaurant car sets were provided for the non-stop 'Flying Scotsman' in 1928, in which the interior decor was modelled by Sir Charles Allom on Louis XIV

lines, whilst a cocktail bar was included in the make-up of the train in 1932. This was followed by the introduction of buffet cars, originally converted from old GNR carriages, which made their appearance of the new, faster trains from King's Cross to Cambridge. The buffet car concept was well received and was extended, new cars being built with facilities for electric cooking. In continuation of his desire to avoid the use of gas on moving trains, Gresley continued to make progress in the electrification of ancillary services, as for example water heating in sleeping cars, as well as the provision of refrigerators, fish fryers and other specialised appliances in kitchen cars, such that generators of up to 20kW capacity were provided. To reduce the need for electricity whilst on the move, facilities were installed at several terminals and layover points at which batteries could be charged and food pre-cooked whilst the coaches were awaiting duty. Experiments were conducted to see if the heaviest loads, ie ovens, could be supplied with an alternative form of fuel, and eventually an anthracite fired system was decided upon. In a comparative statement prepared in 1928 it was stated that the cost of cooking a meal in a kitchen car by electricity was 4d (1.7p), but only 2.8d (1.2p) by gas. However, the price of gas would tend to rise as the consumption of gas for lighting diminished, whilst electricity was safer and enabled cooking to be carried out in better conditions with less smell.

In order to obtain experience with steel panelled coaches as an alternative to teak, two contracts were placed in 1927 for the construction of 34 open thirds and 26 brake vans, generally similar to the equivalent teak panelled coaches. The builders were the Metropolitan Carriage & Wagon Co and Cammell Laird respectively, as the LNER workshops at

that time were equipped only to build timber coaches. Disadvantages of steel construction were the likelihood of corrosion (particularly at window edges), additional weight, a higher noise level, and less flexibility in carriage design since, to obtain the full benefits of large steel plates, compartments with external doors had to be avoided. On the other hand it was considered that longer service life might be obtained, despite the fact that coaching stock tended to become obsolete before it wore out. No further steel coaches were built until 1935, but in 1932 an experimental coach employing cast aluminium panels bolted to steel framing was constructed at Dukinfield. This was an otherwise conventional 51ft composite which took its turn in GER section outer suburban services and which presumably was reasonably successful as it continued in this duty for many years, but the experiment was not repeated.

Important variations in external appearance, in which the traditional varnished teak gave to a coloured livery, were introduced in 1933, although, the principle had been first applied when the steam railcars were introduced for branch line service. The first of these were painted teak, but a more cheerful livery of green lower panels, and cream above the waist, was soon adopted, whilst the cars were personalised by giving them the names of old-time stage-coaches. The new main line coaches of 1933 were specifically designed for excursion working in place of the antiquated stock otherwise frequently used on these services; indeed, authorisation for the first batch was in replacement of a number of old Great Northern four-wheeled coaches. Painted in the distinctive green and cream, each train consisted of 12 coaches, with all third class accommodation

and two buffet cars per train. To minimise the cost, construction was of ¼in plywood panels on teak framing, with straight ends to the roofs, and bucket seats and 'contemporary' decor. These sets proved popular and offered better accommodation than the road motor coaches of the day. Altogether, five trains were constructed for the Great Northern section, two for the North Eastern Area, and three for southern Scotland.

The stock of the 'Silver Jubilee' was of steel panelled sides on teak framing, covered with silver grey rexine; the coaches were articulated in pairs or triplets, and other new features included pressure ventilation and double glazing. To maintain the 'streamline' appearance, underframe fairings were fitted between the bogies, whilst special attention was paid to minimising noise. When the later streamline trains were authorised, experience with the 'Silver Jubilee' sets was put to good use, particularly in the provision of still further improved sound insulation and in the internal decor. A basic alteration in the layout of the coaches was the change from side corridor to centre gangway, but with seating bays partitioned to remove the impression of a wholly open coach. Two kitchen cars were provided, meals being served to passengers at their seats. The 'Coronation' and the 'West Riding Limited' trains were similar, both consisting of four articulated twins, whilst the 'Coronation' had the added attraction of a beaver-tailed observation saloon in the summer months. This matched the wedge-shaped profile of the locomotive but had the disadvantage of having to be turned independently of the train at the end of each journey. These trains, together with a further set built as a spare, were painted dark Garter blue below the waist and light Marlborough blue above.

The speeding up of several important services in the later 1930s did not however result in any extension of the special finishes, and when the 'East Anglian' was introduced in the winter timetable of 1937/38, new teak panelled coaches were built for it. The new 'Flying Scotsman' stock introduced in the summer of 1938 also consisted of teak coaches, but with several refinements following experience with the streamline trains. Money for the 14-coach 'Flying Scotsman' sets had come from the Government 'New Works' programme, under which £½ million was spent on carriages, twice as much as on locomotives. In addition to new construction, the position of the 2,055 gas-lit coaches still running in 1935 was reviewed; it was concluded that there was no point in spending money on those built more than 25 years before, but £152,000 was set aside to convert the remaining 593 coaches, which included a number of bogie carriages still running in express trains.

New construction tailed off rapidly during the war, but steel panelled coaches to Gresley's design were still being turned out in 1943, the last being non-corridor twin articulated sets. No coaching stock at all was built in 1944, but the following year two prototypes appeared which broke away from the Gresley style of elliptical roof by substituting a flat longitudinal profile whilst retaining the bow ends of the 1933 excursion stock. A new, simpler outline was produced, an individual touch being provided by oval windows to the toilets, and whilst the painted and grained teak finish was retained the simulated beading and lining was omitted. In an endeavour to improve passenger movement at stations, compartments were grouped in twos and threes, with short transverse corridors leading to the external doors; windows were larger, but toilets were smaller. Some adverse comment was heard about the utilitarian decor, but this was characteristic of the period. More justified was the criticism of the squared corners of the windows, earlier experience having demonstrated that these would lead to severe corrosion; later, the window corners were given a radius to prevent ingress of water.

Construction of LNER designed coaches continued until 1953, the last to be turned out being for the London, Tilbury & Southend line, this erstwhile LMS suburban extension having become part of British Railways' Eastern Region. However, Gresley's influence on the coaching scene could be discerned for many years yet, particularly when a shortage of buffet cars arose; because of their solid construction, many of his buffet cars underwent a thorough refurbishment, leading to a new lease of life on several important services. Moreover, the Gresley type of bogie was seen on the electric stock of the Southend services, as well as on brake tenders constructed to assist certain diesel classes in braking heavy freight trains. Finally, many Gresley and Thompson brake vans could still be seen in the 1970s, painted rail blue.

In addition to major developments in coaching design, several interesting innovations were made from time to time in efforts to meet passenger needs and to explore possibilities for the future. Amongst these were a hairdressing saloon and a ladies' retiring room on the 'Flying Scotsman' in 1927. Headphones were provided for radio reception for a period of three years, and a pioneer form of television was tried unsuccessfully in 1932. Two coaches were converted into back-projection cinema cars in 1935; featuring news films, this service lasted until the outbreak of war.

When in 1937 the LMS and LNER jointly decided to build a locomotive testing station, it was also agreed that a new dynamometer car would be provided to replace the two older coaches then in use, the LNER coach having been built by the North Eastern as far back as 1906. This new car was designed on a standard 60ft underframe, and construction was put in hand at Doncaster. It became a casualty of the fire which occurred in the works in 1940, and its replacement was not completed until 1951; this meant that when the important BR comparative locomotive trials took place in 1948, reliance had to be placed on then elderly dynamometer cars and their equipment, dating from before the Grouping.

Although Gresley had been appointed to the GNR as Carriage and Wagon Superintendent, when he became Locomotive Engineer he retained his personal supervision of the coaching stock, and this arrangement continued throughout his period as CME of the LNER. For most of this period his Assistant, Oliver Bulleid, worked on special projects, whilst Frank Day and Norman Newsome acted as technical assistants, particularly for design studies of new coaches. At no time did the LNER have an officer specifically designated as Carriage and Wagon Superintendent.

As a postscript to this chapter, it is of interest to observe that almost all LNER coaches were renumbered at least once, and some suffered up to half a dozen alterations to their identification. Each constituent company had its own series, in which coaches were numbered without great regard for order. Further, ECJS and the joint GNR/NER stock were numbered in their own series, new vehicles either taking the lowest vacant number or, in the case of an increase in the total of coaches, the next number on. The first LNER renumbering scheme was introduced soon after Gresley assumed office, and added a suffix to the pre-Grouping number, viz: J for ECJS, Y (denoting York) for NER, N for GNR, E for GER, C for GCR, B for NBR, and S for the Great North of Scotland. A revised scheme was adopted in 1925, a variation of that used for locomotives, in which the original number was retained but prefixed by a digit representing the operating section. East Coast stock was prefixed by 1, North Eastern by 2, North British by 3, Great Northern by 4, Great Central by 5, Great Eastern 6 and GNofS by 7. New stock was given a vacant number in the appropriate series, and when carriages were transferred they were generally renumbered in the series of the receiving section. Little attempt was made to group coaches by type, but under Edward Thomson the renumbering of post-Grouping stock was undertaken in 1946, coaches being renumbered in groups according to type.

NINE

Freight Services

Two-thirds of LNER revenue accrued from freight business — twice as much as from passengers. Moreover, long term contracts ensured a regularity of income not always available from passenger business, apart from season ticket holders usually travelling in peak hours. A 40-wagon fish train rattling its way south brought more joy to a traffic manager's heart than a partly filled passenger express.

Measured in terms of tonnage, the most important class of freight traffic was coal for home consumption and export, but substantial business was also done in moving other minerals, as well as livestock, fish, fresh meat from Scotland, chilled and frozen meat from overseas, grain and seasonal crops of vegetables and fruit, as well as wool, chemicals, sawn wood and pit props, and a variety of manufactured products from factories or docks to customers everywhere. Metal products were particularly important, with iron ore, coal and limestone for primary iron and steel production being transported to foundry and blast furnace, and cast, rolled or fabricated products moved out. Although road competition was to grow increasingly severe, the limited capability of road transport for other than modest sized loads, conveyed over short distances, meant that most of which could not be manhandled went by rail. Sometimes this required the provision of special

wagons, and occasionally, when out-of-gauge loads were transported, needed complete occupation of the line, and even temporary alterations to lineside structures.

Output from Britain's coalfields in 1923 amounted to 273 million tons, over a third being exported; of the total, the LNER moved 102 million tons, each of the constituent companies except the Great Eastern and the Great North of Scotland serving important coalfields. The Great Northern handled much of the coal produced in south Yorkshire, either by direct connections of its own, or by lines in which it had a joint interest; it also had a substantial trade with pits in the east Midlands, for which there was competition between the GNR, the Great Central and the Midland. Both the GNR and the GCR ran long coal trains southward to London, and the Great Central also moved large quantities of coal westward across the Pennines to Lancashire, and eastward to the port of Immingham. The North Eastern handled the bulk of coal movements from

Below:
'K3' No 156 was one of 60 of its class built at Darlington in 1924/5 with the early version of the standard 4,200gal tender, with stepped out copings. *Real Photos*

Right:

New England Class V2 No 879 (originally No 4850), one of only 25 of the class built at Doncaster, is heading a down fitted goods which it will take as far as Peterborough. The train is emerging from Welwyn South Tunnel on the two track bottleneck through the tunnels and over the Welwyn Viaduct c1947. *F. R. Hebron*

Below right:

Class J39 No 4767 (1946 renumbering), shedded at Stratford, is heading a train of international stock off the Harwich ferry, at Mistley, Essex. This engine, previously No 2714, was built at Darlington in 1928 and was one of a batch fitted with the Westinghouse brake, specially for Great Eastern duties. *G. R. Mortimer*

Below:

Another 'J39', No 4810 (orignally No 2784), blowing off whilst held at signals at London Road station, Manchester, watched by a group of youthful train spotters — not in jeans, but wearing sports jackets, grey flannel trousers and school caps. Where are they now, one wonders? *W. R. P. Lees*

the Northumberland and Durham coalfields, except that certain colliery companies possessed their own rail tracks, engines and wagons, conveying their coal direct from pits to staiths independently of the NER. Also, the North Eastern had recently merged with the Hull & Barnsley, which brought coal from south and west Yorkshire to Hull for export. Coal was also moved by the North British from the Fife coalfield to the docks at Methil and Aberdeen. Not all coal loaded on to ships went to overseas destinations, as there was a good deal of competitive coastwise shipping, taking not only coal but general cargo at better rates than the railway could offer. In 1927 it was reported that sailings from Newcastle to London were being increased from two to three a week; there was also a twice weekly service from Leith to the London docks.

The general pattern of freight business changed over the years, with coal losing its dominant position as export markets were lost, notably following the miners' strike of 1926. Even so, by 1930 LNER coal traffic had recovered to 88 million tons; but by 1947 had fallen again to 63 million tons. Losses in the mineral field were partly compensated for by an increase in agricultural products resulting from the burgeoning fruit and vegetable business, particularly in East Anglia where the newly introduced sugar beet made a welcome, though seasonal, addition to traffic. Sugar beet was not confined to the eastern counties, and two factories in Yorkshire, and one in Scotland, were also served by the LNER. Grain, both home grown and imported, provided valuable agricultural traffic, so much so that the Company ran its own sack hire business. New, high volume, block loads arose as a result of new industries being established, such as cement making in several locations; bauxite for the aluminium refinery at Fort William, opened in 1928; and

iron ore from High Dyke, near Grantham, conveyed to the steel works near Scunthorpe and farther afield, even to Clydeside, in wartime.

An important factor in new freight business was the establishment of the Central Electricity Board in 1926, which gave a major impetus to the generation and transmission of electricity on a national scale. New power stations and grid lines were constructed, for which electric machinery and transformers were transported from such firms as Metropolitan Vickers in Trafford Park, Manchester, and Parsons, on Tyneside. Power stations and gas works on the Essex bank of the Thames meant new coal hauls southwards from March, introducing a new dimension to the traffic of the erstwhile Great Eastern. However, a good deal of the coal was brought in by sea from ports on the northeast coast, although of course the North Eastern Area received the benefit of most of the hauls from the pits to the staiths.

Fish was another valuable source of revenue, the LNER moving the greater part of the home waters catch. Overnight delivery was essential, and fast trains from Aberdeen, Hull, Grimsby and other ports ran southwards on the East Coast main line. Seasonal fish traffic sometimes generated additional passenger journeys, as when Scottish fisher girls travelled to Yarmouth and Lowestoft to process the herring catch. Other seasonal traffic occurred at fruit picking time, and in the summer in support of agricultural shows, particularly the Royal Show, involving complex arrangements compressed into a short time as animals, fodder, farm machinery, workers and visitors were transported to and from the show sites.

Exploitation of the benefits of the container marked another new development in the techniques of freight

Left:
Class P1 No 2393, one of two booster-fitted Mikados, working an up coal train at Sandy. The engine is approaching the junction of the up goods line with the up fast, where most coal trains were held until the road was clear for them to pass through the bottleneck through the station. The LMS line from Cambridge to Bletchley is seen on the extreme right, climbing to cross the East Coast main line.
National Railway Museum, Crown Copyright Reserved (NRM)

65

movement. This had been in use on a small scale for many years, but the LMS began to promote the merits of containerisation from about 1928, and the LNER was not slow to follow. By the outbreak of war in 1939, this predecessor of latter-day liner trains was forming an increasing proportion of freight loadings, not only speeding deliveries but also markedly reducing losses from transit damage and pilfering. (Losses from these causes amounted to about ½% to 1% of revenue during the 1920s, and pilferage increased again during the war, goods stolen whilst in transit being a major source of supply to the black market.) In 1926, instructions were issued that more open wagons should be protected by tarpaulin, and that additional closed vans should be built, to lessen the amount of claims.

Business generally deteriorated in the depression years, and picked up again in the 1930s, particularly as additional traffic was generated by increased armaments production. All through the LNER period, however, the increasingly competitive ability of the road hauliers — even having regard to the size of load and distance carried — eroded business which had one time been regarded as uniquely that of the railway, and prevented the Company from holding on to, let alone increasing, its share of a growing market in freight transport generally. This was particularly the case in shorter distance traffic, as for example the carriage of livestock from farm to local market. (Although, early in the LNER period, it was said that an increase had been noted in the transport of sheep, as the number of motor cars on rural roads made it hazardous to walk the

sheep to market.) No fewer than 7½ million animals were carried in 1923, a figure which had halved by 1939. Some relief from the most extreme road competition resulted from the Salter conference of 1932, between the general managers of the four main line railways and representatives of road transport interests. This led to the Road & Rail Traffic Act of 1933, which introduced a road vehicle licensing scheme; this was welcomed by the road interests as it sustained the position of those already well established whilst making it difficult for the smaller operator to move in further. For the railways, it did nothing to recover business

Above:
Raven Class Q6 No 2277 near Plawsworth with a down train of chaldron style hopper wagons loaded with coal, on 28 August 1937. A total of 120 of this useful class were built, between 1913 and 1921, the last 50 coming from Armstrong Whitworth & Co of Newcastle. A Darlington-built example, No 2238, has been preserved and may be seen on the North Yorkshire Moors Railway.
James C. Clark/Lens of Sutton

Left:
Few freight locomotives were kept in a clean external condition in the 1930s, and no identification can be discerned on this Robinson Class Q4 passing through Nottingham Victoria c1930 with a down train of coal empties. Eighty-nine of this class of 0-8-0 were built, and were known as 'Tinies', but they were overshadowed by the more powerful Class O4 2-8-0s. *T. G. Hepburn, Rail Archive Stephenson*

Right:
The long footbridge at Hornsey station gives an excellent vantage point to observe this coal train entering Ferme Park yard, Hornsey, at the end of its journey from New England on a murky winter's day c1930. *IAL*

already lost, nor did it curb the trend for firms to establish their own road transport departments. The LNER strongly opposed the granting of further licenses, whenever these were applied for.

As the years passed, the tendency grew for freight trains to run faster, in response to the challenge of the road transport operator, to give a better service to the customer, and to reduce line occupation. Faster trains called for improved braking, and the number of trains fully or partly fitted with automatic brakes increased, in number and loading, as well as in speed. More powerful locomotives were provided, the first of which was named *Green Arrow*, to publicise a scheme for registered delivery of small consignments. (A similar scheme for packages by passenger train was known as the 'Blue Arrow' service; a cash on delivery service was also offered.) Timetables were published for certain trains, which became well known to customers, who could rely on the advertised arrival times, and indeed, a network of express goods trains was timed to enable a high proportion of consignments to the larger centres to be delivered on the morning after despatch. Notable among these was the afternoon 'Scotch Goods' which in the late 1930s left King's Cross at 3.35pm; this and other similar trains had point-to-point speeds approaching

Left:
An up freight train slowly crossing Manningtree South Viaduct, hauled by an ex-WD Class O7 2-8-0 in the bitterly cold winter of 1947/48. The following easterly wind is causing the exhaust to rise vertically in the air.
G. R. Mortimer

Left:
The railway is dwarfed by the surrounding mountainside along the Mallaig extension of the West Highland line. A down goods is making its way between Glenfinnan and Lochailort on 20 August 1947, hauled by one of the 'K2' class 2-6-0s transferred from the Great Northern section several years before.
B. V. Franey

Above:
The early years of Nationalisation did not see a great change in many services. Class O2 No 63952 (originally numbered 2959) is passing through Spalding with an up freight as late as 1960. Built at Doncaster in 1932 for the Whitemoor to Temple Mills coal traffic, the engine was withdrawn in 1961. *John C. Baker*

Right:
On 17 April 1942 a train of iron ore wagons is approaching Harrogate station, possibly en route from Teesside to Manchester. The engines are Class A8 No 1502, the Starbeck pilot at the time, and Class J39 No 1496. *M. N. Clay, Rail Archive Stephenson*

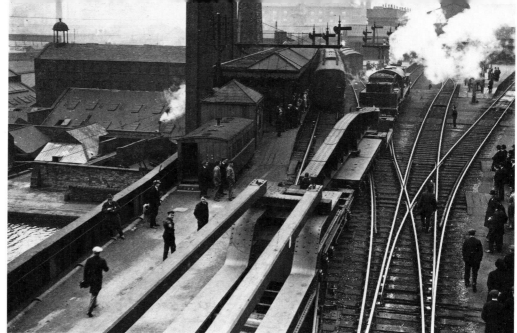

50mph, whilst the overnight up Aberdeen fish train at one time had certain sectional timings faster than the pre-1932 'Flying Scotsman'. Such speeds must have placed severe stress on the four-wheeled vans which made up the trains. Other important fast goods trains ran at half-hourly intervals in the late evening from King's Cross to Manchester, Liverpool, Leeds and Nottingham, and there were corresponding services in the up direction; it is worthy of note that the LNER was able to obtain, and hold, traffic from Luton to the West Riding and Manchester, via Hatfield, in competition with the more direct LMS route. At the more mundane level of coal movement, in a further endeavour to reduce delays on the Great Northern main line, from 1932 two coal trains a day ran between the New England yard at Peterborough to Ferme Park, Hornsey, loaded to 56 wagons only but running to timings half that of the normal 80-wagon trains.

The years just before, and during, World War 2, were of course abnormal, not least in the manner and volume of freight carried. Increase in coal and steel haulage was supplemented by the transport of armaments, whilst a massive volume of building materials — slag, rubble from bombed houses, cement and tarmac in particular — needed urgent delivery as the building of military airfields got under way, often causing the cancellation of less vital services. The war affected LNER freight business in other important ways. Road transport was curtailed as a result of petrol rationing, so that much traffic was thrown back on to the railway, although the volume of non-essential goods declined sharply. Also, the reduction in coastwise shipping diverted coal from ship to rail, with a reversion to normal as the war ended. As an example of the special activities needed in support of the war effort, a 1,000-bomber air raid called for 28 trains to carry the petrol, and another eight for the bombs.

An important feature of freight train operation was the use of yards in which wagons were sorted and marshalled into trains for onward working. A poorly sited or overcrowded yard was a hindrance to efficient operation, and provision of modern yards was given a high priority in the allocation of funds; hence the new yards at March, Mottram and Hull. However, the conventional way of dealing with longer distance wagon loads, by moving them from yard to yard, became to an extent replaced in the

1930s by an increasing number of trains running from originating point to destination, so saving the time spent in remarshalling.

As with passenger traffic, the LNER was reluctant to withdraw goods facilities, any attenuation of the system only being accepted in the face of clear figures of uneconomic working. In the same way, reduction of train mileage had to be considered carefully, since to maintain a competitive service most trains had to be run despite reduced loadings. Efforts were made to concentrate goods traffic in country areas as an alternative to closure, packages being delivered by LNER road vehicles from a railhead, although stations might retain a facility to deal with full wagonloads.

One of the first all-line innovations after the Grouping was the establishment of a freight wagon control centre at York; the first Controller was C. M. Jenkin Jones, who combined the post with that of Superintendent of the North Eastern Area. A daily return was made to York by the major goods depots; by this means surplus wagons at one depot could be despatched to overcome a shortage in another. Periodically, to bring records up to date, a census of wagons would be taken over a weekend, because despite the existence of centralised control, the common-user principle under which wagons were used throughout Great Britain meant that they often went astray. Inevitably there was a shortfall against the recorded numbers, due partly to wagons having been damaged beyond repair without proper notification having been made (instructions were issued to examine the debris after an accident to identify any wagons destroyed), but also it was said due to wagons being 'privatised' by small operators removing railway company identification and repainting in their own livery. The position was also complicated by old wagons being sold out of service.

LNER freight business was delegated to the Divisional General Managers, each of whom had a Goods Manager as a departmental officer, responsible for obtaining the business; trains operation was a matter for the Superintendent. Canvassers were employed at District offices with the specific duties of contracting customers, but the more important ones would be dealt with by the District Goods Manager or his assistant. Where traffic from one customer originated in more than one District, efforts would be made for one office to handle all the business. In view of the importance of freight traffic to the LNER, it is not surprising that many senior posts were filled by men with freight experience; Sir Ralph Wedgwood, for example, had been at one time Chief Goods Manager of the North Eastern Railway.

Below:
The most powerful freight engines on the North British Railway were those classed 'J37' by the LNER, over 100 being built. No 9402 was turned out by the North British Loco Co in 1920, and was photographed passing Inverkeithing in early LNER days with a train of loaded coal wagons.
T. G. Hepburn, Rail Archive Stephenson

TEN

Wagon Stock

At Grouping, the LNER came into possession of some 282,000 wagons, of which fewer than 10,000 were fitted with power operated brakes and screw couplings. There were also 16,000 service vehicles for carrying locomotive coal and for use by the engineer. Many were very old — William Whitelaw said in 1925 that the records showed that the Company owned a wagon built in 1846, although the wagon census had failed to find it. By far the most common type was the four-wheeled open wagon, numbering some 127,000, used for general merchandise, or for agricultural or other products which did not require the security of a closed vehicle, and which could if necessary be protected from the weather by a tarpaulin. Another 99,000 were used exclusively for the carriage of minerals, mainly coal; they were typically of 10 or 12 tons capacity, but there were a number of larger ones, mostly originating on the North Eastern. In addition to the railway-owned wagons a further substantial number, estimated at about 200,000 were owned privately (mainly by coal mining or coal distributing companies) but ran on LNER metals. Rates for carrying coal were lower if the customer provided his own vehicle, and apart from the North Eastern Area this was commonly the arrangement for coal traffic. Consequently elsewhere on the system the typical coal train consisted of a variety of privately owned wagons of various sizes and liveries, some quite bright when newly painted, but which soon became covered in coal dust.

As the NER had arranged with its customers to haul their coal in its own wagons, this system continued in that Area throughout the LNER's existence. It had the merit that larger capacity wagons could be provided and maintained in reasonable condition, instead of the heterogeneous vehicles of the private owners which often ran in less than satisfactory condition and gave rise to breakdowns on the road, not only from failure of grease lubricated axleboxes, but also from partial collapse, despite the watchful eyes of the LNER carriage and wagon examiners. (A lesser known occupation in colliery yards was that of 'wagon patcher', whose job was to keep the wagons running, but no more.) At the outbreak of war in 1939, privately owned wagons were requisitioned by the Railway Executive Committee, on behalf of the Government, and became common user, gradually losing their identity and tending to move away from their original base. Later they were to be purchased by British Railways, the rate for an old eight-tonner being £16 10s. Thus, the typical coal haul of the prewar days

disappeared, the variety of liveries giving way to a grimy anonymity.

The Railway Clearing Houses (RCH) had introduced standard dimensions for components such as buffers and couplings before the turn of the century, but did not succeed in producing a specification for a standard wagon until 1923, whan a 12-ton all-timber design with end doors was evolved; later construction, for whatever owner, was largely to this standard. The LNER was the first of the main line railways to adopt this pattern for its own low capacity open wagon, later changing from a 9ft to a 10ft wheelbase and adopting a steel underframe as an alternative to wood. The RCH specification allowed for either steel or rubber springs on buffing and draw gear; Gresley insisted on rubber, on the grounds that it did not break. Also, from the early 1930s, he preferred his own one-piece cast axlebox to the RCH two-piece, this in turn giving way to a welded type developed at Shildon works.

It was typical of Nigel Gresley that he should campaign for larger wagons, and he made out a strong case in a Paper read before the Institute of Transport in 1923, when Sir Sam Fay was President of the Institute. Gresley argued that the most important factor in merchandise traffic was not tonnage capacity, but cubic capacity; hence if the usual British 16ft open wagon, or 18ft van, could be replaced by the Continental standard of 24ft, there would be an increased capacity of 100% for open and 50% for covered wagons. He acknowledged that there would be difficulties in adjusting terminal facilities such as hoists and tipplers to suit, but he considered that the investment would be worthwhile, and would result in better business for the railways and lower overall costs for the trader, even though rates would have to be increased to cover the provision of the improved facilities. The origin of the low capacity of the British wagon is of course found in history and is the penalty for being the pioneer; early colliery wagons were based on the horse drawn chaldron, and pit and dockside facilities were matched to these small wagons. Later, when the case for larger wagons was proved, finance for replacing the infrastructure was not forthcoming. Elsewhere in the world, profiting from British experience, larger wagons were used from the start, and even some narrow gauge lines abroad employed larger wagons than those on the standard gauge railways in Britain. A. C. Stamer, Raven's assistant on the NER, however expressed the view that whilst he supported an increase in four-wheeled wagon capacity to 20 tons, from an average of 10 tons, he could not agree that 40-ton bogie coal wagons would prove beneficial; land sale coal dealers, for example, preferred to deal in 20-ton lots. However, the bulk of the NER coal trade was seaborne, which explains its hold on the provision of wagons, since this was essentially large scale delivery into the holds of ships. Consequently the NER owned numbers of 20-ton timber built wagons specially constructed for bottom unloading through the staiths at ports on the North East coast. These wagons had no side or end doors, but were of the hopper type, with eight doors in the bottom, and were capable of being discharged in 30sec. Even at inland railheads, such as country stations, the coal was dumped through hoppers.

Since the NER hopper wagons were matched to their terminals, when they became life expired new ones had to be provided of similar pattern. At Grouping, 59,000 were handed over, of which 17,000 were of 20-ton capacity. In 1935 it was decided that replacements should be of steel, but as the LNER did not have the capability for quantity production of all-steel wagons at this time, the drawing office produced an outline diagram and contractors were invited to submit quotations based on their own detailed designs; the successful tenderer was Metropolitan Cammell. This development resulted from the interest of O. V. S. Bulleid, Gresley's assistant, in welding techniques, and saved a ton on the tare weight of a timber built wagon of similar capacity. (The Great Eastern had built steel wagons for loco coal as far back as 1902, but these were of riveted construction and weighed correspondingly more.) Because of the need to replace old hoppers on a like for like basis, construction was continued under British Railways, which even built some 13-ton hoppers, which must have been the last timber wagons to have been built in Britain. Nevertheless, even in the post-World War 2 days, 20 tons was not regarded as an achievable universal standard, and the LNER postwar plans envisaged 70,000 all-steel mineral wagons to be built as partial replacements of private owner mineral wagons, but only of 16-ton capacity.

An important advantage of discharge through hoppers instead of upturning the wagon in a tippler is that there is no likelihood of oil being lost from axleboxes, or damage being caused to the wagon. Other types of hopper wagon were used for the carriage of iron ore, pulverised coal, bauxite and soda ash, but building of very high capacity hoppers had to wait until BR days, when 56-ton bulk ore carriers were introduced for the Consett traffic. However, 20-ton van type grain hoppers, with loading hatches in the roof, were built from 1929 for the carriage of imported grain from Hull to Sowerby Bridge for the Co-operative Wholesale Society, and elsewhere.

Gresley had conducted trials in May 1922 between Peterborough and Boston with trains of wagons loaded with bricks, six 50-ton bogie wagons carrying the same payload as 30 10-ton wagons, which enabled him to argue the case, unsuccessfully as it turned out, for a 50-ton coal wagon. He had already grasped the opportunity to build similar wagons for the Fletton brick traffic between Peterborough and London, 25 being built to his specification by the Leeds Forge Co for the Great Northern, a further 25 being added by the LNER in 1930. However, no special facilities were needed for these, the tedious operations of loading and unloading being carried out by hand, palletisation being unknown in those days. Each bogie wagon carried 20,000 bricks, and was vacuum fitted, normally being marshalled next to the locomotive of an unfitted mineral train to provide additional braking power. Another version of the 50-ton bogie open wagon, of riveted steel construction, was built for sacked ammonium sulphate traffic originating from Imperial Chemical Industries at Billingham-on-Tees.

Turning now to more specialised wagons, an important type was the four-wheeled single or double bolster truck. This was perhaps being marshalled in groups of two or more, depending upon the load, which might be timber, iron or steel products, or even hay or straw in bales. Longer, bogie bolster, wagons were also in use, mostly with five bolsters, but some, 60ft long, had seven. Other versions of special wagons included 30-ton trestle wagons,

Right:
Amongst the many special classes of wagons for the transport of particular loads, an important group were those designed to carry quantities of plate glass. Here is a 'Well Glass O', built around 1939. Note the disc wheels. *NRM*

on which the load, generally steel plates, was carried at an angle to the floor; four were in stock in 1929, when it was decided to build four more. Two further 20-ton well trolley wagons were included in the same year's programme, primarily to convey new narrow gauge locomotives to the docks from such builders as the North British Locomotive Co in Glasgow, and Armstrong Whitworth on Tyneside. The following year a 20-ton flat trolley wagon was constructed to carry buses built by Ransome's of Ipswich.

The NER drawing office at Darlington had a capability for designing wagons for special uses, and a number of types, sometimes consisting of a single wagon only, were built for the conveyance of unusual loads, in particular electrical machinery, ship's propellers and naval guns. Amongst these were the large multi-bolster wagons and a 50-ton trolley wagon; and there was an extremely large trolley wagon which had provision for two flanking wagons to which part of the load could be transferred by means of equalising beams, so spreading the total weight which could reach as much as 370 tons. This 1929 masterpiece was surpassed 10 years later by an even larger vehicle, with a normal load capacity of 120 tons. The imminence of war led to the construction of other large capacity wagons, such as trestle wagons to carry up to 50 tons of steel plate needed for shipbuilding, as well as non-bogie well wagons to carry machinery. Other individual types included longer than normal open wagons for the conveyance of tubes, and well wagons with stanchions and shock absorbers to carry plate glass. In some cases, design effort was shared with the LMS, and wagons of the same pattern were constructed by both companies.

The conventional box van, of which 27,000 were acquired at the Grouping, became more specialised in type. Attention was given to the environmental needs of the traffic — which might be bananas, requiring steam heating by pipes around the roof, so that the fruit became ripened on its journey, or chilled or frozen meat, which called for refrigeration. This was provided not by mechanical means but by double walling, cork insulation and ice packages, later replaced by frozen carbon dioxide,

'dry ice', which had the additional attribute of evaporation and so lessening the weight carried by the van. It was of course important to preserve vehicles for their particular class of traffic, to avoid cross contamination; fish vans in particular had to be kept separate from other wagons, and were provided with ventilation. An exception was that cattle wagons, suitably cleaned, were used for green pea traffic, in bags. Another category was assigned to the carriage of fruit, for which shelves were provided. All these variations were based on a standard 12-ton van, which was of all-timber construction until steel underframes were introduced in the later 1930s, particularly for fitted stock, together with corrugated pressed steel ends. The wartime shortage of steel caused a reversion to all-timber bodies, but using resin-bonded plywood in place of planking.

Wagons for the conveyance of livestock, usually known as cattle trucks (although they were also used for sheep and pigs), were another class built in some numbers in the early years of the LNER. They were subject to official regulations which were intended to prevent injury to the animals whilst in transit, with requirements to ensure that the interiors were devoid of projections, and battens secured to the floor to prevent slipping; usually, limewash was liberally applied as a disinfectant. Many were fitted with vacuum brakes for inclusion in fast goods trains. Horses were almost invariably sent by passenger train, in specially designed horse boxes, with accommodation for a groom; racehorses were an important source of traffic, particularly to and from Newmarket.

Below:
The very large trolley wagon in the centre of this picture was built in 1939 with a normal carrying capacity of 120 tons. However, if the large beams at each end were brought into use to relieve the trolley wagon of some of the weight, the load could be increased by another 40 tons. *Author's collection*

A special class of wagon, seen in increasing numbers after the Grouping, but almost entirely owned by private companies, was the tank wagon. These were primarily for the conveyance of oil, petroleum, bitumen and gases, whilst an interesting development in the 1920s was the glass-lined milk tank wagon, originally four-wheeled and later six-wheeled. The first batch of seven was built in 1928, each holding 3,000gal of milk, for service between Ingestre in Staffordshire and the United Dairies distributing centre at East Finchley; the tanks replaced 2,000 milk churns.

When containers were first introduced, a low-sided open wagon was used to transport them, but a special type of flat wagon was soon developed to deal with this traffic. It was fitted with chocks, suitably positioned to secure the various sizes of container in use; vacuum brakes were provided and the securing chains incorporated shock absorbers. The Railway Catering House drew up standard specifications to cover the variety of containers needed to accommodate particular loads, such as frozen meat (for which the containers were insulated), and for furniture removals. From 1932, arising from the reduction in livestock traffic, 350 vacuum-fitted cattle wagons built in 1924 were converted to container flats. Conversions were also made from the underframes of the four-wheeled milk tanks, which by 1933 had to be on six-wheel underframes to run at passenger train speeds. Another aspect of door-to-door delivery was in connection with road tankers taking vegetable oil from Selby to Scotland, in which six-wheel low sided wagons carried two road tankers, a generator being needed to supply immersion heaters in the tanks, so that the oil could be maintained in the liquid state.

The North Eastern principles of brake van design were included in the standard adopted for group construction, this being of the four-wheeled double verandah style on a 10ft 6in wheelbase, weighing 20 tons and originally with wooden and later with pressed steel lookout duckets. With the increase in speed of many express freight trains, this vehicle tended to give the goods guards a rough ride, and after trials with a Great Western brake van, an amended design was produced in which the standard body was mounted on an elongated underframe with a 16ft wheelbase. This type of van became known to the LNER goods guards as the 'Queen Mary', after the contemporary Cunarder, and was later adopted as standard by British Railways, many hundreds being built in the 1950s. An interesting experiment took place in 1929, when a standard brake van was constructed out of concrete. However, even when lined with cork and provided with a wooden floor, it was unpopular with the guards, whose uncomplimentary remarks were written on the walls of the van, as what is nowadays known as graffiti. Nevertheless it remained in service for many years; the idea was revived during the war as an alternative to scarce timber, but was discarded on the grounds that a concrete van weighed a ton more than its wooden equivalent.

A final category of wagon to be considered is that of service stock, which apart from mineral wagons used for the transport of locomotive coal consisted mainly of vehicles for the use of the engineer for track repairs and renewals. Often, old wagons taken out of service stock would be utilised, but two specialised designs were introduced. These were a hopper ballast wagon, used in groups in conjunction with a conventional brake van fitted with a plough to spread the ballast, and a bogie wagon of low loading height capable of carrying prefabricated sections of 60ft track. Numbers of these useful designs were built and allocated to the various engineering districts.

As with locomotives and coaching stock, an annual programme of wagon construction was authorised by the Board, after the usual discussions at lower levels, but financial considerations often intervened to cause the alteration or cancellation of a programme. The first proposals for wagon construction, submitted in 1923, amounted to 14,000 wagons, or about 5% of the total stock. These ambitions could not be sustained, but even so the 1925 programme contained provision for a further 12,130, whilst in 1927, after considering a detailed programme totalling £1 million, the Locomotive Committee decided to cut it by a quarter, leaving the details to be worked out by the Chief General Manager — another example of the confidence placed in Sir Ralph Wedgwood.

Each of the pre-Grouping companies possessed its own wagon building shops, but in the early days of the LNER, construction was concentrated at Darlington (where new facilities were completed at Faverdale in 1923), Shildon, Doncaster and at the Great Central works at Dukinfield, near Manchester. The first welded steel underframe was built at Dukinfield, but later T. Cruddas (who had been a foreman blacksmith at Doncaster) developed a facility for manufacturing steel underframes at Shildon, including a patented method of fabricating axleboxes, these being despatched to Faverdale for incorporation in wagons assembled there. Cruddas was awarded a special bonus for this work, and appointed Assistant Works Manager at Shildon. It was also the practice for the Company to place quite large contracts with outside firms of wagon builders, there being plenty of competition for such orders. In 1924 no fewer than 26 firms were invited to tender for open wagons; then, the going rate for a 12-ton open wagon was £131, and £181 for a 12-ton van with disc wheels. By 1929 the LNER had so improved production methods that a 12-ton open wagon could be assembled in 12 minutes, with a labour content of no more than 19 shillings (95p).

In the early days of the LNER it was reported that freight trains were sometimes delayed because of a shortage of brake vans, and this no doubt was a factor in the 1923 purchase of 155 brake vans from the George Cohen & Armstrong disposal corporation, acting on behalf of the Government in selling off surplus wartime rolling stock. In the following year 200 30-ton low sided bogie wagons were bought from the same source, for the conveyance of steel plates, as well as 50 45-ton quadruple bogie bolster wagons for carrying rails. The cost was about a third of that of building in the Company's workshops.

The great majority of LNER goods wagons were painted lead grey, with brake vans and fitted stock red oxide, and

refrigerator vans white: service stock was painted blue —
originally a light blue, but later a darker shade appeared —
while wagons fit only to run inside the docks were in
'engine green'. Company identification right from the start
was restricted to the letters 'NE'; originally this was in large
letters on the side of the wagon, but from 1937 small letters
were substituted, in a group together with the serial number
and the load capacity at the lower left-hand side of the
vehicle. Wagons were classified by type codes for
identification and control purposes, but these did not
receive wide or popular recognition, nor were they always
shown on the wagon.

As to numerical identification of wagons, there was no
system of numbering according to class, and new wagons
were numbered in sequence as they were built. At
Grouping, Robinson pressed strongly for the retention of
pre-Grouping numbers with the addition of a letter to
indicate origin, this being held to simplify the task of
number takers and senders of telegrams; but after his
confirmation as CME, Gresley, with the support of

Wedgwood, decided on the system adopted for coaches
and locomotives, although in a slightly different fashion.
North Eastern wagons were to retain their original
numbers, except that some thousands, the number of
which were prefaced by a letter, would be renumbered
from 110001, whilst the other companies' wagons would
suffer the addition of 400000 (GNR), 500000 (GCR),
600000 (GER), 700000 (NBR) and 800000 (GN of SR). It
was accepted that new cast iron number plates would be
needed, but a unique number for each wagon was deemed
essential in view of the introduction of the central wagon
control system. New construction followed the NE series,
which explains the appearance of six digit numbers on new
wagons, ranging from 130001 in 1923 to the low 300000s
in 1947. Unlike coaches and locomotives, Edward
Thompson made no attempt to introduce a rationalised
renumbering schedule for wagons.

By the end of 1947, the LNER wagon stock had been
reduced by about 15% to 250,875 vehicles in all, but the
proportion fitted with vacuum brakes had risen to about a
fifth, reflecting the greater speed of many freight trains.
However, considering the relatively small number of
wagons actually on the move at any one time, it will be
realised that most of their time was spent at rest in sidings,
awaiting loading or unloading, or being marshalled into
trains. This underlines the view expressed by C. M. Jenkin
Jones, based on his experience as wagon stock controller,
that for the goods train operator there is never a shortage of
wagons, only of empty wagons, and appealing for greater
efforts to secure a faster turnround.

Below:
**An ex-Great Northern loco coal wagon is in the cradle and
about to be hoisted to the top of a Mitchell coaling plant. In
the course of time most of the LNER sheds were provided with
mechanically operated plants of this kind, either of concrete
or steel construction, in the largest of which the coal was
transported to the top by means of conveyers. Because of their
height, the concrete plants were prominent landmarks, and
were familiarly known as 'Cenotaphs'.** *Real Photos*

ELEVEN

Pre~Grouping Locomotives

Each of the LNER constituent companies had met its locomotive needs in a different way, due partly to varying traffic requirements, and partly to permanent way limitations, but mainly to the predilections of the engineers concerned. The most popular type for express passenger work, used by four of the companies, was the outside-cylindered Atlantic, which had been introduced to Britain by H. A. Ivatt of the Great Northern in 1898. This was followed four years later by an improved version, the first example in this country of the 'big engine' concept, with a wide firebox and what was for the time a massive boiler. The Ivatt Atlantics provided the main motive power on the GNR until H. N. Gresley introduced his Pacific design just before the Grouping, and they still continued to play an important part in Southern Area workings until well into the 1930s, particularly on the Pullman trains. This resulted from work initiated in the last years of the Great Northern's independence, when Gresley demonstrated that the performance of the Atlantics could be markedly improved by fitting larger superheaters. Also, in 1923, he arranged for one to have a booster engine driving its trailing wheels, with the objective of providing more power at starting and on the steeper banks; but this was not a success in practice as even the large boiler of the Atlantic was unable to provide sufficient additional steam to meet the booster's requirements.

The North Eastern also adopted the Atlantic type, commencing in 1903 with Wilson Worsdell's Class V, followed in 1911 by Vincent Raven's three-cylinder version, Class Z. These were solid machines, adequate for their duties, distinguished by the drive to the trailing coupled wheels and to the leading coupled wheels respectively. Not only did the NER Atlantics haul the through East Coast expresses on their own section of the route, but they also ran onwards from Berwick to Edinburgh over the North British main line. This was due to a long standing arrangement which the North British never liked, but which had the benefit of eradicating the need to stop at Berwick merely for engine changing.

The NBR version of the Atlantic was found primarily on the road northwards from Edinburgh to Aberdeen and southward over the Waverley route to Carlisle. The NBR Atlantics were impressive machines, with large diameter

Below:

Class C7 (NER Class Z) No 706 with LNER dynamometer car No 3591Y under preparation for a test run soon after Grouping. Fifty 'Z' Atlantics were built between 1911 and 1918, No 706 being the first, the contract for the construction of the initial batch having been placed with the North British Locomotive Co of Glasgow. *IAL*

Left:
Raven Pacific, Class A2 No 2402 *City of York* at Haymarket shed, Edinburgh. In early LNER days the NER Pacifics were frequently used on the heaviest Newcastle to Edinburgh expresses, but were gradually replaced by Gresley Pacifics after these had been built in quantity and stationed in the North Eastern Area. No 2402 was withdrawn in 1936 after a life of no more than 12 years. On the right of the picture can be seen the tender of No 2372, a Tweedmouth 4-6-0 of Class B16, which was often working at this time on trains between Berwick and Edinburgh. *IAL*

boilers and Belpaire fireboxes, but were reputedly heavy on coal. Introduced in 1906 by W. P. Reid, at one time the NBR authorities were not too happy about their performance; nevertheless more were built, the final two coming into service in 1921, whilst in the first proposals for new locomotives to be built after the Grouping, a request was made for a further five — met in the event by Gresley Pacifics. The North British and the Great Central Atlantics possessed certain similarities: the GCR design, whilst somewhat smaller, was one of J. G. Robinson's most celebrated classes, capable of good performance and graceful in appearance, and justifying the soubriquet of 'Jersey Lilies' after the actress of the period. Introduced in 1903, they were still in GCR front line service 30 years later.

In 1923 some comparative testing of Atlantics from the three East Coast partners took place between Newcastle and Edinburgh, but the results were not very conclusive, to some extent opposite to what might have been expected, because the Great Northern Atlantic did not show up too well, whilst the NBR representative appeared reasonably economical in operation. To the disappointment of observers the Robinson design was not included in the tests, nor were any comparisons made with 4-6-0s. The reason probably lay in the fact that none of the East Coast lines possessed a modern large wheel design of this type,

Above:
An Ivatt large Atlantic, Class C1 No 4413, outside King's Cross station. This locomotive gained fame on 14 June 1940 when it worked the up 'Aberdonian', weighing over 600 tons gross, into King's Cross, only four minutes being booked against the engine. *LPC*

Above:
Forty-five 4-4-0s in four classes were in Midland & Great Northern stock when the LNER assumed responsibility for operating the Joint line in 1936. All had been built before 1900 and several were in such a rundown condition that they were withdrawn without being taken into LNER stock; those remaining were renumbered into the LNER series by the addition of a cipher. No 025, seen here at Spalding on 11 August 1937, was originally constructed by Beyer Peacock & Co in 1883 and underwent a number of rebuildings before being withdrawn in 1941. Note the tablet catching device fitted to the tender. *T. G. Hepburn, Rail Archive Stephenson*

but since the 4-6-0 was unchallenged on other trunk railways in Britain, notably the Great Western and the LNWR, to have included a Great Central 4-6-0 — or even one from another railway — would have added interest to the tests. Anyway, by then Gresley had ideas beyond the Atlantic type, and the results could only have been of academic interest.

Altogether 241 Atlantics came into LNER stock, and almost all remained in the areas of their pre-Grouping owners. North Eastern classes could however be seen at King's Cross from time to time, particularly when hauling football specials or other excursion trains; the only long-term transfer was of seven GNR Atlantics to the Great Central, the first being as early as August 1923, although on occasion a GCR Atlantic could be seen at King's Cross.

During 1922, the final year before the Grouping, the GNR and the NER each produced a Pacific design. That of the North Eastern was a hastily put together 'stretched' version of the 'Z' Atlantic, but H. N. Gresley, for the Great Northern, had carefully developed an entirely new locomotive over a number of years, one which was to become a classic.

The Great Eastern possessed no Atlantics, S. D. Holden having introduced a class of 4-6-0 which was probably the most successful of its kind with inside cylinders to be built in Britain. They were powerful machines for their size, with a maximum axle load of no more than 15ton 13cwt. This gave them a wide route availability so that not only did they find use on ambulance trains in many parts of Britain during two wars, but also from 1931 several were redeployed in the Northern Scottish Area, where they provided a welcome replacement for withdrawn native 4-4-0s. Others of the LNER's inherited 4-6-0s came from the North Eastern and the Great Central, the NER in fact having introduced the type to England in 1899, and developed it through three further varieties to culminate in a powerful three-cylinder version for mixed traffic duties. Robinson had also produced a series of 4-6-0s for the Great Central, some intended for express passenger work and others for mixed traffic or freight, nine classes in all. Some had outside cylinders, some had inside and others had four cylinders; only his final design, for mixed traffic, was multiplied to any extent. None of the pre-Grouping companies' 4-6-0s compared in performance with the contemporary GWR 'Star' class, and it is an interesting comment on the locomotive practice of constituent companies that so much reliance was placed on Atlantic locomotives, yet differing so much in basic design.

All the constituent companies built 4-4-0s of varying size and competence, the most powerful being the GCR 'Director' class, which maintained a leading place in that section's duties until well in the 1930s; also, in its celebrated 'R' class, the North Eastern possessed a locomotive which had been amongst the most powerful in

Class D10 No 438c *Worsley-Taylor* at Nottingham Victoria with the 2.20pm Manchester to Marylebone express soon after Grouping. The engine is in LNER green, but retains its GCR cabside number plate. The letter 'c' appears to be a later addition to the tender number, probably added when suffix letters were adopted in the interim period before full renumbering took place. This engine, named after one of the Directors of the Great Central Railway, was stationed at Gorton, and worked through to London, the enginemen lodging there and returning next day. *T. G. Hepburn, Rail Archive Stephenson*

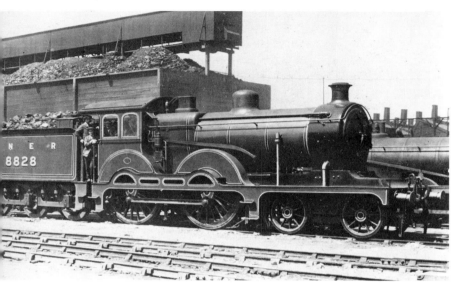

One of the renowned 'Claud Hamilton' 4-4-0s of the Great Eastern Railway, Class D15 No 8828 is seen at Stratford in original condition soon after repainting in LNER livery. Built in 1909, it was provided with a superheater and extended smokebox in 1928, and rebuilt to Gresley's specifications as a 'D16/3' in 1934. *IAL*

the country at the time of its development in 1899. The elegant GER 'Claud Hamilton' 4-4-0s developed into a 'Super-Claud' version, to which most of the originals were eventually rebuilt, whilst the North British achieved the final development of the classic Drummond style in the 'Scott' and 'Glen' classes. On the Great Northern, the 4-4-0 was never seriously considered for the heaviest duties, although Ivatt's three designs provided useful second line locomotives; 100 of the Great North of Scotland's stock of 122 engines comprised successive classes of low powered 4-4-0s. A most useful GER type was the 2-4-0, which because of its low axle load could be used on the lightly engineered East Anglian branches: 100 came into LNER stock, of which 18 lasted until 1947.

Again, there was little inter-section transfer after the Grouping, the most interesting being the employment of GCR 'Directors' turn and turn about with Ivatt Atlantics on the King's Cross Pullman trains between 1927 and 1932, and the transfer of the entire batch of Ivatt's largest 4-4-0s to the North British, to allow obsolescent NBR engines to move to the GNofS, in turn to replace the oldest of the native classes, which were then withdrawn. In the 1930s a number of small GNR 4-4-0s went to Darlington and Hull, and for a time worked over the Stainmore line, but they were not regarded as being successful on this duty and were replaced by ex-GER 2-4-0s.

Only the GCR, GNR and NER had built large locomotives specifically for mixed traffic use — fast or slow freight, secondary express and excursion trains, with the capability of taking over important expresses in emergency. The GCR and NER versions were 4-6-0s, the final developments being powerful multi-cylinder designs. The Great Northern, after many years during which the mixed traffic role was performed by Stirling 0-4-2s, introduced a 5ft 8in 0-6-0 in 1908, but the innovative Gresley followed this by a 2-6-0 class in 1912, with by a larger boilered version entering service two years later, and a three-cylinder design with a 6ft diameter boiler in 1920.

Of all the locomotive types acquired by the LNER, the 0-6-0 was the most numerous, all the constituents except the GNofS contributing a substantial number. Each railway had developed its own style, in which the final version was recognisably a later edition of earlier ones. In 1923 they varied from obsolete machines around 50 years old (one even originated from a design prepared for the Stockton & Darlington Railway) to the most powerful examples of their type in Britain, the final GER class. On the North Eastern the type had progressed through several classes to the 'P3', still to be seen in charge of short haul mineral trains in the 1960s: they were robust machines, characteristic of the North Eastern working environment. The last GNR class, designed by Ivatt and added to in quantity by Gresley, possessed a softer outline, with raised running plates,

Right:
A. J. Hill was responsible for Great Eastern locomotive design from November 1912, and in 1915 introduced his 0-6-2T for Liverpool Street suburban services. This was classed 'N7' by the LNER, and many more were built after the Grouping, mostly to reinforce the original GER stud at Stratford. However, a number, including a batch of 20 built by Wm Beardmore of Glasgow in 1927, were sent at first to King's Cross. One of these was No 2646, seen here at Eastfield shed, Glasgow, on being delivered from the contractors. *T. G. Hepburn, Rail Archive Stephenson*

Right:
Class C11 No 9903 *Cock o' the North.* **Built in 1911 by R. Stephenson & Co, it was renamed** *Aberdonian* **when the first 'P2' took its original name. During its LNER period it was stationed at St Margarets shed, Edinburgh, working to Perth, where this photograph was taken. A Worthington Simpson feed water heater and pump were fitted in 1926.** *T. G. Hepburn, Rail Archive Stephenson*

Right:
Black Duncan, **LNER Class D30 No 9500, was one of the last of W. P. Reid's 'Scott' class 4-4-0s to be built, at Cowlairs in 1920. It is seen after working a stopping train to Dundee when stationed at Thornton Junction in the 1930s. The engine was named after Black Duncan the Mischievous, a character in Sir Walter Scott's novel** *The Heart of Midlothian.* **Note the small letters on the tender — for several years Cowlairs persisted in applying 7½in transfers whereas elsewhere the standard 12in block letters were used.** *T. G. Hepburn, Rail Archive Stephenson*

80

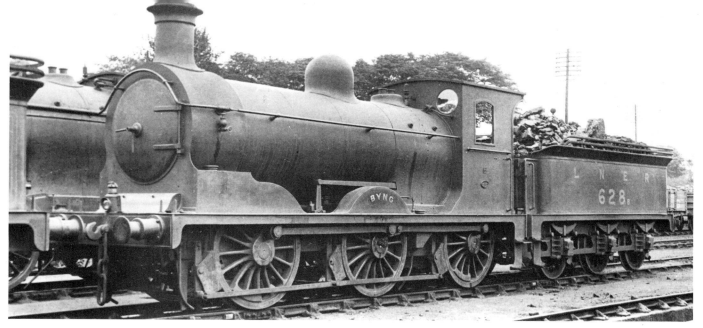

Twenty-five Class J36 0-6-0s of North British origin worked in France towards the end of the World War 1 and their service was commemorated by their being given appropriate names, No 628 *Byng* being one of these. This popular and useful class was long lived, having been introduced in 1888, and of the total of 168 no fewer than 123 saw Nationalisation, the last being withdrawn in 1966. Fortunately one, NBR No 673 *Maude*, had been preserved by the Scottish Railway Preservation Society, and may be seen at Falkirk.
T. G. Hepburn, Rail Archive Stephenson

contrasting with the 0-6-0s of the Great Central which were solidly built in the Gorton tradition. As well as possessing 0-6-0s as powerful as other railways' eight-coupled freight engines, the Great Eastern also owned a lightweight class dating from 1883, with an axle load of no more than 13½ tons, which enabled them to be used almost anywhere on the GER system. The Hull & Barnsley brought two classes of 0-6-0 into LNER stock, totalling over half of the 138 engines of that line which survived to be allocated LNER numbers. Finally, the last North British class was a powerful version of the type, intended for mineral haulage; like the Great Eastern's, they were on a line for which no eight-coupled locomotives had been built, although trials had taken place in 1921 of a number of engines of this type, including a Great Western 2-8-0.

As with mixed traffic locomotives, the GCR, GNR and NER led the way in heavy freight haulage, although it is fair to say that their needs were greater than those of any of the other companies. All three had introduced 0-8-0 designs soon after the turn of the century, the GNR with inside and the others — resulting in a somewhat ungainly appearance — with outside cylinders. The NER variety was developed into a larger machine, and later into a three-cylinder class, whilst the GNR examples, familiarly known as 'Long Toms', were supplanted by Gresley's 2-8-0s, first of a two-cylinder and later of a three-cylinder pattern, but owing little to their 0-8-0 predecessors. Robinson

developed his 0-8-0 into a 2-8-0 with a larger, superheated, boiler, producing a straightforward locomotive, strong, robust and simple to operate and maintain, and which was to be regarded with great affection. The class was selected by the Government of the day for service in overseas theatres in both world wars; large numbers were built to Government order during and after World War 1 to bring the total to 666, of which a large number were to be bought by the LNER.

As the suburban traffic problems of each railway differed, so did the locomotive types provided to meet operating requirements. On the North Eastern, the North Tyneside services were electrified, but other lines continued to be operated by steam. For these, and for branch lines, the usual motive power was an 0-4-4T; for longer distances, such as Newcastle to Middlesbrough, a three-cylinder 4-4-4T class had been introduced, but these suffered from lack of adhesion and were not wholly successful; another class, a 4-6-0T with 5ft 1¼in wheels, was designed for the extremely hilly North Yorkshire coast line. The latter two classes were eventually rebuilt to the 4-6-2T type. On the Great Northern, with a fairly extensive London suburban network, as well as local services around Nottingham and the West Riding, Ivatt built 4-4-2Ts followed by 0-6-2Ts; Gresley revised the latter design to produce a superheated piston valve version which could be seen at King's Cross until well into the diesel area. The Great Central also possessed 4-4-2Ts, which were developed by Robinson into workmanlike 4-6-2Ts which coped well with the outer suburban traffic working into Marylebone. The Great Eastern solution would have been electrification in the early 1900s had not a thorough re-organisation of the steam service taken place. 0-4-4Ts, 2-4-2Ts, 0-6-0Ts and finally 0-6-2Ts worked the smartly timed trains between the closely spaced stations, requiring good acceleration and braking. Finally, in Scotland, the North British possessed two classes of 4-4-2T which dealt adequately with the short distance services from Waverley and Queen Street, whilst the GNofS had nine 0-4-4Ts to work its local trains from Aberdeen.

Freight shunting tanks were mainly of the 0-6-0T or 0-6-2T types, except that there were some diminutive four-coupled tanks used for dockyard shunting, whilst for hump shunting work the GCR had a few massive 0-8-4Ts known as 'Daisies', and the NER a number of 4-8-0Ts. The Great Northern possessed a 0-8-2T class, the tank engine equivalent of Ivatt's 0-8-0 freight engine; originally intended for suburban passenger duties, they were mainly used for trip working in the Nottinghamshire coalfield and empty carriage movement at King's Cross. The North Eastern also had a useful 4-6-2T for short distance freight duties. Of the 0-6-0Ts, on the Great Northern, Stirling and Ivatt had developed a saddle tank design which was taken a stage further by Gresley, LNER Class J50, the saddle tank being replaced by long side tanks which featured sloping tops to the front ends as an aid to visibility when buffering up. In contrast, the Great Central and North British preferred the 0-6-2T, which was also used to bank trains up the Cowlairs incline out of Queen Street station. In some comparative testing which took place in 1924, several classes of 0-6-0T and 0-6-2T shunting locomotives were assessed; it was concluded that the Great Northern's was the best all-round design, and this was adopted as the standard medium shunting tank for future construction.

It can be seen, by studying tables of dimensions, outline drawings, and photographs in particular, that each of the

LNER constituent companies had evolved a distinctive style of its own. The Great Central owed most to J. G. Robinson, who had been in charge of locomotive development since 1900; his designs were solid and workmanlike, and — as exemplified by the Atlantics and 'Directors' — they could be elegant as well. On the Great Eastern, James and Stephen Holden and later A. J. Hill had produced neat inside-cylindered locomotives, powerful for their size, whilst the North British classes reflected the economy of design of the austere Dugald Drummond. Wilson Worsdell on the North Eastern had been the first locomotive engineer in Britain to introduce the three-cylinder system in quantity production: this H. N. Gresley later adopted with enthusiasm, although with derived motion for the centre valves, in contrast to the Worsdell (and later Raven) preference for three independent sets of valve gear. After briefly experimenting with four cylinders, Gresley adopted three cylinders for all except his smallest designs, this constituting one of his most distinctive design hallmarks. He also introduced Walschaerts valve gear to standard British practice, with high running plates exposing the driving wheels, and in addition expounded the principle that all three cylinders should drive on to the same coupled axle. He believed that the more even turning moment imparted by three cylinders, and the consequent lessened hammer blow on the track, more than outweighed the additional weight and cost. However, his conjugated valve gear required good maintenance if it was to be kept in first class order, and this was difficult to achieve during the wartime and after, when skilled labour was not always available. The exhaust sound of a well-tuned Gresley three-cylinder locomotive was unmistakable — as was the irregular beat of one in serious need of adjustment.

Because of the diversion of resources elsewhere, under the stress of wartime, the number of locomotives built by the LNER constituents was relatively few after 1914, and construction did not resume on any scale until 1920, when the emphasis was on meeting requirements for mixed traffic and freight working. A number of tank engines were built for shunting or suburban working, notably on the Great Northern, but few express locomotives were turned out, and these included prototypes. Once the Grouping was seen to be inevitable, the pace of new construction slackened once more, the North British, for example, postponing orders for 30 0-6-2Ts until it was clear that the bill would be picked up by the LNER.

This somewhat discursive summary illustrates the variety of locomotives inherited by the LNER, many of which were obsolescent or out of date; even the one prosperous partner, the North Eastern, possessed some 700 engines — a third of its stock — over 30 years old. In all, 7,423 locomotives of 32 different types and some 232 classes were in existence at the date of amalgamation. By and large the fleet managed to cope with the demands placed on it, but there were important exceptions. In particular there was an urgent need for more powerful locomotives to handle the East Coast and West Riding trains from King's Cross, the heaviest of which had outgrown the normal capability of the Ivatt Atlantics some years before, piloting being needed up the bank to Potters Bar. Also, strong mixed traffic engines were needed in several parts of the system, and new intermediate locomotives in Scotland. These were amongst the first problems to be tackled by the newly appointed Chief Mechanical Engineer, H. N. Gresley.

Below:
North British Railway No 256 (LNER 9256) *Glen Douglas* **was used on special trains for a time after restoration, and was photographed working an RCTS special between Ladybank and Bridge of Earn on 28 August 1965.** *Paul Riley*

Right:

Sir Nigel Gresley was born in 1876 and spent his childhood in Netherseal, Derbyshire, where his father was the rector. Educated at Marlborough, he became a premium apprentice at Crewe, later holding a series of posts on the Lancashire & Yorkshire Railway. In 1905 he moved to Doncaster as Carriage & Wagon Superintendent of the Great Northern Railway, succeeding H. A. Ivatt as Locomotive Superintendent in 1911. Soon after Grouping he was appointed Chief Mechanical Engineer of the LNER, a position which he held until his death in 1941. He was a firm yet kindly man, enjoying the respect of his colleagues and subordinates, and, as a family man, loved by all around him.
From a painting in the possession of Mrs V. Godfrey

Bottom:

The first streamlined Pacific, No 2509 *Silver Link*, is seen at Grantham heading the up 'Flying Scotsman' in June 1937, just before the commencement of non-stop running in the full summer timetable. The engine is in its original silver grey livery, with the name painted on the side of the boiler casing, before receiving the standard garter blue later in the year. Although six of the 'A4s' have been preserved, *Silver Link*, alas, is not amongst them, having been broken up at Doncaster in 1963, 28 years after being turned out of the same works. The train would have been made up of one of the teak 1928 'Flying Scotsman' sets, but the additional luggage brake in the photograph is one of the all-steel coaches built by Cammel Laird in 1927. *Colour-Rail*

Far right:

The third of the LNER trio of steamlined trains was the 'West Riding Limited', leaving Leeds Central at 11.31am and returning from King's Cross at 7.10pm, averaging 68mph in each direction. Here the up train is racing through Hitchin, in charge of Class A4 No 4491 *Commonwealth of Australia*. This Haymarket-based engine hauled the inaugural 'Coronation' from King's Cross to Edinburgh, and was a regular performer on this train; evidently it had been borrowed by King's Cross shed to work the 'West Riding Limited', a duty for which No 4495 *Golden Fleece* or No 4496 *Golden Shuttle* were generally the first choice. *From a painting by George Heiron*

TWELVE

Gresley Locomotives: 1923~1933

When the abortive tripartite merger of the GCR, GER and GNR was mooted in 1909, the proposals were not for full amalgamation but for pooling of receipts and elimination of competition, with continued individual management of the three railways. The question may be posed as to whether this would eventually have led to a single management structure, as happened when the South Eastern and the London Chatham & Dover had merged their operating interests several years before, whilst retaining their separate financial identities. This, in turn, invites speculation concerning the personalities who might have reached the topmost positions in the group, not least in the mechanical engineering field. At that time, S. D. Holden (GER) had not been long in his post and H. A. Ivatt (GNR) was approaching retirement, but J. G. Robinson of the GCR was in his prime and the obvious choice as CME of the group, should one have been appointed. In this event, there would have been no promotion for Gresley; so would he have been content to remain in a subordinate position until Robinson retired, or would he have sought opportunity elsewhere — perhaps as a successor to George Whale on the LNWR, Gresley having served his apprenticeship at Crewe? The intriguing possibility remains that a Robinson Pacific might have been seen on the East Coast main line instead of the Gresley variety. Indeed, an

outline was prepared for such an engine, similar to the later Robinson 4-6-0s, robust in outline but lacking the elegance of the Gresley design.

Such considerations, of course, remain in the realm of fantasy, and the position on the LNER, once Gresley had been appointed Chief Mechanical Engineer, was clear. The new incumbent, now 46 years old, had established himself as a leading practitioner amongst British locomotive engineers, possessing both the engineering practicality and the management ability needed for the post, as well as the inventiveness to ensure that the developing needs of the locomotive department were met. He was to employ all his talents to the full in the years which lay ahead.

The duties of the CME included not only the design, construction and maintenance of rolling stock, but also the provision of gas, electricity and water supplies, of indoor machinery in the workshops and outdoor machinery in coaling plants and pumping stations, machinery in the docks, and road motor vehicles. The workshops employed some 50,000 staff at Darlington, York, Shildon and Hull (NER), Doncaster (GNR), Gorton and Dukinfield (GCR), Stratford (GER), Cowlairs (NBR) and Inverurie (GNofS). The carriage works at Doncaster and York were seriously damaged by fire during the war, but production was resumed after reorganisation of the shop facilities and

Left:
Almost all the steam rail cars were named after old horse-drawn stage coaches. No 2135 *Integrity* was one of the these, and is seen here in 1933 leaving Newcastle Central for North Wylam in 1933. Most of the cars had their engine portion articulated to the coach, but *Integrity* was built as a single unit. It was one of the longest surviving Sentinel cars, lasting until after the end of the War. *Photomatic*

Above:

The engine end of the Clayton steam rail cars was quite different to that of the Sentinels, with an exterior coal bunker and coupled driving wheels. No 44 (later renumbered 43304) *Bang Up* is seen at Doncaster in 1928, soon after entering traffic. Although Gresley originally expressed the view that the Claytons were the better of the two makes, they had comparatively short lives, and all had been withdrawn by 1937. However, this may have been due to shortage of spare parts, as their maker had ceased to trade. *Author's collection*

Below:

Class O2 No 3479, built by the North British Locomotive Co in 1921. Originally provided with a Great Northern type cab with cutaway sides, this was later replaced by a side window pattern, and in 1943 the engine was rebuilt as a Class O1 with Edward Thompson's standard boiler, as used on other classes such as the 'B1'. Stationed at New England, No 3479 worked for over 20 years on the Ferme Park coal trains, until the 'O1s' and 'O2s' were replaced by the WD 'Austerity' 2-8-0s, LNER Class O7. *Gresley Society collection*

priority was given to reconstruction as soon as circumstances permitted.

In his main task, to provide the railway with the rolling stock it needed, Gresley was to be seriously inhibited by the LNER's chronic lack of funds, a situation which was to grow worse as the 1920s progressed, although it is doubtful whether anyone was seriously aware of this threat at the outset of the Grouping. But it soon became clear that any plans for massive replacement of obsolete stock would have to be shelved. As a first appraisal, Sir Vincent Raven, in his report on the Company's workshops, recommended that all new locomotive construction should be concentrated at Doncaster and Darlington, and on the basis of a total stock of some 7,400 locomotives and an average life of 40 years, he calculated that the Company's needs would amount to 185 new engines a year. This number was never to be achieved, except in the last year of the LNER's existence, when 193 new engines entered service.

In the months immediately before the Grouping, meetings of the mechanical engineers of the constituent companies, chaired by Raven, considered the provision of

Above:

The first 10 Class K3 2-6-0s of H. N. Gresley's design also had Great Northern cabs and tenders until modernised with Group Standard tenders and, later, side window cabs. A further 183 were built after the Grouping, by the LNER works at Darlington and Doncaster, and by contractors. No 4007 was built at Doncaster in 1921, and is seen at Grantham on a stopping train c1935. *G. Goslin collection*

Class V2 No 4771 *Green Arrow* is seen heading the afternoon down 'Scotch Goods', one of the tasks for which it was designed. Such was the power and versatility of the class, however, that no fewer than 184 'V2s' were built, finding employment over many parts of the LNER system on heavy passenger and freight trains. *Green Arrow* itself was preserved from scrapping, and has been restored to working order through the efforts of D. W. Harvey; it is now in the care of the National Railway Museum and is one of the small number of locomotives permitted to haul passenger trains over selected BR lines.   *From a painting by George Heiron*

expresses commenced running in May 1932, with a basic formation of three carriages; such was their popularity that loads eventually grew on occasions to 10 coaches or even more. The heaviest trains required Pacific haulage to keep time, but in the middle 1930s the buffet trains were generally in the hands of the large Atlantics of H. A. Ivatt, and here we see the 30-year-old No 4403, clean and green, hustling its train along en route to King's Cross.   *From a painting by George Heiron*

new locomotives in 1923, and three other items of immediate importance: standardisation of brakes and corridor connections, and renumbering of rolling stock. These topics have been discussed in Chapter Eight, but whilst the renumbering of locomotives and coaches followed the same principles, there were differences in application. As with coaches, an interim decision was taken to add a suffix letter to locomotive numbers, except that in the case of North Eastern engines, it was 'D' (for Darlington). This plan was superseded in 1924 by a scheme under which NER locomotives retained their original numbers, and those of the GNR were increased by 3000; GCR by 5000; GNofS by 6800; GER by 7000; and NBR by 9000. New locomotives were generally allocated numbers at the end of the North Eastern block, or, if they were to be stationed in that Area, taking vacant numbers within the NER series. There were many exceptions to this practice, particularly in later years, and in any case few attempts were made to number locomotives within a coherent class grouping until a wholesale renumbering scheme was introduced in 1946. Nevertheless, a comprehensive system of classification was introduced, following Great Northern practice, under which a locomotive class was denoted by a letter indicating the wheel arrangement, followed by figures representing the particular series concerned. Thus, 'A1' denoted the original Great Northern Pacific, 'A5' the Robinson 4-6-2T, and 'J27' the largest NER 0-6-0. In addition, power or load classifications were applied, but these differed in each Area, no attempt being made to standardise these; a route availability classification too was commenced in 1940, this becoming an all-line practice in 1947.

The 126 locomotives built in 1923 were all of pre-Grouping designs, having been authorised by the constituent companies and confirmed by the LNER board. As soon as Gresley was appointed as Chief Mechanical Engineer, plans began to be drawn up for a centrally controlled building programme for the following year; Gresley designs were to be built for various parts of the system, but certain pre-Grouping classes were also included. In 1925 the practice was instituted of preparing an annual building programme of locomotives and other rolling stock, which was presented to a joint meeting of the Locomotive and Traffic Committees and subsequently to the Board in November of each year.

Following the comparative testing of three classes of Atlantics, a more important trial took place in 1923, in which the Raven and Gresley Pacifics were compared. It would have been remarkable if the North Eastern design had demonstrated such superiority as would recommend it for adoption as a standard design, and whilst on the evidence of performance there was not a lot between the two, the Gresley design clearly had more development potential. Indeed, it marked one of the most important stages in British steam locomotive design, introducing a combination of large, well designed boiler and wide firebox, enabling plenty of steam to be generated and used, combining these with three cylinders and Walschaerts valve gear. It was a logical step forward from Ivatt's large Atlantic of 1902 and incorporated a number of important features from American practice, notably the 'K4s' Pacific of the Pennsylvania Railroad. Gresley's Pacific was a classic steam locomotive, powerful, fast and elegant, and without doubt one of the outstanding British designs of all time. Its principal features were adopted, with variations in proportions and in component design, not only in later Pacific designs on the LNER, but also in those on the LMS, Southern and British Railways.

Twelve Gresley Pacifics were built in 1922/23 to the orders of the Great Northern Board, one of which was the immortal *Flying Scotsman*, and a further 40 in 1924/25 with cut down boiler mountings and cab roofs to permit

Below:
Two hundred and eighty-nine 0-6-0s of Class J39 were built between 1926 and 1941, being employed on relief passenger and excursion trains, as well as general freight duties. Apart from those working from Stratford, which had a large allocation, they were rarely seen in the London area, none being permanently stationed at King's Cross or Neasden. No 1930 was built at Darlington in 1938. *IAL*

their use on the North British section. Most of the class were given names of racehorses, generally classic winners with splendidly appropriate names such as *Flying Fox* and *Royal Lancer*, but others commemorated horses which had borne names like *Spearmint* and *Sandwich* which in the minds of the non-racegoing public would appear to be inappropriate for such imposing locomotives. No satisfactory explanation has been discovered for the manner of choice of the names.

The new Pacifics met the immediate demands for increased haulage power on the main East Coast services, and released an equivalent number of smaller engines, mainly Atlantics, for lesser duties, in turn enabling older engines to be withdrawn. But new 4-4-0s were needed in Scotland, and, lacking a Gresley design for this type, the Robinson 'Director' class was selected in preference to the NBR 'Scott', 24 being built by contractors for the Southern

Scottish Area in 1924. At the same time, to meet the need for competent mixed traffic locomotives, Gresley's three-cylinder 2-6-0, Class K3, was turned out in quantity from Darlington, 60 being built there in 1924/25. The first of these had NER type cabs with low side windows, but later production was fitted with a pattern more in keeping with Gresley lines. The 'K3' class continued to be built until 1937, and 193 in all were turned out, to find their way to most parts of the system. Over half of the first Darlington production run was allocated to the Great Northern section, which enabled the transfer away of many of the earlier, less weighty, 'K2' class locomotives, these finding useful work on such services as the Southend trains from Liverpool Street, and the West Highland line from Glasgow to Fort William and Mallaig.

A new group standard design of tender was introduced with the third 'K3' to be built, holding 4,200gal of water

91

All Derby or St Ledger winners!

Top:
The inside cylinder 4-6-0s designed by S. D. Holden for the Great Eastern Railway were highly regarded as powerful for their size and for their low axle weight, which allowed them a wide route availability. After the introduction of the 'Sandringham' class in 1928, 'B12s' were made available for regular work on the Southend line, and here No 8532 is seen on the ashpits outside Southend shed in 1938. Built at Stratford in 1914, No 8532 was one of 55 of this class later fitted with the French ACFI type of feedwater heating equipment, which was eventually removed. Two years after this photograph was taken, the engine was transferred to Aberdeen, to begin a new life in the Northern Scottish Area.
Colour-Rail

Above:
Edward Thompson's Class B1 4-6-0s were seen in all parts of the LNER system, and here at Newcastle Central No 1100 is ready to leave with the 4.20pm train to Carlisle. Passenger workings on this cross-country line were in the hands of Gateshead shed, and the 'B1s' would normally carry out two round trips each day. No 1100 was one of a large number of this class built by the North British Locomotive Co, and entered service in November 1946. *Colour-Rail*

Above:

A typical 1930s LNER express, with a green engine and teak carriages, Class B3 No 6166 *Earl Haig* is seen leaving Aylesbury with an up restaurant car train from Manchester to Marylebone in December 1938. The engine is one of J. G. Robinson's majestic 4-6-0s of the 'Lord Faringdon' class, and, despite the introduction of 'B17' 4-6-0s of the 'Footballer' series to the Great Central section from 1936, the Neasden-based 'B3s', of which No 6166 was one, continued to take a share in the working of the heavier long distance trains. The standard LNER corridor stock had provision for three roofboards, although often only the centre one was used. However, because of the number of stops en route, Great Central trains often needed all three, giving clear indications of the train's destination and the principal stations served. *Colour-Rail*

Above left:

William Reid, Locomotive Superintendent of the North British Railway between 1903 and 1919, introduced two well-known classes of 4-4-0, with driving wheels differing in diameter but otherwise virtually identical. The 'Glens' were the smaller-wheeled version, and several including No 9035 *Glen Gloy*, were stationed at Eastfield shed, Glasgow, to handle traffic on the West Highland line to Fort William and Mallaig. At its home shed in August 1939, No 9035 is nicely turned out in black livery, lined out in red; in the background can be seen an old NBR six-wheeled coach, part of a breakdown train. Glen Gloy itself lies near Loch Lochy, the nearest station being Invergloy platform, closed when passenger services on the Fort Augustus branch ceased in 1933. *Colour-Rail*

Left:

Built at York carriage shops in 1937, Buffet Car No 51769 typifies the very best of LNER coachbuilding craft. Body framing was of teak, on a steel underframe, with teak panelling and roofboards of deal covered in canvas. The teak panels were varnished, with carefully lined out beading, and transfers used for the lettering and numerals. This coach was allocated to the Great Central section for services between Manchester and Cleethorpes and was one of some 25 new buffet cars constructed following the success of the original ones used on the Cambridge trains, which were conversions of older Great Northern open thirds. The new coaches included a small kitchen, a bar and seating for 24 passengers. It is seen here as restored on the North Norfolk Railway. *Brian Fisher*

Top:
The classic Gresley Pacific: Class A1 (later rebuilt to Class A3) No 2549 *Persimmon,* **built at Doncaster in 1925 and stationed at Grantham during most of the LNER period. The racehorse after which the engine was named was owned by the Prince of Wales, later King Edward VII, and won the Derby and the St Leger in 1896.** *Locomotive Publishing Co*

Above:
Pacific No 2581 *Neil Gow* **on 7 May 1932, under the Mitchell coaling plant at Doncaster Carr shed. This was one of the 20 Pacifics built by the North British Locomotive Co in 1924, which (until their appearance became altered in later years) could be distinguished from those built at Doncaster by the distinct bends in the sheeting where the firebox met the running plate, and at the foot of the casing over the steampipes.** *Neil Gow* **was stationed in the North Eastern Area until it was withdrawn after 39 years of service.**
T. G. Hepburn, Rail Archive Stephenson

and 7½ tons of coal. It was built in large numbers until the end of locomotive construction to LNER designs, the only external alterations being the substitution of straight sides for the original stepped-out coping, and higher fronts to those built after 1937. Not all new locomotives were provided with the 4,200gal tender, however; the principal exceptions were the Pacifics, which had an eight-wheel, 5,000gal tender, originally with coal rails but later with straight sides up to the limit of the load gauge, some of these being provided with corridors to enable the crew to be changed en route. There was also a smaller, 3,500gal tender for freight engines engaged on short haul work, whilst on occasion new engines were provided with tenders from withdrawn locomotives.

The LNER was not to need to build new eight-coupled locomotives for mineral traffic for several years, as large numbers of Robinson's 2-8-0 class had been turned out to Ministry of Munitions orders but were surplus to requirements, so that altogether 273 were purchased between 1924 and 1927, the last batch costing no more than £340 each. The Great Central had handed on 148 (including 17 with larger boilers, later replaced by the standard pattern), so the total on the LNER became 421, the most numerous class ever to run on the system. They served not only in their own territory of the Great Central, but were also allocated to such depots as March, Hull Dairycoates, and Thornton Junction, in Fife. Ninety-two were requisitioned by the Government for service in Egypt and Palestine. However, before the decision was taken to buy the 2-8-0s, Gresley obtained authority to build two Mikados, Type 2-8-2, Class P1: these were each fitted with a booster engine which could be used to drive the trailing wheels in the same way as that fitted to one of the Atlantics. Like the Pacifics, they had several features in common with the equivalent 2-8-2 class on the Pennsylvania Railroad and were designed to haul 100-wagon mineral trains between New England yard, Peterborough and Ferme Park, Hornsey. Unfortunately, because of operating difficulties with trains of this length the potential of this powerful design could not be exploited fully. The first 'P1' was turned out in time to take part in the parade held at Darlington in 1925, to mark the centenary of the Stockton

Left:
Great Western Railway No 4079 *Pendennis Castle* **leaving King's Cross for Grantham and Doncaster with the 10.10am train on 27 April 1925, during the exchange of GWR and LNER locomotives. The leading coach will work through to Sheffield Victoria, and is still in Great Northern livery. It is a brake composite built in 1906, one of Gresley's earliest coach designs.**
BBC Hulton Picture Library

& Darlington. Also brand new at this time was a 2-8-0+0-8-2 Beyer-Garratt locomotive, virtually a double Gresley 2-8-0 with a single massive boiler, the idea having originated with Robinson who had discussed the idea with Beyer Peacock & Co several years before. It may have been the case that the Garratt was intended to haul coal trains between Wath and Immingham, but in the event it spent its working life on the Worsborough Bank, near Barnsley, until electrification took over, when it was transferred to similar duties on the Lickey Incline on the LMS system.

Although they were powerful machines with a good turn of speed, the original Gresley Pacifics were not particularly economical on fuel. This was perceived to be due to the throttling effect of short travel valves, but although advice was submitted to the CME that he should consider an experimental redesign, he was reluctant to act. In 1925 trials were arranged with the Great Western under which GWR 'Castles' and LNER Pacifics were to exchange duties. The Pacific's task on the GWR was to run nonstop from Paddington to Plymouth over a sinuous, undulating road, alternating with a 'Castle', whilst the comparative stretch on the LNER was between King's Cross and Doncaster. The Pacific's performance on the Great Western improved as the trials progressed and the driver became more familiar with the route, but on the Great Northern main line the 'Castle' gave a much superior performance, not only from the point of view of timekeeping but also in fuel consumption. The way in which the trials were initiated has remained a subject of controversy, one school of thought holding the view that they were set up by the recently promoted Divisional General Manager, Alex Wilson, who was immensely proud of his new charges and wished to show them off to the rival Great Western; another theory has it that the matter was manoeuvred so that the superior valve performance of the 'Castles' could be brought home to the CME. Whatever the basis, the trials attracted wide public interest, and LNER partisans were disappointed at the outcome.

Most importantly, the lessons were learned, and first an improved valve design, with longer travel, was introduceed; later another feature of the 'Castles' was followed in the application of higher boiler pressure. All the 52 Gresley Pacifics in service in 1925 were converted to the new valve arrangements by 1931, but only five received the higher pressure boilers during this period, the remainder having to wait until their boilers were no longer capable of repair, mostly in the early 1940s. A further 27 were built with both of these improvements, the last appearing early in 1935, and being classed 'A3', those with the original boilers remaining as Class A1.

The modified valve design considerably increased the fuel efficiency of the Pacifics, so much so that it became possible to run nonstop from London to Edinburgh without running out of coal; this would have been an impossible task for one crew, so the corridor tender was devised, permitting the driver and fireman to be changed half-way along the run. Nonstop running of the 'Flying Scotsman' was inaugurated on 1 May 1928, although the timing remained at 8¼ hours until the 1932 accelerations.

At the end of 1929 a remarkable experimental locomotive emerged from Darlington works, with a 4-6-4 wheel arrangement, and classed 'W1'; given the number 10000 it earned the soubriquet 'Hush-hush' because of the secrecy surrounding the project. Its principal feature was a water tube boiler with a pressure of 450lb/sq in, constructed by the shipbuilder Yarrow & Co, of Glasgow; this was mounted on an elongated Pacific frame and provided with four-cylinder compound propulsion. Special attention was given to the problem of smoke clearance, and an overall steel sheeting fitted, the front end of which was designed following wind tunnel experiments. One of the reasons for secrecy was that Gresley and Sir Henry Fowler of the LMS were engaged in personal rivalry at the time, each producing his own version of a high pressure locomotive; as it happened, both the engines were exhibited to the press within days of each other. Of the two, the Gresley version was the more successful, as the LMS engine, named *Fury*, did not enter revenue earning service, and after a fatal explosion was withdrawn and later rebuilt. The novelty of many features of No 10000 brought problems which were expensive to overcome, and it was never sufficiently reliable to be fully accepted by the operating department, although it worked scheduled

Left:
Gresley Pacific No 4474 (later to be named *Victor Wild*) passing Laira with the down 'Cornish Riviera Express' during the exchange of 1925. The longer wheelbase of the Pacific restricted its maximum speed on the curving downhill stretches of the Great Western main line, and hard uphill work was required for time to be kept. Nevertheless No 4474 performed better on the GWR than did its shed companion No 2545 on the Great Northern. *BBC Hulton Picture Library*

95

Above:
No 2564 *Knight of Thistle* was not only built in Scotland, by the North British Locomotive Co, but was stationed in Scotland for most of its LNER period. Although one of the small number of Haymarket Pacifics provided with a corridor tender for working the non-stop 'Flying Scotsman', No 2564 was not often seen south of Newcastle, and was recorded in London on only three occasions, one being on a football special. Originally named *Knight of the Thistle*, new plates were cast in 1932, with an incorrect rendering of the name, an error which was never put right. The engine is seen outside Haymarket shed in August 1937.   *Colour-Rail*

Two examples of LNER poster art

Above:
Anna Zinkeisen was a well-known portrait painter, and an exhibitor at the Royal Academy. Her poster advertising the delights of Harrogate comprises a splendidly stylised group of visitors to the spa town in the 1930s, retaining its freshness and zest half a century after it was painted. It is not just a prestige advertisement, but one carrying a strong message: people so obviously enjoy themselves in Harrogate that who could resist travelling there by LNER?
Crown Copyright: National Railway Museum

Right:
The LNER Variety Programme was an amusing, yet to-the-point way of presenting specific travel information. On the lines of the traditional music hall poster, the headlines played on the titles of well-known productions in London's West End at the time. 'While Parents Sleep — they can travel in comfort by LNER' promote   an overnight return to Scotland for £2,

including sleeping berths. Also featured were details of excursions to race meetings, and to the FA Cup fifth round tie between Sheffield Wednesday and Chelsea. (The match was drawn, and in the end the cup was won by Newcastle United, so the LNER should have done well from football specials in that year, 1932.) *Crown Copyright: National Railway Museum.*

Left:
**Two Class P1 2-8-2s were
built at Doncaster in 1925,
and for a number of years
hauled 100-wagon coal trains
between New England and
Ferme Park. No 2393 took
part in the Stockton &
Darlington Centenary
Parade, and like its
companion was fitted with a
small booster engine
operating on its trailing
wheels (note the
Westinghouse pump to
provide compressed air to
cut the booster in and out).
The booster was removed
soon after this photograph
was taken, at Welwyn on
19 March 1938.**
H. C. Casserley

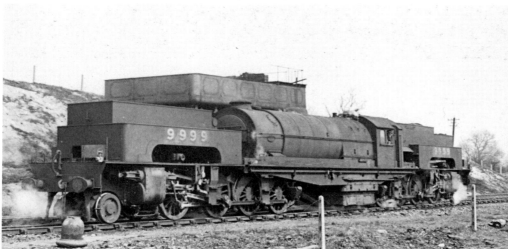

Below left:
**The Beyer-Garratt Class U1
took part in the Stockton &
Darlington Centenary
Parade. It is seen here at
Wentworth Junction on
18 April 1947. It was formerly
No 2395 but renumbered
under the 1946 scheme.**
H. C. Casserley

services on occasion, including the nonstop 'Flying Scotsman', and was displayed at several exhibitions of rolling stock. In 1937, after spending a large part of its life in workshops or in store, No 10000 was reconstructed along more conventional lines as a three-cylinder Simple.

At the other end of the passenger locomotive spectrum, Gresley's attitude towards suburban tank locomotives is of interest in that he did not impose his own classes on to other lines unless he considered they would be appropriate for the job. The LNER constituents which handled London suburban traffic had evolved three classes of locomotive for this work — the small-wheeled Great Eastern 0-6-2T, capable of rapid acceleration between closely spaced stations, the Great Central 4-6-2T designed for longer distances and higher speeds, and the Great Northern 0-6-2T somewhere between the two. So, more of the Gresley design, Class N2, were built for the King's Cross services, releasing older Ivatt 'N1s', which left for Nottingham and Yorkshire to replace 4-4-2Ts which in turn went to country branches to take the place of Stirling 0-4-4Ts, which were then withdrawn — such could be the cascade effect of introducing a new batch of locomotives. But 'N2s' were also drafted to Scotland, as an improvement on the NBR 4-4-2Ts, and for several years took a major part in the operation of suburban services from Glasgow, Edinburgh and Dundee. A small number of 'N2s' were used for a time on the Great Eastern outer suburban trains, but the major reinforcement of the Liverpool Street tank

allocation came from additional construction of the local product, LNER Class N7, no fewer than 112 being built to LNER orders. As for the Great Central, the services from Marylebone were adequately dealt with by the large Robinson 4-6-2Ts, LNER Class A5, no more being needed here. However, the North Eastern Area was short of powerful tank engines, and rather than construct more of the unsatisfactory 4-4-4Ts, Gresley decided on the only suitable class at his disposal, the 'A5s'. These were well received on Tyneside, but after an order for 13 had been executed, no more were built; instead (although not for 10 years), the 4-4-4Ts were themselves rebuilt as 4-6-2Ts, with commensurate improvement in performance.

Gresley made a number of proposals for larger tank engines, including 2-6-2T and 2-6-4T designs for the Great Northern, but these were turned down either because they would have been too long for the platforms at Moorgate station or unnecessary for outer suburban work as there were still plenty of Atlantics and 4-4-0s available. A further proposal for a 2-6-4T for the Great Eastern, with 6ft 2in wheels, was rejected in favour of additional tender locomotives. Nevertheless, in 1930 his 2-6-2T, Class V1, finally appeared, a neat and compact design which eventually totalled 92, including a later version with higher boiler pressure, a standard to which most of the class were eventually to be rebuilt. These found their way to the Great Eastern section, the North Eastern Area, and to Scotland to replace the 'N2s'.

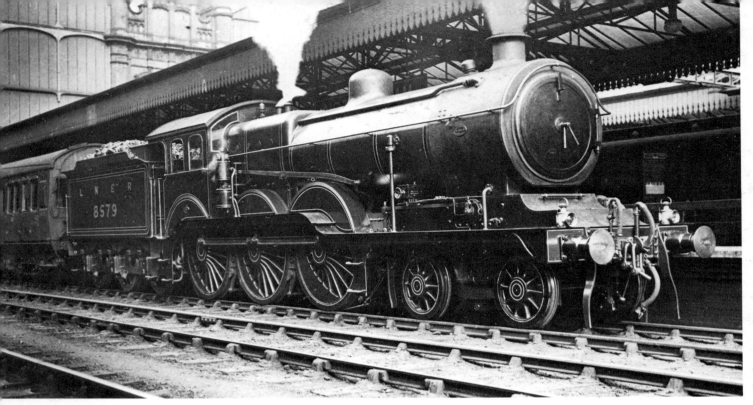

Above:

Class B12/2 No 8579, new from Beyer Peacock, at Nottingham Victoria with a Manchester to Marylebone express in 1928. Each of this batch of 10 'B12/2s' was kept at Gorton for a short period until run in, and used on Great Central section trains as far as Sheffield and Leicester. The drive to the Lentz poppet valves can be seen above the bogie, but this refinement did not fulfil its early promise and long travel piston valves were fitted when No 8579 was rebuilt with a larger boiler as Class B12/3, no more than four years after entering service.
T. G. Hepburn, Rail Archive Stephenson

The first steam rail cars, introduced in efforts to find a low cost solution to the problem of branch line operation, were bought from the Sentinel Co in 1926, and despite questions of unreliability and lack of capacity to deal with overloads, altogether 92 of various designs were acquired. Most were powered by two-cylinder 100hp engines, but there were also a few more powerful ones, and an articulated pair, as well as a number built by the Clayton Wagon Co. Sentinel also supplied 58 small shunting engines, including some for departmental use in the workshops and stores.

As the 1920s progressed, needs became pressing for new passenger locomotives, smaller than the Pacifics, to replace older engines due for withdrawal, and to provide more power to work the main Great Eastern expresses which were assuming greater importance with the increasing prosperity of the region. A new 4-4-0 class was designed at Darlington, embodying the Gresley precept of three cylinders; in this case they could be made to drive on to the leading coupled wheels, so enabling the conjugated valve gear to be mounted behind, instead of in front, of the cylinders — an advantage in that the linkage was less likely to be affected by dust and cinders from the smokebox.

Thirty-six were built at Darlington between 1927 and 1929, bearing the names of Shires in England and Scotland. One of the class was sent to King's Cross for a period when new, and worked turns normally allocated to an Atlantic, but the Great Northern was not then in need of further secondary passenger locomotives and none of the class, 'D49', was ever stationed permanently in the Southern Area. Later variations of the class, named after Hunts, were fitted with poppet valves in place of the usual piston valves, with different forms of drive.

A new 4-6-0 was required for the Great Eastern, but Gresley's design principles could not readily be accommodated in a design which kept within the strictures laid down by the civil engineer, having regard to the limitations imposed by a number of weak underbridges on that section. In the event matters reached a crisis: Doncaster was not making progress with the design, and new locomotives were badly needed. So, in a compromise, 10 new engines of the now obsolescent Holden class were built by Beyer Peacock, and the North British Locomotive Co was given a 'design and build' contract for the new 4-6-0s. By dividing the drive, so that the centre cylinder drove the leading coupled wheels, thus shifting weight on to the bogie, the axle loading was reduced to a level acceptable to the Engineer; the first batch of 10 was completed by the end of 1928. Despite the involvement of the North British Locomotive Co, the class has always been regarded as one of Gresley's, and further examples were built, mainly at Darlington, to make 73 in all. They were named at first after country estates in East Anglia and the northeast, and the earlier batches were known as 'Sandringhams', the first of the class bearing the name of the King's country residence in Norfolk; the LNER classification was 'B17'. At first used almost exclusively on Great Eastern services, from 1936 they began to be

allocated to the Great Central section, new engines built at that time being given the names of football clubs, and popularly known as the 'Footballers'. Unlike the 'D49' 4-4-0s, the 'B17s' did not normally venture north of York, and whilst on more than one occasion it was proposed to build a batch for service in the North Eastern Area, the class did not appear to have been welcomed there, and locomotives of other classes, such as the 'K3', were built instead.

The LNER possessed a continuing need for 0-6-0s as maids-of-all-work, and Darlington evolved a design for a class with 5ft 2in coupled wheels, which in course of time found its way to most parts of the system, 289 being built altogether, plus an additional 35 (the first batch to be built, in fact), having 4ft 8in wheels specially for mineral hauls in Scotland. The latter were classed 'J38' and the larger wheeled version 'J39', these being regarded as useful locomotives, not only for all kinds of freight duty but also for shorter distance passenger and excursion working, for which they possessed a fair turn of speed.

New locomotive construction reached its lowest ebb in the early 1930s; no more than 34 engines were completed in 1932, and only 17 the following year. Amongst interesting proposals which were cancelled around this time were two designs of 2-8-2T, primarily intended for short haul mineral traffic in the Nottingham area, to replace Ivatt 0-8-2Ts on similar duty. A number of important rebuildings took place, however, the most interesting being of two North Eastern Atlantics which were fitted with a booster incorporated in a bogie articulating the locomotive to the tender, a larger boiler being provided. These features were intended to correct two of the deficiencies — rough riding and lack of steam — which marked the conversion of the Great Northern Atlantic, but with more Pacifics entering service there was less work for the converted Atlantics than

would have been the case in earlier years. On the Great Eastern section, Edward Thompson, then Mechanical Engineer at Stratford, initiated a number of improvements to the native 4-6-0s and 4-4-0s, which were reboilered and generally updated on Gresley lines; also, more than 50 of the 4-6-0s were fitted for some years with ACFI feedwater heating equipment — the associated hardware detracting from the Edwardian lines of the engines — whilst some were provided for a period with Lentz poppet valves in place of the conventional piston valves.

Gresley also authorised studies to examine possibilities in other than conventional steam engines. One of these was a proposal, in 1928, to convert one of the electric locomotives used between Shildon and Newport to diesel-electric propulsion for use on the New England to Ferme Park coal trains; the second, in 1932, was to alter an Ivatt 0-8-2T to diesel-compressed air operation. Each of these was seen to suffer engineering deficiencies as the designs were refined, and neither progressed beyond the drawing board. In early trials of diesel-engined motive power developed by outside builders, two locomotives and four railcars were tested, but none proved to be mechanically satisfactory.

Finally, in further demonstration of his willingness to add to a pre-Grouping class where one was suitable, rather than go to the expense of designing afresh, Gresley built five 4-8-0T heavy shunting engines of an old Wilson Worsdell class in 1925, and in 1932 Gorton turned out a pair of 0-8-4Ts of Robinson pattern, in this latter case fitting a booster engine to the trailing bogie. But whilst these two locomotives were being turned out to obsolescent designs, Doncaster drawing office was in the early stages of developing a completely new eight-coupled passenger class, which was to turn out to be one of Gresley's most advanced designs.

THIRTEEN

Gresley Locomotives: 1934~1941

The all-round success of the 'A3' Pacifics prompted Nigel Gresley to consider extending the principles of the design to other types, and as a result two particular applications were identified. One was for a small number of substantially more powerful locomotives for the Edinburgh to Aberdeen road, as since the introduction of third class sleeping coaches in 1928 the overnight trains to Aberdeen had consistently loaded beyond the point at which even the Pacifics had to be piloted. The other need was locomotives for fast freight and mixed traffic service, more powerful and capable of longer point-to-point running than the 'K3s'. An abortive design had already been prepared for this, in which — following the rebuilt North Eastern Atlantics — a 2-6-0 with 6ft 2in driving wheels was to be articulated to its tender. Two of these had in fact been authorised in 1932, but had been cancelled in favour of a more radical solution.

Below:

An 0-6-0 and three generations of Great Northern express locomotives leave the plant at Doncaster in July 1938, after overhaul. They are Class J2 No 3073, Ivatt Atlantics Class C2 No 3254 and Class C1 No 3280, and Gresley Pacific No 4472 *Flying Scotsman*. The latter still retains its 180lb boiler but has acquired a non-corridor streamline type tender. Note the lining on the *back* of the tender, and on the buffer beam.
T. G. Hepburn, Rail Archive Stephenson

At this time Gresley had formed the opinion that the Lentz poppet valve system possessed advantages over the conventional piston valves, and had also been impressed by the smoke lifting ability of the unconventional sheeting fitted to No 10000. Consequently two designs were developed, both with a new wheel diameter of 6ft 2in — a 2-8-2 for the Aberdeen trains, and a 2-6-2 for fast freight services: each was to have the wide firebox of the 'A3s' (enlarged to 50sq ft in the 2-8-2) and a boiler with the 6ft 5in maximum diameter of the Pacifics, but shortened by 2ft in the 2-6-2. Originally both were envisaged in conventional form, but when the first 2-8-2 appeared from Doncaster Works in May 1934 it had boiler cladding based on that of No 10000, and Lentz valves. Classed 'P2', and provocatively named *Cock o' the North* it made a great impression when it first ran trials from King's Cross. Larger and more powerful than any other contemporary British express engine, arrangements were made for it to be sent to the French testing station at Vitry sur Seine, at which useful information was gained about draughting proportions. The second of the class came out in October 1934 and reverted to piston valves driven by Walschaerts gear, with derived motion for the inside valve; four more were built two years later, these being streamlined overall, with wedge-shaped smokeboxes instead of shrouding, the two original examples later being modified to the same outline. The

'P2s' were certainly powerful machines, and could deal adequately with any task normally presented to them, but the anomalous situation existed that they were often too big, and too heavy on coal, for much of the work, as apart from the sleeper trains few of the loadings were sufficient to justify such large locomotives; on the other hand they were masters of their work and all those who operated the 'P2s' paid tribute to their capabilities.

Before the 2-6-2 design could be finalised, developments took place in a new direction when, in contrast to the normal design task of the Pacifics of hauling heavy trains at average speeds of around 50mph, trials took place of lighter-weight trains running at much higher speeds. In November 1934 *Flying Scotsman* itself achieved 100mph — the first time this magic figure had been reached in fully authenticated conditions — and shortly afterwards an 'A3', *Papyrus*, reached 108mph in the course of running a seven-coach train from Newcastle to King's Cross in under four hours. The driver on each of these high speed occasions was W. Sparshatt, who had been regularly employed on the Pullman link with Great Northern Atlantics; he was well known for his ability to get the most out of an engine, and on his last day before retiring in 1936 it was reported that his train arrived at King's Cross on time when most other trains were running late.

Four more 'A3' Pacifics were included in the locomotive building programme for 1935, but Gresley decided to modify the design in three important ways. The boiler was shortened by a foot, with a corresponding increase in the length of the combustion chamber, and at the same time the pressure was raised to 250lb/sq in, whilst the entire exterior was covered in a silver grey cladding, including valances over the motion and coupled wheels. So was evolved the streamline form of the 'A4' class, the first of which was given the name *Silver Link*. To meet the requirement for the new high speed 'Silver Jubilee' train to commence running at the beginning of the 1935 Winter Timetable, *Silver Link* was turned out from Doncaster in no

more than 11 weeks, just in time to meet the operating deadline. At the inaugural press run, 112½mph was recorded, an average of 100mph being maintained continuously for 43 miles; no steam locomotive had ever before achieved such a performance. For the first three weeks, *Silver Link* ran the double journey from King's Cross to Newcastle and back without incident or failure, 537 miles in 24 hours, until the second of the class, *Quicksilver* was completed.

The Government's new Works Programme of 1935 enabled the LNER to allocate more money to build locomotives, and 43 were included in the expenditure arising from this, replacing a similar number of older machines which were withdrawn for scrapping; these included the North British Atlantics and most of the small Great Northern variety. The list of new engines included 17 further 'A4s' as well as 11 'B17s', 10 'K3s' and five of the new 2-6-2s. The 'A4s' were turned out from Doncaster in 1936/37 and were followed by a further batch of 14, to make 35 in all. The first of the new construction was painted green, but in 1937 five were painted Garter blue to work the 'Coronation' service and were named after the major countries in the British Empire. The streamlined outline was primarily intended to save horsepower at higher speeds, but a further important advantage emerged when it was found that the new shape gave considerably improved lifting of the exhaust, so that 'A4' drivers suffered less from obscured vision than did drivers of the earlier Pacifics. Two of the 'Sandringham' class operating the 'East Anglian' express were also given streamline form, but in this case the treatment was largely cosmetic, to gain publicity, as the train ran below the level of speed at which much benefit would accrue from the streamlining; moreover, the coaches were standard teak, not following the lines of the East Coast streamline trains.

When No 10000 was rebuilt in 1937 to work alongside the 'A4s', it too was provided with a streamline outline, but although it was the most powerful 6ft 8in locomotive in

Left:
A corner of Top Shed, King's Cross, in February 1938, with Class K2 No 4659 and two Class A1 Pacifics, No 2555 *Centenary* and No 4472 *Flying Scotsman*. *Centenary* was not named after a racehorse, but was the first locomotive to be completed at Doncaster Works in the centenary year of 1925. It had several moves around the sheds of the Great Northern section, and was based at Copley Hill, Leeds, at the time of the photograph.
C. C. B. Herbert

The Three Phases of *Cock o' the North*

Above:

Class P2 No 2001 *Cock o' the North* was a source of immense pride to the Doncaster staff who were responsible for building it. In this photograph, taken on 12 May 1934, can be seen (left to right): R. A. Thom, Mechanical Engineer, Doncaster; E. Windle, Chief Locomotive Draughtsman; J. S. Jones, Assistant Works Manager; J. Eggleshaw, Works Manager; two chargehand fitters and the foreman of the erecting shop; and, on the extreme right, the paint shop foreman. *NRM*

Centre right:

When first turned out, with shrouded front end and Lentz poppet valves, No 2001 was the subject of several test runs, as well as visiting the French locomotive testing station at Vitry sur Seine. Here it is seen at Grantham, with a shelter fitted in which engineers rode to observe the gauges and obtain indicator diagrams. *A. C. Cawston*

Bottom right:

Commencing with the third of the class, No 2003, a profile similar to that of the 'A4's was adopted, and *Cock o' the North* was rebuilt in this form in 1938. Here we see No 2005 *Thane of Fife* photographed at Eastfield, Glasgow, in July 1939, its home shed at the time being Dundee. The 'P2s' only occasionally appeared on passenger trains between Edinburgh and Glasgow, and the engine may have been visiting Cowlairs works for minor attention. *C. Lawson-Kerr*

service in Britain, it did not show any superiority over the 4-6-2s, and no further development of the type took place. Also in this period an outline drawing was prepared of an Ivatt Atlantic with a streamline profile, but this cannot have been considered seriously as by then the Atlantics had been superseded on the Pullman duties by Pacifics and were around 30 years old.

The final prewar development of the Pacifics was the fitting of a Kylchap double exhaust system and chimney to four of the last 'A4s', improving the emission of steam and exhaust gases, and so lessening back-pressure in the cylinders. Taking advantage of the long downhill stretch of line from Stoke summit, Driver Duddington and *Mallard* achieved a world record for a steam locomotive of 125mph. Gresley was informed by his staff that the Kylchap system was the main factor in enabling this speed to be reached, the best that the rival LMS having achieved being 114mph. However, the LMS did not possess an equivalent racing ground, without restrictions on such high speed.

The final development of the new 2-6-2 design had to wait until the first 'A4s' had been completed. After considering and discarding alternative outlines based on No 10000 as originally built, with Lentz valves, or streamlined as the 'A4s', the new class emerged clearly as a shortened 'A3'. The 'V2s' had a group standard 4,200gal tender and detail modifications such as a 'banjo' steam collector instead of a dome (originally introduced on the last batch of 'A3s') and, following the 'P2s', a wedge-shaped spectacle plate. Another feature was a monobloc casting for all three cylinders and valve chests. The first was given the name *Green Arrow*, the style under which a new freight service was operated, but only seven others of the class received names. Eventually 184 'V2s' were built, the last in 1944, compared with 113 Gresley Pacifics; the class must be regarded as one of the most successful multi-purpose designs anywhere, coping with all classes of traffic from slow freight to emergency substitute on a streamline express. They took over fast freight services from the 'K3s' and often ran turn about with the Pacifics, as well as finding an increasing role in replacing the various classes of Atlantics.

New batches of 'B17s' constructed in 1936/37, the 'Footballers', had their centre splashers painted in club colours, the first being named *Arsenal*. They were drafted to the Great Central section, but did not possess the reserve of power needed to cope with the increasing weight of the Marylebone expresses, and although a few remained, later in 1938 new 'V2s' and a small number of older Pacifics

Above:
Cock o' the North was finally rebuilt by Edward Thompson to the 4-6-2 wheel arrangement, with the streamline covering removed and small smoke lifters welded to the smokebox on each side of the chimney. It is seen here in BR days as No 60501, wearing the 50A shedplate of York shed, where it spent the last 10 years of its life until withdrawal in 1960, mainly working fast goods trains. *IAL*

Below:
Except for two brief periods, Class A4 No 4492 *Dominion of New Zealand* was stationed at King's Cross for all its life, and was a well-known performer on East Coast expresses both before and after Nationalisation. Its most notable exploit was in the summer of 1937, when it worked the non-stop 'Flying Scotsman' for 44 consecutive days. *Gresley Society collection*

Bottom:
Class A4 Pacific No 2512 *Silver Fox* being turned at King's Cross shed, shortly after the installation by Cowans Sheldon of a vacuum operating mechanism for the turntable, this being connected to the main hose of the engine and the ejector opened. *Silver Fox* possessed an additional embellishment in the form of a stainless steel fox, supplied by Samuel Fox & Co; at the time of the photograph the engine was still in silver grey livery, with the name on the sides of the boiler. *IAL*

Above:
The immortal *Mallard*, still in LNER blue but with its new owner's name on the tender. Renumbered 22, it is seen at Barton Mill, near Basingstoke, with the down 'Atlantic Coast Express' on 8 June 1948 in the course of the locomotive exchanges of that year. The leading coach is the ex-NER dynamometer car. *Mallard* is now in the possession of the National Railway Museum, York. *M. W. Earley*

displaced on the Great Northern section by 'A4s' made their appearance on GCR sheds. The Great Central line accepted the 'V2s' without difficulty, but their high axle loading of 22 tons debarred them from the Great Eastern section. For the same reason they were unable to be used on a number of other lesser main lines; they did however perform creditably on the difficult Waverley route between Edinburgh and Carlisle.

Many drawings exist of locomotive outlines prepared at Gresley's request, but which were not proceeded with. One of the most enigmatic of these abortive proposals was that for a 4-6-0 of greater power than the 'B17', but the only details which are known show that it would have been a powerful machine, potentially in the same class as the GWR 'Castles' and the LMS 'Royal Scots'. The maximum axle loading indicated that it would not have been permitted on the Great Eastern, even though a number of bridge improvements had been completed in 1935, the date of the drawing. The proposal in fact appears to have been made as a hedge against the possible inability of the 'V2s' to deal with fast passenger trains, but Gresley was confident that this class, although primarily introduced to deal with fast freight work, would also be engaged in hauling passenger trains, and this turned out to be the case, Nevertheless, at the time of the development of the 'V2' there was some hesitancy about the use of a leading pony truck instead of a bogie on locomotives hauling passenger trains which might average 60mph over long distances, and until the class had been proved in service, the 4-6-0 design was kept in reserve. A proposal in 1937 for an additional 32

'B17s' was qualified by the CME, stating that he contemplated the substitution of an improved type, which in the end turned out to be the 'V2', 28 being built with the money allocated for the 32 'B17s'.

During the mid-1930s the LNER acquired a number of secondhand locomotives, few of which formed useful additions to its fleet. Eighty-five old 4-4-0s, 0-6-0s and 0-6-0Ts were bought for £50,879 after the Midland & Great Northern Joint was taken over operationally by the LNER in October 1936; mostly of Midland design, 25 were in such poor condition that they were not taken into stock, and all except the shunting tanks were withdrawn within a few years. The following year 18 steam locomotives previously owned by the London Passenger Transport Board were acquired when the LNER took over the operation of steam trains from the Metropolitan Railway; these were reasonably modern tank engines, but all had gone by 1947.

Following the success of the 'A4s', Gresley began preparations for the next generation of his locomotives by

Top:
The first five Class V2 2-6-2s, popularly known as the 'Green Arrows', were built at Doncaster in 1936, the second to emerge being No 4772. It was allocated to York and is seen here at Neasden on 9 October 1937, probably after working the last stage of the overnight Glasgow to Marylebone fast goods. *G. T. Stamp, G. Goslin collection*

Above:
The final 25 Class B17 4-6-0s were given the names of prominent football clubs, the first being that of the leading team of the day, *Arsenal*. One of the Robert Stephenson batch of 1937 was No 2864 *Liverpool*, here seen at Manchester Central station on 10 June 1937. This engine was initially stationed at Gorton, later transferred to Colwick shed, Nottingham, and finally went to the Great Eastern section. *A. R. Price*

proposing to fit a 275lb/sq in boiler to the next batch of Pacifics, to give a greater reserve of power to cope with expected increases in the weight of the streamline services, Details exist of both this 'Super A4', and of an 'A3' elongated to a 4-8-2, with 6ft 8in coupled wheels, but it is unlikely that this latter subject was fully explored, as studies of the proposal throw into doubt a number of features, notably the ability of a single fireman to feed the large firebox. Given his energetic approach to matters of design, no doubt Gresley would have devised solutions to these problems, should so large a locomotive have been needed to deal with the heaviest non-streamline services.

Gresley's last designs were not for fast passenger trains, but were for mixed traffic work. A new 2-6-2, Class K4, came from Doncaster in 1937/38; with 5ft 2in wheels, specifically designed to work the heaviest trains on the West Highland line, only six of the class were built. Finally, in 1941, the 'V4' appeared, a scaled down version of the 'V2' with 5ft 8in wheels, 250lb/sq in boiler pressure, and a wide firebox. This relatively lightweight engine, with a maximum axle load of only 17 tons, was able to run over most of the system, but it is questionable whether the three cylinders or the wide firebox were essential on a design which, if multiplied, would have found itself on many minor duties for which a simpler, less expensive, design would have sufficed. As it happened, only two were built, the first being appropriately named *Bantam Cock*. On the same occasion as this locomotive was unveiled to the press, the prototype electric design for the Manchester to Sheffield electrification (as described in Chapter Fifteen) was also seen for the first time, presaging the beginning of a new era in British locomotive practice.

H. N. Gresley was knighted in 1936, becoming Sir Nigel, and the 100th Pacific to be built was named after him, an honour bestowed on few CMEs, and never before on one still in office. The later 1930s until the outbreak of war were to be his finest years, with the new streamline locomotives entering service and the LNER leading the world in high speed travel. The war abruptly interrupted this heyday, and after a brief period during which the 'A4s' were withdrawn from traffic, LNER motive power was fully put to work in handling the greatly increased volume of traffic generated by the war effort. Passenger trains became fewer, heavier and slower, and freight movements were increased substantially, so that the entire LNER stock of 'big engines' was pressed into service more or less indiscriminately. It was in these circumstances that Sir Nigel Gresley passed away, on 5 April 1941, a few weeks before his 65th birthday.

He was not to see the completion of a project for which he had campaigned for many years. This was the establishment of a properly engineered locomotive testing station, and, after trying in vain to get the support of the Government and locomotive industry generally, the LMS and LNER decided to set up their own station, at Rugby. This was delayed by the war, and was not opened until 1948, too late to be of any real value in the further development of the steam locomotive.

In retrospect, the 'A4' and 'P2' classes must be regarded as Gresley's masterpieces. The 'A4s' were probably the only locomotives in the country capable of achieving 100mph in everyday service, whilst they were equally at home on long distance trains averaging 60mph with 500-ton loads. The fact that the 'P2s' were not always economically used in their day-to-day employment should not detract from acknowledgement of their proficiency as machines; if they had been used to a greater extent on the East Coast main line south of Edinburgh, their load hauling ability would have been utilised much more effectively.

Had Nigel Gresley remained in office, particularly if peacetime conditions had continued, one can only speculate as to how matters might have turned out. Undoubtedly the very successful 'A4' design would have been developed further, and there is a strong possibility that the 4-8-2 would have been seen as well. But to what extent the 'V4' would have been replicated, or whether a less costly 4-6-0 would have been seen instead — as was the case on the Great Western and the LMS, and which was to be produced in large numbers by his successor — is yet another uncertainty. These imponderables are part of the continuing fascination of any study of Sir Nigel Gresley and his work.

Below:
Construction of the more powerful 'K3s' permitted the transfer to Scotland of several 'K2' class 2-6-0s, and by 1925 14 were at Eastfield shed, Glasgow, for work on the West Highland line. No 1782 *Loch Eil* was built in 1921, and it is of interest to compare this, which was virtually Gresley's first design, introduced in 1912, with the accompanying 'V4' there being almost 30 years between them. *C. Lawson-Kerr*

FOURTEEN

Post~Gresley Locomotives

At no time did Nigel Gresley have a nominated deputy, the nearest person to fill this role having been Oliver Bulleid, who was his senior headquarters assistant until Bulleid became CME of the Southern Railway on 1 September 1937. The next occupant of this post was D. R. Edge, who had previously been manager of the Carriage and Wagon shops at Doncaster, but who was not regarded as a likely successor to Gresley; in fact his position was mainly in the co-ordination of the various tasks falling within the CME's department. The title of Assistant Chief Mechanical Engineer had been borne by A. C. Stamer, who had been Raven's senior assistant on the NER, and who remained in charge of mechanical engineering in the LNER North Eastern Area until his retirement in 1933, when the title of Assistant CME was allowed to lapse. Elsewhere, Mechanical Engineers had been appointed in each Area, possessing delegated managerial authority for activities in their Areas, including the operation of the locomotive workshops, and the carriage and wagon workshops. Consequently, on Gresley's death, there was no obvious successor to the position of Chief Mechanical Engineer; this is perhaps indicative of Gresley's intention to remain in office after his 65th birthday, which, although contrary to the Company's general policy, would have been acceptable in wartime.

In the event, the Board selected Edward Thompson who was then Mechanical Engineer, Southern Area (Western Section), at Doncaster, and the senior of the Mechanical Engineers; he possessed broad experience of engineering management in all branches of rolling stock and, pre-Grouping had served with the Great Northern and North Eastern Railways. Thompson was a severe individual not noted for his tact when dealing with his staff, and in many ways was the antithesis of Gresley. He was 60 when appointed, so could not have had great expectations of succeeding Gresley, had the latter decided to continue in office. Thompson took over at a time when train services were seriously affected by the war, and the workshops were engaged in a variety of tasks from bending rails to form tank traps, to the fabrication of major components for aircraft, guns and armoured fighting vehicles. Darlington was still turning out 'V2s' but at a much reduced rate, and there were outstanding orders for 'J50' tank engines and 'O2' mineral locomotives. Despite official preference for the Stanier Class 8F 2-8-0, which had been adopted for service with the armies overseas, the 'O2s' were completed in 1942/43, whilst 'V2' production continued until 1944.

Other orders were cancelled, Thompson strongly expressing a view which had not been publicised during Gresley's lifetime; he considered that the policy of three cylinders with conjugated valve gear was misconceived, and advocated the use of two cylinders for all but the largest locomotives, on the basis of simplicity of construction and maintenance. Further, where three cylinders were essential, each should have a separate set of Walschaerts gear. In this he was supported by many who were responsible for locomotive operating; as periods between overhaul lengthened under the stress of wartime conditions, the conjugated valve mechanism became increasingly out of adjustment, and the shortage of skilled fitters exacerbated the situation. Thompson expounded the benefits of a more standardised approach to locomotive construction, and produced a plan under which he proposed to concentrate on a limited number of classes of new or rebuilt locomotives, an approach which Gresley had never

Above:
Edward Thompson, LNER Chief Mechanical Engineer 1941-46. *Railway Gazette*

adopted. This was basically a sound intention, but Thompson alienated many of his subordinates by his cavalier approach to the task, in particular in moving away from influence on design matters those who had been closest to Gresley in the past. Since he was already located at Doncaster, and the LNER headquarters departments had been evacuated from London to various country locations, he established the CME's office at Doncaster. Edge, as well as B. Spencer and N. Newsome, Gresley's personal technical assistants in the locomotive and carriage and wagon fields respectively, were transferred to other posts, whilst E. Windle was promoted to Chief Draughtsman, with special responsibility for locomotive design. To replace himself as Mechanical Engineer at Doncaster, Thompson moved A. H. Peppercorn from the similar position at Darlington, at the same time reviving for him the title of Assistant Chief Mechanical Engineer.

When Thompson's plans were published, they were regarded as sound, placing emphasis on the advantages which would accrue from standardisation of components, particularly expensive items such as boilers and cylinders. The most interesting locomotive in the list was a medium powered mixed traffic 4-6-0, the equivalent of the Great Western 'Hall' and the LMS 'Black Five'; in Thompson's view, the 2-6-2 'Bantam Cock' was not the type for this work, and he set about producing his engine, the 'B1' as far as possible from standard parts. He took the boiler from the 'Sandringham' class, strengthened it to withstand a pressure of 225lb/sq in, and using an existing coupled wheel diameter of 6ft 2in and the outside cylinders of the 'K2' 2-6-0 (although new patterns had to be made) he produced a nicely proportioned locomotive which gained

general approbation. The first of the class appeared in December 1942 and was named *Springbok*, and although not to be remarkable for their speed or agility, all but one of the first 41 were given the names of species of antelope, one unfortunate engine being called *Bongo*.

Thompson was anxious to prove his points in a larger locomotive, and was aware of the operating difficulties with the 'P2' class 2-8-2s; the next month one of these appeared rebuilt into a 4-6-2 type, which earned him a good deal of justified criticism. To retain the existing short connecting rods, the leading bogie was positioned in front of the cylinders, resulting in an ungainly appearance and completely destroying the elegance of the Gresley design. Moreover, time was to show that the overall wheelbase, longer even than that of the 'P2', reacted to the engine's disadvantage, whilst the reduction in adhesion weight made the rebuild notoriously light on its wheels. Nevertheless Thompson was satisfied — initially at any rate — and with Board approval rebuilt the remaining five of the class, as well as amending the design of the last four 'V2s' on order, so that these too appeared as 4-6-2s, also in rather ungainly form. These 6ft 2in hybrids were used as the basis for a new design of mixed traffic Pacifics, of which 15 were built at Doncaster in 1946/47, the first being named *Edward Thompson*. The CME earned the further opprobrium of LNER enthusiasts by rebuilding the first Gresley Pacific, *Great Northern*, in similar form, retaining the 6ft 8in wheels, with the intention of building a new class on the same lines.

With the boiler and cylinders developed for the 'B1', Thompson also derived a 2-8-0, Class 'O1', using the frames and wheel centres of the Robinson 'O4'. Further,

Right:
Edward Thompson's Class B1 4-6-0 is regarded as his most successful locomotive, a neat and straightforward design which was replicated to a total of 410. No 1005 *Bongo* **was completed at Darlington in 1944 and allocated to Stratford shed. It is seen here at Parkeston, being prepared for a return working to Liverpool Street.**
C. C. B. Herbert

with a shortened version of the same boiler, a 'K1' 2-6-0 appeared, reconstructed from a 'K4', and also a new design of 2-6-4T, Class L1, both of these having 5ft 2in coupled wheels. For a medium power 0-6-0, Thompson took the largest Robinson class, and rebuilt it with piston valves and a higher pitched boiler; otherwise it was little changed from a design which first saw the light of day as far back as 1901. A further rebuild was of an obsolete Robinson 0-8-0 mineral class into a 0-8-0T, Class Q1. This was an ingenious conversion which made use of materials already to hand for a batch of 0-6-0T shunting engines, together with the robust frames of the Gorton engine; at the same time the original tenders, still serviceable, were re-allocated to new

locomotives and so saved steel, which was very difficult to obtain at that time.

These classes were to be multiplied under Thompson's plans by new construction and continuing conversion of old locomotives, and he also proposed to maintain in service a number of existing classes. However, he also experimented with other rebuildings; but in only one case was more than a single engine converted. These included an inside-cylindered version of a 'D49' 4-4-0 and a two-cylinder rebuild of a 'K3' 2-6-0, both retaining the original boilers. Examples of two classes of 4-6-0 were also rebuilt with the 'B1' boiler and cylinders; these were the GCR 'Valour' class, one only of which was so dealt with,

Above:
The 'K1' class was originally conceived in LNER days, one engine having been rebuilt in 1945 to meet Thompson's specification for a medium power goods engine. However, the quantity order for the class was not placed until 1947, and the contractors, the North British Loco Co, did not effect delivery until 1949/50. Compared with the 'B1s', note the cutting away of the footplating to provide improved access to the steam chest covers. *Rev J. B. Bucknall*

Below:
Thirteen of the Great Central 'Q4' 0-8-0s were rebuilt by Thompson in the form of 0-8-0Ts, and reclassified 'Q1'. No 9927, originally No 6139, is seen at Eastfield shed, Glasgow, where it spent its working life from 1943 until withdrawal in 1956. Note the 'LNER' plate, the 'not to be moved' signs and the graffiti chalked on the tank side. *IAL*

and the Gresley 'B17', of which class ultimately 10 were converted. Such radical alterations to the locomotives, involving new cylinders, valve gear and other components, were extremely expensive, and the justification is not easy to grasp. Renewal of a boiler by one of a different type however is another matter, if the conversion is relatively simple, and applying the standard boiler to other classes when the original boilers fell in was a reasonable course to follow: this was the case with a number of GCR and GNR 2-8-0s and 'B17' 4-6-0s.

Thompson visualised a postwar building programme comprising 1,000 locomotives, but his retirement at the end of June 1946 came before he had time to do much more than lay the foundations of the programme. In the event, in addition to rebuildings, the total of postwar locomotives entering stock as a result of LNER design initiative or purchases from outside amounted to 952, so that Thompson's plan can be said to have been virtually carried out to completion. There were a number of

alterations to his original intentions, particularly as the availability of low cost freight locomotives from the Ministry of Supply enabled the Company to purchase quantities of these, as had been the case after World War 1, so saving substantially on the cost of new construction. 200 of a design inspired by R. A. Riddles and dubbed 'Austerities' were acquired in 1946/47, and 75 saddle tanks were similarly purchased in the same period. Unlike the Robinson 'O4s', however, neither of these two classes were related to any previous LNER design, but they filled an urgent need. Even under BR auspices the planned total of 400 further 'B1s' was achieved, the last being delivered in 1952, by which time the BR standard Class 5 was entering service. Most of the 'B1s' came from the North British Locomotive Co, the Vulcan Foundry and Darlington, but none from Doncaster — it is a surprising fact that until a batch of Class 5s was commenced in 1955, Doncaster had never built any 4-6-0s.

Thompson was followed as Chief Mechanical Engineer by A. H. Peppercorn, who had also made successive moves up the mechanical engineering ladder; an amiable, outgoing personality, he set about maintaining the impetus of Thompson's programme. At the same time he restored the Pacific design to a more conventional outline by moving the outside cylinders forward to the usual position between the wheels of the bogie; however, he did not revert to Gresley's conjugated valve gear, and continued to provide the new Pacifics with three sets of Walschaerts

Below:
An up Cambridge express at Hadley Wood station in 1946. The locomotive is Class B2 No 1671 *Royal Sovereign* (originally No 2871 *Manchester City*), rebuilt by Edward Thompson from Class B17 in 1945. It was later used for royal train workings between King's Cross and King's Lynn, en route to Sandringham. *C. R. L. Coles*

Below:

Arthur H. Peppercorn, LNER Chief Mechanical Engineer 1946/47. *Railway Gazette*

gear. Also, he introduced a new profile to the cab. The final versions of the LNER family of Pacifics were powerful machines, 15 being built with 6ft 2in coupled wheels before a 6ft 8in version was introduced, of which 49 were built at Darlington and Doncaster within two years. They were given the classification 'A1', the second time this had been used. The class was reputed for running very high annual mileages, with lengthy intervals — averaging 100,000 miles — between heavy repairs; five were fitted with roller bearing axleboxes, which had the effect of adding another 20% to the interval between heavy repairs.

Thompson's programme did not include any diesel or electric locomotives, but Gresley's proposal for the Manchester to Sheffield electrification went ahead as part of the blanket authorisation for this project, whilst he had also inaugurated plans for four 350hp diesel-electric shunting engines, which were authorised in February 1941 but not completed until 1944/45. They were built at Doncaster, using English Electric equipment, and are of

Below:

Peppercorn Class A1 No 60161 *North British*, the last but one Pacific to be built at Doncaster. It was stationed at Haymarket for all its working life, except for two brief spells at the ex-Caledonian shed at Polmadie, Glasgow, when it worked trains on the West Coast main line. Note the hand-painted coat of arms on the nameplate. *IAL*

interest in that they were fitted with provision for ready adaption as static power plants to provide a limited supply of electricity should this have been needed in a wartime emergency.

After Thompson's retirement, studies were made of the possibilities for wide scale employment of diesel propulsion, and the LNER promulgated the most ambitious main line diesel programme of all the main line railways. Not only were 176 diesel-electric shunting engines to be purchased, but proposals were drawn up for 25 diesel-electric locomotives, to be used in pairs on services between King's Cross and Scotland, and for the necessary maintenance establishments to be constructed at each terminal. However, although tenders were received from six manufacturers, nothing further was done, because the end of 1947, and of the LNER's existence, was approaching; the nationalised administration was content to run trials with the few locomotives then in being or on firm order, the policy of the Railway Executive being to give steam an Indian summer before what was thought to be the onset of electrification. Had the LNER scheme gone ahead — preceding 'the Deltics' by 10 years — valuable information would have been obtained and in all probability the BR conversion from steam to diesel traction would have taken place earlier, with less expense being incurred on unsuccessful designs. Investigations also took place into the feasibility of multiple-unit operation, following trials with a GWR railcar in the Newcastle area, and outline drawings were prepared of railcars and trailers, but without any firm decisions being taken.

An important post-Gresley activity was the complete renumbering of the locomotive stock on a block basis, with most powerful express locomotives occupying the lowest numbers. The first proposals for such a scheme had in fact been discussed in 1936, but it was not until 1943 that details were finally worked out. This was not an opportune time to put in hand a wholesale renumbering programme, and it was not until 1946 that the scheme was fully implemented; even so, a number of changes were made to the original proposals, and some interim renumbering took place.

Despite the abberations introduced by Edward Thompson, the LNER series of locomotive designs retained much of the elegance which was a feature of the Gresley era, and the last class, the 'K1' 2-6-0, was a recognisable successor to Gresley's first 2-6-0 of 1912. Fortunately, thanks to the efforts of a small number of enthusiasts, several LNER locomotives have been preserved, notably *Flying Scotsman* and no fewer than six 'A4s', two of which are across the Atlantic Ocean, but *Sir Nigel Gresley, Bittern, Mallard* and *Union of South Africa* may be seen in this country. Others include the first 'V2', *Green Arrow*, and examples of the 'N2' and 'K4' classes, whilst from the Thompson period there is a 'K1' and a couple of 'B1s'. Unfortunately very few LNER locomotives found their way to Woodham's at Barry, practically all having been withdrawn by the end of 1966. No Gresley racehorse Pacifics remain, although there is a steady business in their nameplates. We are fortunate,

therefore, that in a number of private collections, as well as at the National Railway Museum, the Gresley style of locomotive engineering can still be seen, and on occasion, heard.

In 1923, Sir Vincent Raven had estimated that the LNER would need 185 new locomotives each year, to keep the stock up to date. In fact, during 30 years from 1923 until the construction of locomotives to LNER orders ceased in 1952, some 2,900 locomotives were built or bought; representing a yearly average of less than 100. By the end of 1947 the total steam stock had fallen to 6,545 engines.

Apart from the inevitable changes in upper management consequent on nationalisation, the division of the LNER into three Regions did not have an immediate effect on locomotive policy or allocations. It is important to note however that the first BR Standard locomotives to be built were allocated to Stratford and Norwich, to provide a long overdue boost to services on the erstwhile Great Eastern; 13 of the first batch of Class 7 Pacifics went there, including *Britannia* herself.

Arthur Peppercorn, the last CME of the LNER, retired at the end of 1949, to be succeeded at Doncaster by J. F. Harrison, a Gresley stalwart who rose to become Chief Engineer (Traction and Rolling Stock) of British Railways. LNER influence continued in this position when T. C. B. Miller, another Gresley premium apprentice, was appointed Chief Mechanical and Electrical Engineer of British Railways, to be instrumental in the development of today's InterCity 125 HSTs, the successors of the LNER high speed trains of the 1930s.

Above:
J. F. Harrison, Assistant Chief Mechanical Engineer of the LNER. He was later Chief Engineer (Traction and Rolling Stock), British Railways. *IAL*

FIFTEEN

Electrification

Around the turn of the century, when rapid progress was being made in the development of electricity, Newcastle-upon-Tyne was a centre of expertise in this new branch of engineering. Charles Parsons applied the steam turbine to electricity generation, and the work of Joseph Swan led to the widespread introduction of the incandescent electric lamp. During the same period the Newcastle Electric Supply Co was active in extending its distribution mains, and in 1899 Charles Merz founded the firm of consulting engineers Merz & McLellan, who acted as electrical advisers to the North Eastern Railway. In this general atmosphere it is understandable that the NER should become the leader in the field of railway electrification in the provinces, converting the North Tyneside suburban lines to third rail multiple-unit operation as long ago as 1904, following this the next year by an overhead system on the short, steeply graded line down to Newcastle Quayside.

In 1915, as a proving ground for more ambitious schemes, 18 route miles were electrified between Shildon and the Erimus yard near Newport, this time at 1,500V overhead. A mineral line, then with heavy occupation, it conveyed coal from the pits in the interior of County Durham to Teesside for use in the steelworks, and for export; 10 1,100hp Bo-Bos were built for this service. Experience with the Shildon to Newport line, combined with the favourable light in which electrification was viewed in the region, and supported by the fact that the North Eastern Railway would probably have had no difficulty in raising the money, encouraged the NER Board to consider electrifying its main line from York to Newcastle, also at 1,500V dc. Eighty-seven freight and 20 passenger locomotives were postulated, one of which was actually built, a 1,800hp 2-C-2. It was constructed before the line was ready for it, and apart from trial outings or at exhibitions, it was never seen in public. (Incidentally, Sir Vincent Raven did not visualise electrification extending beyond Newcastle; his Pacifics would be used onwards to Edinburgh.)

So, at Grouping, out of 6,307 total route miles, the LNER possessed 58 route miles of electrified track in three separate sections, all inherited from the North Eastern, plus 126 multiple-unit motor coaches and trailers, and 13 locomotives in three classes. In addition, there were the 4½ miles of the Grimsby District Light Railway, opened in 1912 by the Great Central Railway to serve the new port of Immingham. This would be more correctly regarded as a tramway, and, running on its own trackbed, had no physical connection with the main line. Sixteen single-deck tramcars were provided, operating at 500V dc from overhead conductors. Four cars were withdrawn in 1934, and the line was closed in 1961.

Although this was the sum of the electrified portions of the LNER system at Grouping, this is not to say that other constituent companies had not given serious thought to electrification. In the early years of the century, both the Great Eastern and the Great Northern had considered the conversion of at least part of their suburban systems, and indeed the GER had obtained Parliamentary powers in 1903, but in neither case was it considered that the expense would be justified. Moreover, there was strong opposition in many quarters — not least from the Mechanical Engineers, Holden and Ivatt, each of whom indicated that they could match anything put forward by the protagonists of electricity, and built special locomotives to prove their case. Unfortunately neither Holden's Decapod nor Ivatt's 0-8-2T lived up to its designer's hopes, but by the time their failings had been demonstrated the impetus for electrification had been lost, and season ticket holders travelling to Liverpool Street and King's Cross continued to be served by steam for another half century or more.

With the strong North Eastern influence on the LNER Board, it is surprising that nothing more was heard of the York to Newcastle proposal, but there is no evidence that it was ever considered again. Raven was a strong advocate of electrification, and in this he was supported in principle at least by Gresley, who was broad-minded on the subject, on one occasion reminding members of the Institution of Locomotive Engineers that they were not the Institution of *Steam* Locomotive Engineers, but that all kinds of locomotives were their concern. (And, at a lecture given by Raven to a GWR Debating Society, even C. B. Collett was heard to remark that South Wales coal should be used for generating cheap power for railway supplies, and that he for one would be glad to be relieved of the responsibility for high pressure locomotive boilers.)

A simplistic contemporary argument in favour of electrification was expounded by H. A. Watson, General Superintendent of the NER: with steam one has to cater for trains moving at seven different speeds, but with electricity only three — 60mph for express trains, 30mph for fast goods and stopping passenger, and 15mph for slow goods.

Above:

New stock for the north Tyneside suburban system was delivered by Cammell Laird in 1937, and the original NER-designed coaches were transferred to the newly electrified south Tyne services. In 1941 a new colour scheme of blue and grey was adopted, and ex-NER driving trailer third coach No 23791 is seen in this livery. Note the LNER totem on the coach sides. *NRM*

Right:

Car No 1 of the Grimsby District Light Railway at Corporation Bridge station, Grimsby, in April 1947. *A. F. Cook*

Below:

Two classes of electric locomotive, one for mixed traffic and a second for passenger services, were specified by Gresley for the Manchester, Sheffield and Wath electrification. One of those built in BR days for passenger work, No 27002 *Aurora* is seen approaching the western portal of the new Woodhead Tunnel. Note the Thompson coach in the foreground.

John Clarke

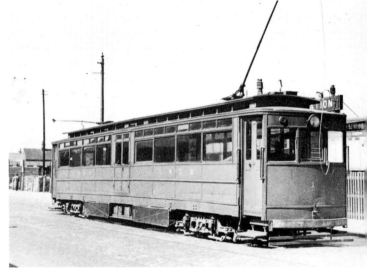

Raven went on to say that with electrification 60% savings could be made in coal consumption, and the coal could be of the lowest quality, not the high grade needed for steam engines. He compared an 0-C-C-0 electric locomotive with a steam engine, on the basis of 60,000lb tractive effort. The electric locomotive could be contained within the load gauge, and be driven by one man, but the steam engine — he outlined an 0-8-2 tender locomotive — would stand 14ft 6in high with a 7ft 1in boiler and would need a team of firemen to feed the 76sq ft grate.

In the 1920s three Government-sponsored committees considered electrification of the railways. In 1920, and again in 1927, when Gresley was a member of the committee, recommendations were made that future electrification should be at 1,500V dc overhead, or 750V dc third rail, according to the circumstances. The most important of the three committees was that chaired by Lord Weir, of which Sir Ralph Wedgwood was a member, and which was charged with making recommendations for main line electrification. Weir commissioned Merz & McLellan to cost a scheme for the LNER main line from King's Cross to Doncaster and Leeds, together with the major branches, eg to Nottingham and to March; this was calculated to cost £8.6 million, producing a 7.22% return on investment. In its final report, in 1931, the Weir Committee concluded that a comprehensive programme of electrification should be aimed at, and this was supported by a separate, more broadly based, report by a Royal Commission on Transport, which advocated the electrification of all suburban lines.

It is clear that although it ignored the claims of the North Eastern, the LNER Board addressed itself to the question of electrification as one of its first considerations, priority being given to the London suburban lines of the Great Northern. A Technical Committee was set up in 1923 (with Raven in the chair, and Gresley a member), to consider the subject, and a report was compiled outlining a scheme for electrification as far out as Hitchin, at 1,500V dc, but at 650V for the inner suburban services, so that these would be compatible with the Metropolitan system. Apart from express passenger and fish trains, which would be operated throughout by steam, a changeover point would be established at Hitchin; 20 electric locomotives were envisaged, replacing 60 steam engines.

Financial stringency caused the plans to be shelved, but they were revived in 1930 when the Board resolved to undertake the electrification of the main line to Welwyn Garden City, together with the High Barnet and Hertford North branches, but with the proviso that an adequate grant should be received from the Government. Perhaps the Government considered that it had done enough at this stage, by remitting Passenger Duty and passing the 1929 Development Act, but if it had been thought that these measures would stimulate the railways into electrification, that was not how the LNER looked at it. Neither Weir, nor the Royal Commission, prompted the Government to act quickly, but perhaps the influence of the latter can be seen in the establishment of the London Passenger Transport Board, which, under the leadership of Lord Ashfield, maintained the progress already being made in extending the London Underground system. The Piccadilly Line reached Cockfosters in 1933, and whilst tapping new housing areas, undoubtedly encroached on LNER territory; indeed, despite the relief the new extension would afford to the overloaded LNER system, the inevitable loss of revenue was viewed with concern. However, the growth of the outer London suburbs generated an increasing amount of traffic into London, and clearly the LNER was unable to cope with this influx. So a programme was evolved under which the High Barnet branch would become part of the Underground system, and work was completed in 1940. The establishment of a scheme of pooling receipts partly compensated the LNER for the traffic which had been lost.

In the meantime, further reviews had taken place of the problems of the Great Eastern suburban lines, and in 1927 outline plans were considered for a £7.5 million scheme, returning 5.1%, for electrification between Liverpool Street and Shenfield, on the Colchester main line (with a new station at Crowlands), and of the Ongar branch. It is of interest to note that the report was compiled by Fred V. Russell, then in the Divisional General Manager's office, but who earlier in his career had been instrumental in the design of the Decapod in 1902. Two years later a scaled down plan was costed at £4.9 million, with a better return amounting to 11.9% after 10 years, in which allowance appears to have been made for increased traffic; savings were made by cutting back the electrification to Gidea Park, and reassessing the need for new stock. Each of these projects called for major civil engineering works, including widening, and a flyover at Ilford.

As with the GNR scheme, the ultimate solution lay in accepting that the London Terminus, Liverpool Street, had to be relieved of part of its traffic, and so the Central Line of the Underground system was extended to take over the Ongar branch; main line electrification eventually reached Shenfield in 1949, at 1,500V dc overhead.

Elsewhere, and going back in time, a new suburban electrification had been initiated in 1931, when the Manchester, South Junction & Altrincham line was converted to 1,500V overhead supply. This was owned jointly with the LMS, and the coaching stock was to LMS design. Later, in 1938, the Tyneside electrification was extended by 10 route miles to South Shields, the prewar stock used on the North Tyne lines being refurbished for this service, whilst the original system was provided with new all-steel coaches, 128 being supplied in articulated pairs, together with four motor parcels cars. Originally painted a cheerful red and cream (reviving a short lived NER livery), they were later repainted blue and grey and were at first compared unfavourably with the earlier stock of North Eastern design, the bucket seats — similar to those provided in the new tourist coaches — coming in for particular criticism. The Tyneside system was de-electrified in stages in 1967/68, much being incorporated in the Tyne & Wear Metro system of 1980. The Shildon to Newport line had already reverted to steam in 1935; traffic had fallen to 15% of the 1913 level, and money needed for system renewals could not be justified. The 10 Bo-Bos were placed in store.

The 1935 New Works provisions gave the opportunity for spending on a more expansive scale than the Company had previously enjoyed. Consequently, and after much consideration of alternative proposals, it was decided to electrify the Great Central route across the Pennines between Manchester London Road and Sheffield Victoria, and Wath Yard, near Mexborough. The heaviest traffic comprised coal trains travelling westward to the industrial areas of Lancashire, but this important link also carried a respectable amount of passenger traffic which had to be interspersed with the slow-moving freight trains. The increase in line capacity offered by electrification and the end of steam operation through the long bores of Woodhead Tunnel were the prime reasons for the priority given to this scheme, which was originally estimated to cost £1.6 million, to return 10%. This was before it was realised that a new tunnel would have to be bored.

The original expectation was that 25 passenger, 64 freight and 32 banking and shunting engines would be needed, 10 of which would be provided by the conversion of the Shildon Bo-Bos: 196 steam locomotives would be replaced. Great attention was given not only to the haulage of the heavy unbraked coal trains, but also to the problems of slowing down and stopping them: 41 40-ton brake vans of a special design were envisaged to supplement the electrical and mechanical braking systems on the locomotives. However, it was found in trials that better and safer operating would result from running shorter trains, which removed the need for the banking engines and brake vans. A. G. Hopking and A. H. Emerson of the electrical engineer's staff, in conjunction with leading British manufacturers, developed specifications for a Bo-Bo mixed traffic locomotive of 1,868hp, followed by a 2,700hp Co-Co for the higher speed passenger services. In the event, one prototype mixed traffic locomotive was completed just before Gresley's death in 1941, so that he had the satisfaction of introducing to Britain the first main line electric locomotive since Raven's 2-C-2 of 1922 — a similarity existed between the two in that each was built before the track was ready for it. Gresley's locomotive successfully passed acceptance trials on the Altrincham line, and was employed on the Netherlands railway system between 1947 and 1952; as a result of this extensive testing several modifications were made to the original design before the production locomotives — reduced in number to 57 — were completed. These were followed by the larger Co-Cos, of which in the event only seven were found to be necessary. On the withdrawal of passenger services between Manchester and Sheffield in 1968, they were sold to the Netherlands Railways. As had been the case with the Shildon to Newport line many years before, railborne coal traffic declined severely, such that the MS&W line became redundant, and was closed in 1981, after only 29 years of electrification.

In addition to his other investigations, Sir Vincent Raven, as Technical Adviser to the Board during 1923, was asked to report on the organisation of electrical engineering work. He recommended that large schemes of electrification should be in the hands of the CME, but that signalling should be separately controlled under a signals engineer. Gresley did not at that time possess an electrical engineer of sufficient experience, and as a result H. W. H. Richards was recruited from the Southern Railway at the end of 1924. Before Grouping, Richards had been Traction Engineer with the London Brighton & South Coast Railway, having been involved with the 6.6kV overhead electrification schemes of that company. Despite the financial stringency of the period, his staff was increased in 1928 to deal with the preparation of new schemes, and in 1936, with definite prospects in sight for the Shenfield and Manchester to Sheffield conversions, the group was further strengthened by the appointment of H. H. Swift as assistant to Richards; previously he had been with English Electric. A. H. Emerson, one of only three LNER premium apprentices in both mechanical and electrical engineering, was a technical assistant at the time; his LNER training was to lead to his eventual responsibility, in BR days, for the Euston to Gretna Green electrification.

On Edward Thompson's appointment as Chief Mechanical Engineer, Richards became Chief Electrical Engineer, and his position was made independent of Thompson; instead, he now reported direct to the Chief General Manager. Swift was appointed Assistant Electrical Engineer, and after nationalisation rose to become CMEE of the Southern Region. Richards retired at the end of 1947, without having had the satisfaction of seeing any of the projects on which he had laboured for so long coming to fruition, although they were all completed, and more, by British Railways. But, some 70 years after the NER announced its intention to electrify from Newcastle to York, conversion of this stretch of line is still awaited. The 13 ex-NER electric locomotives were still extant at nationalisation, but did not survive much longer. They, together with the MS&W prototype and two Southern Railway locomotives built in 1941, were the only electric locomotives to pass into BR stock. Despite all the hopes and the planning, it is a sad commentary on official attitudes towards railway electrification during the period of the Grouping that, in contrast to the countrywide increase in the use of electricity during the interwar period, there was less electrified route mileage in the LNER system in 1947 than when the Company commenced operations in 1923. It has been said that had Sir Herbert Walker, General Manager for many years of the Southern Railway and an outright advocate of electrification, been in charge of the LNER, he would somehow have raised the money to electrify the Great Northern main line at least as far as Peterborough. But it would be wrong to attribute any anti-electricity attitudes to the LNER management: when a clear case was made, and the finance was available, as in the Manchester, Sheffield and Wath scheme, the plans were pushed ahead.

SIXTEEN

Train and Traffic Control

For many decades prior to the Grouping, the railways in Britain had followed the practice of using semaphore signals to inform drivers of the condition of the road ahead, the arm falling to a lower quadrant position to indicate authority to proceed. Arms were painted red, and at night a red light showed that the signal was 'on', ie at danger, and a green light indicated 'off'. Although common basic principles were followed, railways differed in the detail of the signalling systems they had adopted. The North Eastern Railway, for example, was noted for the complexity of its signalling arrangements, and large gantries carrying multiple arrays of semaphore signals were a feature of its important stations; these were to be simplified by the LNER as opportunity offered. Great Northern signals were distinguished from those of other LNER constituent companies in that the arms were pivoted at the centre instead of at one end, and were known as 'somersault' signals. This dated from 1876, when a signal in a slotted post became frozen in the 'off' position, so precipitating a serious collision. No other major British railway employed this type of signal, although it could be seen in South Wales and in Australia and New Zealand.

Signalmen were in contact with their colleagues in neighbouring signalboxes by means of a telegraphic bell code, supplemented by visual reminder block instruments which indicated the current status of each line. In foggy weather detonators would be placed on the rails to warn drivers that signals were against them, but no recognised method of communication existed between a locomotive in motion and a signalbox or station other than the use of the whistle. However, by 1923 more modern technology could be seen in a number of instances, particularly in the adoption of track circuiting in selected locations, which gave the signalman evidence of line occupation and prevented him from allowing another train to enter that section. As for the signals themselves, the NER had introduced electro-pneumatic operation before World War 1, with installations on the main line between Alne and Thirsk, and at Newcastle Central, and the Great Central used pneumatically operated signals between Manchester London Road and Ardwick; the GCR had also planned a trial installation of automatically operated electric colour light signals on the 1.9 miles of line between Marylebone and Camfield Place, this being completed by the LNER in 1923.

After the formation of the LNER, organisation of the engineers concerned with communications was for many years devolved to the Areas, each of which had a Signal and Telegraph Engineer and a small staff, as part of the Engineer's Department. Thus, until J. C. L. Train became

Right:
The interior of the manually operated signalbox at St Ives. The main signals appear to be 'on', so it would seem that a shunting movement is in progress, and the signalman is waiting for a track circuit to clear before replacing the lever on which he is leaning.
IAL

HULL PARAGON

Chief Engineer in 1942, signalling matters lacked overall guidance, and indeed differences of opinion became apparent on occasion. Apart from the technical features, the signalling function required close collaboration between the signal engineer and the Operating Department, and although in general a high degree of harmony was achieved within an Area, problems sometimes arose at the boundaries. Nevertheless, despite variations in practice (generally for historical reasons), certain matters of standardisation were adopted, often following recommendations by the Institution of Railway Signal Engineers later adopted as mandatory by the Ministry of Transport. Thus, the arms of distant signals were distinguished by being painted yellow, and a yellow light was shown after dark, whilst it was also decided that somersault and other lower quadrant signals would be replaced by upper quadrant ones as opportunity offered. Modification of distant signal arms and spectacle glasses took place fairly rapidly, but older type signals lingered on for many years, only being

replaced when the mechanism had worn out. Examples of somersault signals could still be seen in Lincolnshire in the 1980s.

Post-Grouping practice in modernisation of signalling functions took two forms. One was the replacement of semaphores by colour light signals, usually in a strategic situation such as in the neighbourhood of a major station, but the line from York to Northallerton was completely resignalled with colour lights in 1933, and this was extended to Darlington by 1939, to give the longest continuous stretch of colour light signalling in Britain at that time. Another resignalling took place from Gidea Park to Shenfield in conjunction with track development. The second major form of updating was the introduction of power-operated systems in place of hand-operated equipment, often in conjunction with line modernisation, which led to the concentration of signalling systems and the closure of signalboxes made redundant. This was an effective way of achieving economies, but modernised equipment required a reliable dc power supply. Hence, progress was aided by the spread of electricity supply networks and the development of the metal oxide static rectifier.

Power-operated systems, combined with route diagrams indicating the presence of trains, were installed in 1933 at King's Cross and Thirsk; the latter was of particularly advanced design, and unique in the world at the time, incorporating a route setting facility which automatically

moved points and signals to the desired position. Other still more advanced installations were later commissioned at Edinburgh, Northallerton, Leeds and Hull Paragon, in which electrical relay interlocking replaced mechanical methods; in these installations the equipment was supplied and installed by specialist contractors, notably Westinghouse, and Siemens and General Electric. The postwar plans envisaged further improvements in signalling systems, including the complete installation of colour light signals on the East Coast route.

These widely scattered examples of modernisation of signals systems indicate the limited amount of money which was spent on this function, although the 1930s was the period when modern signalling practice, based on route setting with relay interlocking, became established. More rapid progress was to take place after the war, as the economics of modernisation, particularly following the development of electronics, became more attractive. Nevertheless the LNER, particularly in the North Eastern Area, could be seen to be taking at least limited advantage of new techniques as they became available.

It is perhaps surprising that, particularly in the early years of the Grouping, and with North Eastern influence as strong as it was, more concern was not felt about cab signalling, bearing in mind the much higher incidence of fog and smoke haze in those days. Moreover, the NER already possessed a system of this nature, and the GCR had one in the development stage, in which the driver was given

audible notification of the position of distant signals, and making a partial brake application if the signal was 'on'. The North Eastern system was credited to Vincent Raven and C. Baister, who commenced trials as far back as 1894. It was applied to the main line between York and Alnmouth, and in 1920 the North Eastern Board decided to extend it to the remainder of its network, apart from minor branches, but this was deferred because of the imminence of the Grouping. During the next 10 years, locomotives working on the main line, including those stationed elsewhere, were fitted with the operating mechanism, but following the introduction of colour light signalling the system was withdrawn in 1933. The GCR device, known as the 'Reliostop', was prone to mechanical damage, and development work on this ceased after the Grouping.

In the meanwhile the Great Western extended the use of its own simple system which employed a ramp between the rails to give an indication in the locomotive cab of the state of a distant signal, and claimed that this was instrumental in its network's relative freedom from accidents. It was not until the war was approaching that the LNER gave serious attention to the subject, when authority was given for a trial installation on the main line between Edinburgh and Glasgow of the Hudd system, which employed electromagnetic cab signalling gear. Then, circumstances prevented any progress being made, nor was any specific proposal for cab signalling included in the postwar plans, though it would be wrong to suggest that the management was unduly dilatory; cost, and the lack of a proved system which would meet all requirements, were major delaying factors. Moreover, one school of thought held the view that money spent on replacement of semaphore signals by colour lights would give better results in terms of safety.

The LNER produced a number of eminent signal engineers, notably A. F. Bound, who, coming from the Great Central, was appointed Signal and Telegraph Engineer of the Southern Area at Grouping, but lacking promotional prospects on his own railway joined the LMS as Chief Signal and Telegraph Engineer in 1929. Another was A. F. Tattersall, who commenced his career on the Great Northern, moving to the North Eastern Area after Grouping, where he claimed to have removed a redundant NER signal for every working day he was there; he later

became Assistant Chief Engineer (Signals) when civil engineering was made an all-line function.

As distinct from systems of sectional safety control, appreciation of the operating advantages to be gained from a greater degree of overall control of train movements, coupled with improvements in telephone communication, led a number of railways to look carefully at such systems. The Midland Railway had pioneered a form of control in 1907, in efforts to minimise trainmen's working hours, and the idea was picked up by other railways. By Grouping the NER had instituted control on the East Coast main line between Shaftholme Junction and Newcastle, as well as on Tyneside and Teesside, for mineral traffic, and the NBR had also introduced a system of control for traffic from the Fife coalfield.

Early systems were based on a geographical layout on which information regarding trains was placed, or on a 'time board' on which the progress of trains was noted. An interesting variation was installed at York, which used moving bands driven by clockwork at speeds appropriate to the trains concerned. Later, a card system was introduced in the Southern Area of the LNER, but the

Above:
Ex-Great Northern somersault signals silhouetted against the sky at Harringay. There was quite a variation in the angle at which signals of this type adopted the 'off' position.
Photomatic, G. Goslin collection

Right:
Multiple aspect searchlight type colour light signals on the North Eastern main line between York and Darlington. *Real Photos*

122

Above:
Electro-pneumatically operated signals in the main gantry at the east end of Newcastle Central station. Note the cast manganese crossings in the foreground. *IAL*

North Eastern Area standardised on graphs on which paths were recorded on a time/distance basis in different colours according to the class of train. Each system had its merits; the card system enabled the same working to be compared on a daily basis, to investigate the cause of regular hold-ups, but the relationship between trains was less easy to determine. As a protagonist of the card system, V. M. Barrington-Ward (who had received his early training on the Midland Railway), when Superintendent in the Southern Area, differed from C. M. Jenkin Jones, who was responsible for the introduction of graphs to the North Eastern Area; possibly the differences in the systems led to delays which sometimes occurred to traffic passing from one Area to the other.

Control was delegated to District Control Offices, and was effectively in the hands of a number of section controllers, who received information about the amount of traffic to be moved, and how the booked trains were running in other sections. On the basis of this knowledge the controllers decided on the running of trains in their sections, conveying information by telephone to signalmen and shunters, the objective being to get goods traffic moving expeditiously. Passenger trains were reported to Control, but were not necessarily controlled to the same extent as goods trains. An important aspect of a controller's duties was to match locomotives to loads, hence the need for him to be aware of the capabilities of the various locomotive classes, and to have an intimate knowledge of the section of the railway he was controlling.

It was inevitable that despite the care taken in installing and operating signalling systems and other forms of control, human or mechanical failure would on occasion lead to disasters on the railway, and the LNER record discloses a number of these. They had few common features, but many could probably have been avoided had the strictest regard been paid to the rules governing the control and working of trains. The LNER Rule Book contained no fewer than 240 rules, of which one of the most important was Rule 55, requiring a member of the train crew (generally the fireman) to report to the signalman if his train was delayed for more than three minutes, in clear weather. Lapses on the part of the devoted body of railwaymen, drivers and signalmen in particular, were few indeed, particularly when reckoned in terms of passenger miles per casualty, whilst extenuating circumstances such as severe weather conditions were present on many occasions. An important factor in saving life when an accident occurred was the use of the buckeye coupler and Pullman type vestibule on coaching stock; these often enabled coaches to remain upright after a crash, and prevented telescoping. At many official enquiries into the cause of accidents, the Inspector commented favourably on the presence of buckeye couplers, but regretted the absence of cab signalling.

A considerable organisation was brought into being to deal with the aftermath of a crash, involving first aid treatment and evacuation of casualties, clearance of the line and diversion of following trains. This was the overall responsibility of the Operating Department, but with considerable assistance from the engineers. Special trains and equipment were kept in reserve, notably 72 breakdown cranes which came into LNER ownership and were stationed at strategic places around the system. Only four new ones were added to stock before 1938, but another eight were obtained during the war years, all from

123

specialist manufacturers such as Cowans Sheldon; many other, smaller, units were withdrawn, leaving 57 in stock in 1947.

The first severe collision after the formation of the LNER occurred at Retford, on a misty day in February 1923, when an Atlantic hauling an up East Coast express ran into the rear of a goods train; the footplate crew lost their lives but the presence of modern coaching stock led to minimal damage to the train. In April the same year a suburban train ran into the buffers at Liverpool Street, bringing to light a strange operating procedure. A large chalk mark on the platform indicated the point at which the final brake application should be made, but so many passengers were waiting on the platform that the mark was obscured and the driver applied his brake too late.

A head-on crash took place in February 1927 when a train leaving Hull Paragon station ran into an incoming train, 12 passengers being killed. Both drivers were held to be blameless, the main factor being a fault in the mechanical interlocking system. The following year, at Darlington, the driver of a parcels train misread signals and moved to a position fouling the main line, where he was

run into by an excursion train passing through the station at speed: 25 passengers were killed. When the Board considered the report of the occurrence, concern was expressed about its causes, particularly as it was due to the negligence of the Company's servants. Two hundred claims for compensation were received from passengers in the excursion train, who were travelling on tickets which stated that the Company was not liable for any injury, however caused. Nevertheless, it was decided that the claims should be recognised, and settled 'on the best terms possible'.

Scotland saw two severe accidents. One occurred at Haymarket, Edinburgh in July 1924, when five persons were killed in a rear end collision, but the second was the LNER's worst crash. This took place at Castlecary, near Falkirk, in December 1937, when in conditions of heavy snow and poor visibility an express from Edinburgh ran into a stationary train at 60mph after overrunning signals. Thirty-five people were killed and the damage to the locomotive, a Pacific named *Grand Parade*, was such that it was scrapped, a replacement being built at Doncaster bearing the same name and number.

What might have been an even more disastrous mishap occurred near Northallerton in September 1935. The down 'Yorkshire Pullman' was approaching the junction with the East Coast main line from the Ripon direction at the same time as the 5.30pm from King's Cross to Newcastle, on the main line. The route was clear for the Pullman, but the driver of the Newcastle train misread the colour light

Below:
Clearance work beginning after the Castlecary disaster in December 1937. Pacific No 2744 *Grand Parade* is buried in the wreckage of an Edinburgh to Glasgow train.
Railway Gazette

signals, which were sighted for left-hand driving whereas his engine was driven from the right. Believing he had the road, he burst through the points, which were set against him. Only the presence of mind of the Pullman driver, seeing in the darkness the lights of the Newcastle train on a convergent course, enabled him to pull up in time to avert a side-long collision. Had there been a crash, not only would there have been severe casualties, but doubt would have been cast on the wisdom of running the high speed 'Silver Jubilee', due to be inaugurated within days of this near miss.

Serious rear end collisions took place at Welwyn Garden City in June 1935, due to a signalman's error, and at Hatfield in January 1939, when in severe weather a driver, despite having been warned about the conditions, drove too fast and ran his train into the back of another. The Welwyn collision caused the deaths of 13 people, and led to the introduction of a special sequence of interlocking arrangements before 'line clear' could be given, known as 'Welwyn control'. Rear end collisions also occurred on a stretch of line signalled by colour lights. These were at Ilford in January 1944, when again it was disclosed that the lights were sighted for left-hand viewing whereas the locomotive was being driven from the right; the other was three years later at Gidea Park, once more in fog.

Two crashes involving servicemen took place in 1942. The first of these occurred when the corresponding train to that in the Castlecary disaster, the 4pm from Waverley, collided with a troop train at Cowlairs, blackout paint on

the windows of the signalbox preventing the signalman from having a clear view of the track. In the same year, an incorrectly loaded steel plate on a passing freight train cut into a troop train, killing 14 soldiers. Also during the war, in 1941, a number of boys returning to school were flicking lighted matches and started a fire which killed six of the boys and destroyed three coaches. And in 1947, near Bridlington, an army lorry carrying soldiers and prisoners of war stalled on a crossing and was demolished by a train, resulting in 12 deaths.

A somewhat bizarre incident took place at King's Cross in February 1945, due to a 17-coach Leeds train headed by Class A4 Pacific *Silver Fox* failing to mount the 1 in 107 up through Gas Works Tunnel and sliding backwards into the station, the driver being unaware of what was happening because of the darkness inside the tunnel. It had been the practice since December 1943 for trains of such weight to be assisted out of the station for the first 100yd or so by the engine which had brought in the empty coaches, but on this occasion no assistance had been provided as the train had been backed into the platform. Two passengers were killed and it took a fortnight to restore services to normal.

In 1946 two derailments occurred near Hatfield, attributed mainly to defects in the track, but partly to the design of the pony trucks of the 'V2' locomotives, the class involved; as a result, the 'V2s' were fitted with a new design of pony truck in which side spring control was substituted for the previous arrangement with swing links.

Four other serious occurrences took place in the last years of the LNER. The first was at Ferryhill in June 1945, when a sleeping car train ran into derailed goods wagons, a freight train having broken in two because of a defective 30-year-old wagon, the runaway part catching up with the main train. The second was at Potters Bar the following year, when a railwayman's nightmare occurred: one train was derailed and two others ran into the wreckage. Mercifully only two passengers were killed, both soldiers. The third took place at Doncaster in August 1947, when 18 lost their lives in another rear end collision, attributed to a signalman's error; whilst the last, in October, was also one of the worst. Track repairs were in progress at Goswick, south of Berwick-on-Tweed, when the driver of an up East Coast express failed to exercise proper caution when his train was diverted to a relief line. The locomotive and three coaches fell down an embankment, 27 persons being killed.

Left:
At Potters Bar, in the late evening of 14 June 1946, an up suburban train hauled by Class N2 No 2679 should have halted on the slow line outside the station, before entering the two-track section. However, it ran on to the buffer stops and became derailed, fouling the through lines, so that it was run into by Class V2 No 4826, heading the 9.45pm down express from King's Cross to Glasgow. Seconds later the 5.00pm up from Bradford to King's Cross, with No 4833, ran into the wreckage. *Railway Gazette*

SEVENTEEN

Ancillary Services

From the earliest times, railways had regarded the road as a natural feeder of traffic, and horse-drawn vehicles of all descriptions conveyed passengers and goods to and from the railway stations. After the steam-hauled train had shouldered the stage-coach aside, the road was not regarded as a competitor until the introduction of the internal combustion engine and the tarmacadam road surface, and even then mechanical unreliability was for many years a limiting factor on the expansion of road transport. Nevertheless, the railways appreciated the potential of the road for improved local feeder services, and experimented with mechanical transport for goods deliveries, even venturing into motorbuses; the Great North of Scotland provided an example as early as 1904 in a service from Ballater to Braemar, an extension to the Deeside line which the railway had been unable to complete. As the 1921 Act did not forbid the railways to operate road services, several took advantage of this gap in the legislation, but to establish their legal right to run on the road, the LNER and the other main line companies in 1928 obtained formal powers under which they were enabled to purchase shares in road transport businesses. An important feature of the situation then achieved was that the railways undertook not to operate road passenger services in their own names. However, this did not apply to the transport of goods, the LNER operating both under its own name and indirectly through cartage companies.

No time was lost by the LNER in buying into road interests, and by 1931 £2¼ million had been invested, bringing in an income of £145,000. The main passenger concerns included such well known firms as the East Yorkshire and the United Automobile Services, as well as, jointly with the LMS, Eastern National and the Scottish Motor Traction Co. In an alternative administrative arrangement, in which the interest of the railway was not immediately obvious, the well known cartage firm of Thompson McKay, which had been a part of the GCR and had become a wholly owned subsidiary of the LNER, took under its wing certain small bus companies in which the LNER had acquired share capital: one of these was Emmersons, which operated a service between Newcastle and Carlisle. In 1935 the LNER, in concert with the other railways, acquired Carter Paterson and the Hays Wharf Co, which included the removal firm of Pickfords. After then, little change took place in the total investment in road company ownership, but the outlay became increasingly

profitable; in 1946, on an investment of £3¼ million, receipts amounted to £836,000.

Railway officers were appointed to the Boards of the bus companies, on which they were expected to further the interests of the company concerned, rather than attempt to act where they thought the railway's traffic might benefit; however, committees were set up jointly between the railway and the bus companies to co-ordinate services where this was deemed to be desirable, and to decide on the interchangeability of tickets. Nevertheless, the LNER attitude towards bus competition was always somewhat ambivalent, possibly because of its inability to operate services entirely on its own. There were no extensive moves to close down rail services and leave the traffic entirely to the road companies — which probably generated their own business anyway from the convenience they offered from village centre to village centre, whereas railway stations were often at a distance from the village after which they were named. The railway was of course quicker between towns. The conclusion one comes to is that the LNER regarded its part ownership of bus companies as a defensive measure against too blatant a degree of competition, whilst accepting the dividends as a welcome addition to net revenue.

Freight road transport was approached in a somewhat different manner, as collection and delivery of goods by road was an integral part of the total rail operation. Customers could, of course, use their own transport, or use other carriers to and from the railhead, but the LNER delivery van or lorry was a familiar sight on the streets of the cities and towns served by the railway. Company-owned vehicles increased substantially over the years. In 1923 there were 20 steam, 25 electric and 153 petrol vans and lorries, together with 29 buses and 58 cars — a total of 285. By 1947 this had grown to over 4,000. Delivery vehicles were broadly of two kinds: the 'mechanical horse', a tow vehicle articulated to a trailer, replacing the horse drawn dray or rulley for shorter journeys in congested areas, and the conventional van or lorry for longer journeys, often on a fixed route. The mechanical horse was introduced in 1930, and was built in more than one size; originally the Karrier Cob, later the Scammell, was the favoured make.

The design and technology of road vehicles improved considerably during the LNER period, with more powerful engines, better gearboxes and pneumatic tyres replacing solid rubber. It was customary for the LNER to purchase

Above:
A small Karrier omnibus of the late 1920s. Numbered s1 and registered in London, presumably it was used for transporting guests between railway station and hotel. *IAL*

Below:
An advanced design for its day, with pneumatic tyres and an almost wholly enclosed cab, No 247 was one of many Albion two-tonners in use c1928. Note the pre-Gill lettering. *NRM*

chassis and engines from the manufacturers and build the bodies itself at one of the carriage works. A small number of battery electric vehicles were employed at the beginning and end of the LNER period, for limited mileage runs on which the low running costs of these vehicles could be exploited.

Organisationally, the Suburban and Road Traffic Committee considered road transport matters on behalf of the Board, whilst operations were within the purview of the appropriate Passenger or Goods Managers. Sir Nigel Gresley's staff included a Road Motor Engineer for the Southern and North Eastern Areas, but he does not appear to have taken a close personal interest in road vehicles, except to oppose for a time the purchase of mass produced vehicles with short lives.

Horse transport was an important, although diminishing, factor in the LNER's road services. In 1923, 6,989 horse drawn vehicles were in service, together with 5,189 horses, of which 547 were employed for shunting on the railway. Even by 1946 the figures had only declined to 3,369 vehicles and 1,398 horses, 118 still being used for shunting. Probably the cheapness of horse transport militated against a faster replacement by mechanised methods; the prewar cost of a horse, driver and two rulleys was no more than £200 a year. The logistics of caring for such a large horse population, including the supply of provender and disposal of the noisome refuse after mucking out, must be a study on its own. An interesting insight into the intricacies of horse management is contained in a note from the Chief General Manager in 1926, seeking Lord Faringdon's views on the method employed for the purchase of horses. Evidently horses cost £44 in the northeast, but as much as £55 in London and in Scotland; the working life averaged 5½ years, but was eight years in Scotland. The practice was to buy from dealers, horses being selected by the horse superintendent and brought together for inspection by a Director. Bringing horses together for this purpose often led to their catching a cold or even pneumonia, a number dying as a result soon after they had been purchased. The matter was resolved by authority being given to the horse superintendents to buy animals at country fairs, or from farmers, so saving dealers' profits and removing the need for a number of stablemen.

Air transport was, of course, an alternative and not a supplement to the railways, but to protect their position, in 1929 the four main line railways each obtained powers to own aircraft, to establish and work aerodromes and to operate services within specified areas. For the LNER, this meant within its own boundaries and into the Continent as far as 20° east — an arbitrary limit which would have permitted the Company, had it wished, to serve Budapest and Stockholm, but not, by a few miles, Warsaw. Again, these powers were largely defensive, commercial air transport at this time being neither reliable nor profitable; nevertheless, a company known as Railway Air Services was formed by the railways. Some routes were introduced from 1934, but none were in direct competition with LNER services, except that a traveller could leave Croydon Airport at 9.30am and arrive in Glasgow at 1.40pm, the return fare being £9 10s (£9.50). The aircraft employed were the 'latest four-engine de Havilland type, provided with every modern wireless and other device, and double manned, carrying both a captain and a first officer'. The routes were operated by Imperial Airways (of which, in yet another metamorphosis, Sir Eric Geddes was now Chairman), the railways taking the receipts and paying the airline on a route mile flown basis. A competitive service was introduced by North Eastern Airlines in 1937, operating between Croydon, Doncaster, Newcastle and Perth, tickets being interchangeable with first class rail. GPO mail services were introduced the following year.

In 1944 the four railways again presented a plan for a collaborative arrangement to cover internal air transport, as well as to the principal cities of Europe, this being introduced to the House of Lords in 1944 by Lord Balfour of Burleigh, an LNER Director. The postwar political climate of nationalisation however, led to the creation of British European Airways, which took over the obligations

A 1944 poster illustrating the railway companies' plans for postwar air services. The routes described indicated not only a desire to serve the main centres of Europe, but also to fly routes within Britain, even over as short a distance as from London to Bristol. *IAL*

and aspirations of Railway Air Services; the LNER postwar plans did not visualise any investment being made to enable the railway to take to the air.

The involvement of the LNER in alternative forms of transport indicates that those who directed the affairs of the Company, although conscious of their responsibilities as railwaymen, were not wholly constrained by that consideration. Looked at from the broader view of transportation, they would have done better for their shareholders had they gone still further into road transport by exploiting the growing customer preference for travelling by road, and closing unprofitable rail services in favour of the road. But opposition would have been generated to such moves, not least in official circles, and the Company would have been told that if any money was going spare, it should be invested in improvements to the railway system, and not on excursions into other forms of transport.

An important ancillary to travel is catering for the rest and refreshment of travellers, and all the LNER constituent companies recognised the benefits of investment in hotels, restaurants and refreshment rooms. At Grouping, the Company owned and operated no fewer than 23 hotels, plus one (at Perth) owned jointly with the LMS; in addition, eight small hotels, mostly in Scotland, were owned and let to tenants. The largest hotel by far, with over 400 rooms, was the North British Hotel at Edinburgh, which dominated the view over Waverley station. The next largest were the Felix, at Felixstowe, and the Great Eastern Hotel at Liverpool Street, each with 250 rooms. Others included the Great Northern at King's Cross, the Royal Victoria at Sheffield, and the Royal Station Hotels at Newcastle, York and Hull, whilst amongst the smallest was that at Cruden Bay, north of Aberdeen, mainly catering for visiting golfers. Hotel ownership by no means extended to all the major towns and cities on the system, and the LNER made no attempt to enlarge the chain. Most survived until 1947 (an early closure was the Great Eastern Hotel at Harwich, in 1923) although several were requisitioned for use by the

Forces in the war. During the 1930s a fair amount of money was spent on modernisation, such as the provision of lifts and private bathrooms, as well as general refurbishment in line with current trends. Only one, however, was completely modernised and extended; this was the Royal Station Hotel, Hull, the work being hastened by the knowledge that the foundations and much of the structure were in a poor state.

The hotels were regarded not only as a useful adjunct to the rail system, but also as profit earners in their own right. Many had originally been built as part of a station complex, whilst in certain instances — the Felix was an outstanding example — the presence of a railway-owned hotel enhanced the attractions of a resort. Railway hotels were generally of a good class, often the best in the locality. One important hotel which the LNER did not own originally was the Great Central Hotel at Marylebone, where the annual meetings of shareholders were held until 1940: in 1945, whilst it was owned by Frederick Hotels but under requisition by the War Office, the Company purchased it for £500,000. The intention was to move the Southern Area traffic and other staff there, so centralising them in one building, but in a change of plan in 1947 it was proposed as a hostel for railwaymen, to be run by the LNER on behalf of the other four main line railways. This project was abandoned on nationalisation, and the building was taken over by the Railway Executive, to be known as 222 Marylebone Road.

Restaurants were, of course, a feature of the hotels, and many stations had refreshment rooms (there were over 150 in all), sometimes let to outside caterers, whilst the LNER catering organisation also had charge of the feeding arrangements in restaurant and buffet cars. Station buffets tended to be sombre in appearance and slow in operation, in contrast to today's 'fast food' in bright surroundings, but a programme of improvement was commenced in 1945. The LNER was not able to escape criticism of the quality of its buffet food, the sandwich under the glass dome being an example of what could have been better, but those were the days before the introduction on a wide scale of the refrigerated cabinet. Set meals in restaurants generally represented excellent value, although perhaps the variety of menu was less than would be expected today. A three-course meal might cost three or four shillings (15p or 20p) and a pint of locally brewed draught bitter one shilling (5p). The prices were higher at the Great Eastern Hotel, which was renowned for the excellence of its catering and of its wine cellars, the Abercorn Rooms, in particular, being in demand for party functions and banquets. At the other end of the scale, contractors supplied vending machines for station platforms, typically offering a bar of Nestlé's Chocolate or Sharp's Kreemy Toffee for one (old) penny.

The Directors had a divided interest in hotels, a committee of the main Board considering the affairs of those in the Southern and North Eastern Areas, the hotels in Scotland coming under the Scottish Local Board. Long hours of duty characterised the staff working in hotels, who in return often received food and lodging as part of their emoluments. Hotel managers in particular were expected to be on the job virtually 24 hours a day, and in addition to their salaries they received full board on the premises; often the manager's salary would take account of the services of his wife as housekeeper. A good salary had to be paid to attract a first class chef, as for example the incumbent at the Great Eastern Hotel, who was paid £700 a year plus his food. This may be contrasted with the train staff travelling on the 'Northern Belle', for each of whom the Hotels Superintendent allowed 15 shillings (75p) for food for the week.

Although most purchases were left to the local management, the Directors required all requisitions for wines and spirits to be referred to them for confirmation. Possibly this arose from a discovery in 1923 that an inferior brand of Scotch was being stocked; instructions were given to dispose of several gallons of 'NE Special Whisky' at a special price of 13s 1d (66p) per proof gallon. William Whitelaw took a personal interest in the purchase of spirits, and 'new whisky', ie, in bond, straight from the distillery and not aged, was bought on the authority of the Chairman for 2s 7d (13p) a gallon for grain, and 5s 7d (28p) a gallon for malt. Bottled Scotch, duty paid, was bought at £5 11s 7d (£5.58) a dozen, and Hock, £1 5s (£1.25) a dozen. As a personal benefit, authority was given for Directors and Officers to purchase wine and cigars at cost price plus 10%.

An innovation in 1933 was the camping coach. An old passenger carriage would be parked in a country siding after having been converted to provide family living accommodation. This proved to be increasingly popular, such that by 1939 over a hundred were sited in selected positions, painted green and cream, and offering a week's self-catering holiday for six from £2. Finally, although the LNER did not regard itself as being in the entertainment business, it owned the South Pier at Lowestoft, as part of its inheritance from the Great Eastern.

A separate account was prepared for hotels, refreshment rooms and restaurant cars, in terms of net revenue, and incorporated in the final accounts. In 1923 a profit of £300,000 accrued from turnover of £2,146,000; the level of business did not vary greatly as the years passed, but profits became harder to earn, £175,000 being made from just under £2 million turnover in 1930, and £132,000 from just over the same sum in 1938.

Right:
Marylebone station was rather overshadowed by the imposing Great Central Hotel opposite, the two entrances facing each other across the courtyard of the station. Owned and managed privately, the hotel was requisitioned during the war but purchased by the LNER before Nationalisation with the objective of converting it to house a number of London offices. After 1948 it became the Headquarters of the Railway Executive, and is well known as 222 Marylebone Road. *IAL*

EIGHTEEN

Shipping and Docks

Unlike longer distance road and air transport, which were essentially alternatives to rail, seagoing operations — until the age of the drive-on, drive-off ferry — were almost wholly regarded as extensions to the rail network, passengers and freight being conveyed to their port of embarkation by train and continuing their journey by ship. The Great Central, Great Eastern and North Eastern all possessed important North Sea shipping interests, whilst the North British operated a number of paddle steamers on the Clyde; only the Great Northern and the Great North of Scotland had no involvement in shipping. The LNER also came into possession of some river ferry and canal interests, but no part was taken in coastwise shipping. However, the extensive deepwater docks owned by the pre-Grouping companies went to make the LNER the largest dock-owning railway company in the world.

The GER had for many years been developing shipping services from Harwich to the Hook of Holland, commencing with paddle steamers as far back as 1867, whilst in 1887 the Company opened its own port facility, Parkeston Quay, named after the then Chairman, Sir Charles Parkes; this became the embarkation point for its Continental services to the Low Countries, the traveller completing his journey on the European railways. Most of the passenger traffic to and from Eastern and Central Europe went this way, despite competition from the Tilbury-Dunkirk route, and the Channel crossings. For some passengers the shorter sea passage from Dover or Folkestone was preferable to the longer route via Harwich, and consequently the Great Eastern provided a high standard of accommodation on its ships, particularly on the night crossings, with cabin availability. Soon after the Grouping a new form of competition was seen, the newly formed Imperial Airways advertising flights from London to Berlin in seven hours, compared with 23 hours by surface transport; first class fare by air, at £8 10s (£8.50), was only £1 more than the equivalent by rail and sea. But civil air transport was not yet to be relied on, and patronage during the LNER period was slow to build up.

In 1923 the LNER acquired nine passenger and two cargo ships from the Great Eastern, the oldest having been built in 1894. Three newly-built vessels, the *Antwerp*, *Bruges* and *Malines*, each of almost 3,000 tons gross and with accommodation for over 750 passengers, were employed on the main Parkeston Quay services to the Hook of Holland, the older ships sailing to and from Antwerp as well as running a cargo-only service to Rottderdam. In 1924 a notable innovation took place in the shape of a freight train ferry service between Harwich and Zeebrugge; this employed three wartime ships originally used to transport men and stores from Richborough in Kent to Dunkirk. A subsidiary company was formed to operate the service, jointly with the Belgian State Railways, and known as 'La Société Belgo-Anglaise des Ferryboats'; it was bought out by the LNER in 1933. A terminal was specially built at Harwich and opened by Prince George (later to become the Duke of Kent and husband of Princess Marina). The three ships were prosaically named *Train Ferry No 1*, *Train Ferry No 2* and *Train Ferry No 3*, and were pressed into War Department service again during World War 2; two were sunk, the only one returning to LNER service being *Train Ferry No 1* which was renamed *Essex Ferry*. A new ship, the *Suffolk Ferry*, was launched in 1947. The ferries were of some 2,600 tons, making 12kt.

A major success was recorded in 1927, when, after a disagreement with the Southern Railway, the Zeeland Shipping Co transferred its English base from Folkestone to Parkeston Quay, so enabling a day and night service to be provided to Holland, the Zeeland Co berthing at Flushing. Increased pressure on the facilities at Parkeston was such that an extension was built in 1934, and the original section reconstructed; also in that year a Danish company commenced a service to and from Esbjerg.

A new cargo ship, the *Sheringham* of 1,088 tons, entered service in 1926 to replace an older ship sold for scrap, and three new passenger vessels, the *Vienna*, *Amsterdam* and *Prague*, were built for the Hook of Holland route in 1929/30. Larger and more commodious than their predecessors, with accommodation for only 716 passengers, the new ships provided a still higher degree of comfort; they replaced *Antwerp* and her two sisters, which were transferred to the Antwerp service. Only two of the new vessels were needed to maintain the nightly sailings to the Hook, and a beginning was made in pleasure cruising by employing the third ship on this work, a move which proved sufficiently successful for *Vienna* to be specially adapted for cruising. Only *Prague* of these three ships survived the war to re-enter LNER service when sailings to the Hook were resumed in November 1945 after the necessary rehabilitation work had been completed, Parkeston Quay having been a naval base and the Hook a German fortress. Sadly, *Prague* was not to remain afloat for

Three Generations of LNER North Sea Ferries

Above:
St George, built in 1905 for the Fishguard and Rosslare service, and sold to Canadian Pacific in 1913. Later a hospital ship, it was bought by the GER in 1920. Its tonnage was 2,676, it carried 396 cabin passengers and could make 22kt. *LPC*

Right:
Vienna, built in 1929 for the LNER. Its tonnage was 4,227, it had accommodation for 716 passengers, and could make 21kt. *LPC*

Below:
Arnhem, of 4,891 tons, was built on Clydeside by John Brown & Co in 1947. It had accommodation for 422 passengers and could make 21kt. *IAL*

much longer, as she was broken up in 1948 after sustaining severe fire damage whilst in the course of a refit. Changes in mercantile design were seen in 1947 when a new ship, the *Arnhem*, appeared, with one-class accommodation for no more than 422 passengers in a displacement of 4,490 tons. She was built by John Brown on the Clyde, and was a superb ship for her day, providing a welcome contrast to the surrounding postwar austerity. The launch was a diplomatic and social occasion, guests being taken from London in a special coach attached to the end of a service train; such was the quality of the meals provided that the curtains were drawn whilst the train was in York station, to avoid complaints being made by less well-fed travellers, in those days of rationing.

The Great Central fleet operated out of Grimsby to Antwerp, Rotterdam and Hamburg, the first railway-owned sailings having been inaugurated by the Manchester, Sheffield & Lincolnshire Railway in 1865. In contrast to the fast, relatively luxurious ships of the Great Eastern passenger fleet, those of the GCR were smaller, around 1,400 gross tons, with a speed of only 12kt; some were primarily cargo vessels, with only a small allocation of space for passengers. None had been built since 1911, nor did the LNER build any new ships for its Grimsby fleet. The most important route was the Royal Mail and passenger service to Hamburg, taking 30 hours; other sailings took place once or twice a week to Antwerp and Rotterdam, mainly with cargo.

The North Eastern did not own any ships in its own name, but held shares in two shipping lines. One was Wilson's & North Eastern Railway Shipping Co Ltd, in 1923 the owners of seven small cargo ships, all except one having been built before 1914. Of the company's £165,000 capital, the NER owned half, the remainder being in the hands of the Ellerman Wilson Line, the principal shipowners in Hull. The other venture, in which the NER held practically all the shares, was the Hull & Netherlands Steamship Co Ltd, which owned two small vessels and had three others on charter, one dating back as far as 1874. For many years Wilson's & NER contributed little or nothing to the LNER net revenue account, but the returns from the Hull & Netherlands were generally satisfactory. The North Eastern had also obtained powers to operate steamship services to Scandinavia but did not take advantage of these; instead, sailings to Denmark and Norway were undertaken by other concerns, the most important being from the Tyne.

Trading conditions deteriorated during and after the years of depression, amongst the causes being the fluctuations in currency values, imposition of import tariffs, and later specific embargoes as a result of the growing political differences between Britain, Germany and Italy. This led the LNER to review its Humber-based operations together with the LMS, owner of competing services sailing from Goole; consequently the four lines in which the railways had an interest — Wilson's & North Eastern, Hull & Netherlands, LNER (ex-GCR) and LMS — in 1935 formed a consortium known as Associated Humber Lines,

which rationalised the services and managed the ships, the owners sharing the proceeds. Quite extensive sailings were maintained, eight Continental ports being served from Goole, Grimsby and Hull, but fewer ships were employed than before.

The North British fleet consisted mainly of six small paddle steamers operating on the Clyde, all of which bore names associated with Sir Walter Scott, and two ferry services across the Firth of Forth — from Leith to Burntisland, and at Queensferry, in the shadow of the Forth Bridge. In addition, half a dozen paddle steamers on Loch Lomond were owned in equal shares with the Caledonian, and these became joint LMS/LNER property at the Grouping. Two new vessels were provided for the Clyde sailings, to replace ageing boats which had been in service for many years; these were the *Jeanie Deans* which entered service in 1932, and the *Talisman* of 1935, a pioneer in diesel electric propulsion, the speed of the ship, as well as its direction, being directly under the control of the bridge. Another paddle steamer, the *Waverley*, was completed in 1947 as a replacement for one lost in the war. Paddle steamers were also built as replacements on the ferry service across the Humber, between Hull and New Holland; these were *Tattershall Castle* and *Wingfield Castle* in 1934 and *Lincoln Castle* in 1940.

A house flag was introduced in 1923, consisting of a St Andrew's saltire with 'LNER' in the centre. In the dexter canton (ie next to the mast) distinctive emblems represented each port — a bat's wing for Harwich, a white star for Grimsby and a thistle for the Scottish services. These emblems were discontinued in 1932. Funnel colours remained as pre-Grouping, yellow for the Harwich steamers, white for Grimsby and red with a narrow white band for Scotland.

The ships passing into LNER ownership in 1923 numbered 22 vessels of over 250 net registered tons, and 18 smaller ones, plus a miscellany of tugs, dredgers and other small craft, as well as the six shared with the LMS and those in the subsidiary companies. Several were sold out of service or for scrap before 1939, whilst 11 additions were made to the fleet, including the ex-Government train ferries. Most were requisitioned for service in 1939, and their number was decimated during the war period. Of particular note is the career of the *Amsterdam*, which after taking part in the Dunkirk evacuation was converted to a landing ship for service in the Normandy landings, finally being employed as a hospital ship before being sunk by a mine. By 1946 only 13 large and eight small ships remained in LNER ownership, whilst the Loch Lomond squadron had been reduced to two. Three more new vessels were added before the end of 1947.

Port installations owned by the GER included not only the Harwich and Parkeston Quay facilities, but also the fish docks at Lowestoft. The largest docks vesting with the LNER were those farther north, notably on the Humber. Here, the Great Central had owned extensive docks at Grimsby, primarily for the import of fish and timber (including pit props), and for the export of coal. These were

supplemented in 1922 when Immingham was opened, incorporating also a dry dock run by the Humber Graving Dock & Engineering Co Ltd, in which the LNER held shares; much of its ship overhaul work was carried out there. Grimsby docks were enlarged in 1934, £1.7 million being spent on a new fish dock. On the north of the estuary, the NER and the Hull & Barnsley were in possession of substantial multi-purpose docks capable of handling not only coal and timber but also general cargo, and oil and grain imports. Additional fish facilities were provided at St Andrews dock and a further oil terminal was constructed at Salt End in 1928, whilst in 1930 the obsolete Queen's Dock was sold to Hull Corporation, who filled it in and built the Hull Civic Centre on the site.

Farther north, on Teesside, the North Eastern owned Middlesbrough docks, and in County Durham Hartlepool docks served the Durham coalfield by exporting coal and importing pit props, as well as sawn timber. Similar facilities were available at Tyne Dock, near Jarrow, where iron ore was imported for the Consett steelworks. As part of their plans for developing installations along the river, the Tyne Improvement Commissioners expressed interest in acquiring Tyne Dock, and it was sold to them in 1936. The NER also owned staithes at Dunston and Blyth, and improvements were made to these in the first year of the Grouping. The North British too was a substantial dock owner, particularly at Methil to serve the Fife coalfield, with smaller installations at Burntisland, and farther up the Forth at Bo'ness and Alloa; there was also a tidal harbour at Silloth

on the Solway Firth, served by a branch line from Carlisle and well inside LMS territory. Altogether, in 1923, 400 acres of water area and 41 miles of quayside came into LNER ownership, the latter figure reduced by only five miles by the time war broke out; almost a third of the docks were in Hull. Wartime damage to the docks installations, much of them timber built, was severe, and little had been done by way of rehabilitation by the time nationalisation arrived.

The LNER also inherited no less than 285 miles of canals, mostly in the Midlands, where the largest, the Chesterfield Canal, extended to 45½ miles; in Scotland there was the Edinburgh & Glasgow Union Canal, 31¼ miles in length. Other long stretches were in the name of the Sheffield & South Yorkshire Navigation Co, in which the LNER owned virtually all the ordinary shares, standing in the books at £540,000; the last dividend had been paid in 1899. Only the minimum of maintenance was carried out on these waterways, but even this cost up to £50,000 a

Left:
The Orient Line operated summer cruises to the Norwegian fiords, using 20,000-ton vessels such as the *Orford* and *Orontes*. These berthed at the Eastern Jetty at Immingham, which protruded into the River Humber and consequently could take larger vessels than Immingham Dock itself. A boat train is seen pulling away, headed by a Class B3 4-6-0, c1927. The clerestory coach in the foreground appears to have been overhauled after transfer from East Coast main line duties. *R. Milnes collection*

year. Toll clerks and lock-keepers were employed to regulate the traffic, but in 1923 tolls amounted to only £12,000 and declined steadily thereafter. Twice as much income was received by rents from canal premises as from tolls, but in a typical year anything up to £50,000 was lost on the canals account. William Whitelaw complained about the encumbrances of the canals, but it would have needed at Act of Parliament — unlikely to be obtained — to have got rid of them; he would, he said, be glad to give them away if anyone could be found to accept them. On the canals were a few Company-owned narrow boats, said to have been known on the Great Central as 'Sir Sam's Navy'. Whether any of them bore the LNER's initials is not known.

The LNER did not attempt to operate its maritime interests as a single entity, although A. L. Gibson, the Continental Traffic Manager, was of chief officer status. Master mariners were appointed as marine superintendents at Harwich and Glasgow, and the CME had a docks machinery engineer on his staff, whilst a Chief Engineer for Docks (NE and GC Sections), for many years A. Tulip, had his office in Hull and reported to the divisional general managers concerned. Otherwise, operations were in the hands of the Area staffs. Gibson was one of the characters of the period, esteemed as a 'great gentleman', and was very well known in Continental traffic circles.

The multiplicity of large and small dock installations and the miscellaneous fleet of ships, which comprised the maritime interests of the LNER, were not greatly profitable, in contrast to the money earned from investment in road transport. There were many poor legacies from earlier days, and little was done by way of renovation in many instances; where there was clear evidence that profits could be made, internally generated funds were made available for new ships and port facilities. Each year throughout the peacetime LNER period, the gross income from the docks was of the order of £2.5 million to £3 million, but net revenues fell from £661,000 in 1923 to £82,000 in 1938. The shipping brought in less, income from passengers and freight generally grossing just under £1 million, the passenger traffic forming an increasing proportion. But despite the endeavours of the Company to attract more business, net revenue declined until by the outbreak of war a small net loss was recorded. As there were no Government restrictions on through freight rates to the Continent, it might be thought that more realistic rates could have been charged, but the pressure of competition, particularly from the London docks, was such that with a limited amount of business available, rates had to be held down or negotiated privately on a 'one occasion only' basis.

Depending upon which end of the country the journeys took place, the abiding memories of passengers on LNER steamships were either of pleasant voyages down the Clyde, or of the excellent services offered by the *Amsterdam*, *Prague* or *Vienna*, when the rail/sea combination was the normal way of travelling to the Continent, before the day of the jetplane and the packaged holiday.

NINETEEN

Public Relations

The pre-Grouping companies had long appreciated that there was more to informing the public about their services than simply publishing timetables, and the Great Central and Great Northern in particular had been conscious of the value of good publicity in attracting custom. The Great Northern made a feature of cheap trips to the Lincolnshire coast resorts, and the figure of the bounding fisherman in the poster 'Skegness is so bracing' earned the Company, and the artist, justified approbation, whilst the Great Central was amongst the first British railways to establish a publicity department as a specialist unit under the General Manager. The LNER followed suit at the outset, and as a member of the small team of NER officers brought to London by Ralph Wedgwood, W. M. Teasdale, the NER Advertising Manager, was appointed to a similar position with the LNER. He was expected to mastermind all LNER advertising, although much material of immediate impact was necessarily produced locally. His terms of reference were somewhat ambiguous, as he was 'to be responsible for the whole of the trade and traffic advertising of the railway, subject to the Divisional General Managers for work affecting their respective Areas'. This was amplified before long in a circular from the Chief General Manager, which set out the organisation of advertising, with the Advertising Manager having offices in each Area, and relations between Head Office and the Areas clarified — 'on urgent matters the Advertising Manager will be at liberty to communicate with District Officers and Stationmasters'. Clear and detailed instructions were given on the handling of advertising, down to such detail as the mixing of paste for posters.

An interesting appointment was made in July 1923, when S. T. Burgoyne, a one-time assistant to Sir Eric Geddes, was recruited from the Ministry of Transport to be Industrial Agent, with the objective of persuading industrial concerns to establish new plants on the LNER system. A year later he returned to the North-East as Assistant Goods Manager, whilst in 1928 Teasdale was promoted to Assistant General Manager, to deal with Parliamentary matters, combining this position with that of Industrial Agent. As an indication of the effectiveness of this contact with industry, the Chairman said in 1932 that 24 firms had been attracted to the LNER in a period of three months, although nearly all were south of the Humber. Teasdale was succeeded by C. G. G. Dandridge, who had orginated on the Great Central and whose first exercise was to

reinforce previous instructions on advertising by issuing a hardback booklet entitled *Selling LNER Transport by the help of the Advertising Department*. This was primarily aimed at stationmasters, and set out instructions on the ways to get the best results from advertising. Teasdale resigned in 1932, to join Allied Newspapers, whilst Dandridge later became Southern Area Passenger Manager. The LNER's last Advertising Manager was A. J. White, promoted from Commercial Advertising Agent.

Public relations in the broad sense was a matter on which the Chief General Manager exercised considerable personal control, as no committee existed to direct this important aspect of LNER administration; Wedgwood, with the confidence of his Directors, played a free hand successfully in the Company's interests. His appreciation of sensitive issues may be seen in 1934, when the Board had decided to place orders for relatively large numbers of new locomotives; he counselled that 'the press should not get wind of our intention to order 30 or 40 engines in one batch', evidently being concerned that the Government, then considering the New Works provisions, should not be given the idea that the LNER had that much money to spend. However, certain decisions of principle were remitted to the Board, as, for example, the colours of rolling stock and the adoption of the letters LNER in preference to L&NER.

The British Empire Exhibition at Wembley gave the LNER an early opportunity to show off its wares to an impressionable public, and *Flying Scotsman*, in immaculate condition with its driving wheels slowly revolving, was exhibited in 1924 and again in 1925. Later, exhibitions were staged by the Company in several centres; generally a small number of the latest locomotives was on display, whilst on occasion goods wagons were featured as part of a presentation to freight customers. However, it was in 1925 when the opportunity occurred to mount a major public relations exercise in celebration of the centenary of the first steam worked public railway, the Stockton & Darlington Railway having been opened on 27 September 1825. To capitalise on the public interest in steam locomotives — this still being the era in which they were regarded as being amongst the best of contemporary technology — an exhibition of rolling stock and equipment was held in the newly-built Faverdale works, and 53 new and old locomotives and trains travelled in procession from Stockton to Fighting Cocks, near Darlington. Some of the

District engines taking part in the procession found a home in the Railway Museum at York. This was established by the NER in 1922 and continued under the LNER, although on a small scale compared with the present National Railway Museum.

Another anniversary took place in 1938, 50 years after the inauguration of the 'Flying Scotsman' as a named train. Patrick Stirling's 8ft Single No 1 was restored to working order and a number of Howlden's Victorian coaches, still in service, were assembled to represent the 'Flying Scotsman' of that period, the train venturing as far as Cambridge, and later being featured in a number of exhibitions of rolling stock.

Each of the Big Four railways, and the Metropolitan, contributed towards the development of the advertising poster as an art form by commissioning posters from leading artists of the day, but the LNER probably did more than the others, being responsible for many posters which conveyed a strong advertising message, in addition to standing up well artistically. Amongst the well known painters who produced work for the LNER were Austin Cooper, Frank Mason and Frank Newbould. Subjects featured were particular resorts or regions or named trains, whilst a postwar subject by Terence Cuneo entitled 'Giants Refreshed', depicting two Pacifics in the paintshop at Doncaster, served as a powerful reminder of East Coast locomotives at their best. A variation on the pictorial theme was a representation of a music hall bill of the 1930s, featuring special offers such as cheap excursions, and

providing other information. From time to time exhibitions of LNER posters were held, at such venues as the Burlington Galleries.

In addition to large quantities of publicity leaflets, booklets were produced on such subjects as *Expressing Freight*, whilst each year saw an updated *Holiday Handbook*, typically extending to over 1,000 pages and costing 6d (2½p). This described the holiday areas served by the LNER, region by region, and carried literally hundreds of advertisements offering accommodation from hotels to camping sites. Also, magic lantern slides were available on loan, and were reported to have been very popular.

An informative booklet entitled *Locomotives of the LNER Past and Present* was published in 1929, illustrating all recent classes of engine and listing those which were named, but it was by no means a comprehensive survey of all locomotives. Nothing was available in those days on the lines of the Ian Allan 'abc' series.

From 1929 the LNER deliberately began to introduce a house style based on a distinctive typeface created for the

Below:
An exhibition of rolling stock was held at Ilford, on 2 June 1934. The two main exhibits were *Cock o' the North* in original condition, only a fortnight after completion at Doncaster, and *Flying Scotsman*. *E. R. Wethersett*

Monotype Corporation by the sculptor Eric Gill. Known as Gill Sans because it lacked the serifs prominent in Roman characters, it was elegant and clear, and it stimulated a trend which was to become worldwide. The sum paid for the use of the typeface has never been disclosed, and the matter was the subject of some criticism at the time, it being claimed that the Company's draughtsmen could have done as well at much less cost; but it is unlikely that the same orginality would have been displayed by an employee, however well trained in drawing office practice. Gill Sans was gradually adopted throughout the LNER for timetables and most other printed matter, in advertising and wherever station names and directions were displayed. Soon after Grouping, a neat device was standardised for publicity material, in which the letters LNER appeared enclosed in a border, but this was later supplanted by Gill Sans letters appearing within a cigar-shaped lozenge.

Some latitude was allowed to Gresley, as CME, in the use of Gill Sans, as rolling stock continued to display block characters on locomotives and heavily serifed ones on coaches. Minor changes were introduced gradually, the new typeface being introduced for locomotive nameplates and carriage roof boards, and later the streamline trains and selected locomotives were given elegant stainless steel letters and numerals. After the war, locomotives displayed unshaded Sans characters, but the teak coaches retained the traditional style until BR days. The LNER totem, although featured in advertising, never achieved the prominence given to the London Transport bullseye, and was only seen on two classes of locomotive — the Thompson 'Q1' shunting tank and the prototype Bo-Bo electric for the Manchester to Sheffield electrification.

Dirty buildings and coaches were a common cause of complaint, but in the age of steam it was an impossible task to maintain cleanliness, although some brightness was introduced as stations were repainted — Marylebone being given a green and cream treatment, whilst Cambridge was repainted light blue, in deference to University wishes. Railwaymen had always taken a pride in the appearance of their stations, particularly the smaller ones, where the efforts of local staff often led to a blaze of floral colour in summer time. Prizes were awarded for the best kept stations, for which the competition was very keen.

By the late 1930s the railway companies were losing patience with the Government's dilatoriness in removing restrictions which prevented them from competing on an equal footing with other forms of transport, and mounted a combined exercise with the objective of marshalling public opinion to influence the Government to repeal the anachronistic legislation. Sir Ralph Wedgwood is credited with being the driving force behind the campaign, and for having coined the 'Square Deal' slogan under which it was mounted. As might be expected, the British Road Federation actively opposed the campaign, pointing out that if the railways wanted a square deal, then the roads needed a new deal, the amount of money being spent on the roads, compared with that raised by taxation, falling short by £30 million. However, there were signs in 1939 that the railways' message was getting home, but the events of that year put the whole subject of the regulation of the railways into a different context.

Promotional advertising ceased with the war, publicity being generally confined to the negative 'Is your journey really necessary?' style of message, and nationalisation arrived before very much could be done to restore the prewar situation. Some prestige advertising took place in a forlorn hope that the Government takeover might be averted, Sir Ronald Matthews being intent on demonstrating that the LNER was preparing for the future by publicising the two-stage £50 million plan for postwar reconstruction. Details were set out in a booklet entitled *Forward: The LNER Development Plan*, the cover of which displayed the front end of a streamline locomotive bearing the nameplate *Enterprise*. The booklet was produced by Michael Bonavia, well known as a transport historian, who was at that time Assistant to the Chief General Manager, with special responsibility for public liaison. Bonavia was also responsible for drafting a formal alternative to full nationalisation; conceived by Sir Charles Newton, and adopted by the Board, it was known as the 'Landlord and Tenant Scheme', and proposed that the Government should assume ownership of the railway system and its infrastructure, leaving the companies free to run the services. But the Minister of Transport, Alfred Barnes, was in no mood for half measures, and the LNER scheme was dismissed out of hand.

One chapter is missing from this account of the LNER: it would have been entitled 'The Passengers'. But strangely there is little of recorded note from this source. There were no consultative councils in LNER days, and passengers with unrequited complaints had to make them personally through the medium of correspondence to railway officers, or to the press or their Member of Parliament — to quote some of the avenues open to them. One is left perhaps with the conclusion that, in the standards of the day, the passenger generally got his money's worth; certainly management and supervisors were aware of passengers' needs, and did their best to meet them. But the frequently overcrowded suburban peak hour trains, and the delays which all too often followed some breakdown in service, were the subjects of many complaints. 'LNER stands for the Late and Never Early Railway' and 'Suffolk is a county cut off on one side by the sea and on the other three sides by the LNER' were gibes which were at least partially true, and which could not be ignored. But it was beyond the Company's financial ability to do more than attempt to ameliorate many of the causes of complaint, and no amount of money spent on public relations would have put matters right. What was done was to make the very best of those situations which were to the Company's credit, and to publicise its services effectively. Those professionally engaged in LNER publicity achieved a great deal, not least in the boldness of treatment of advertising, the efforts to express a corporate image through the use of Gill Sans typeface, and for raising the standard of poster art to a high level.

Above:

George Stephenson's *Locomotion* at the 1925 Centenary celebrations, hauling a train of chaldrons containing passengers dressed in period costume. The drive was by means of a petrol engine in the tender, oily waste being burned in the firebox to produce smoke. The tank locomotive in the background is believed to be Class F8 2-4-2T No 205D. *IAL*

Below:

The 50th anniversary of the 'Flying Scotsman' was commemorated by a number of trips by Patrick Stirling's renowned No 1, seen at Hitchin on 30 June 1938, flanked by No 4498 *Sir Nigel Gresley* on the adjoining platform. Sir Nigel himself can be seen by the tender of No 1, wearing a light suit and a Homburg hat. R. A. Thom is standing by the station nameboard, whilst Cecil J. Allen is in the centre foreground, facing the camera. L. P. Parker, the respected District Locomotive Superintendent at Stratford, is in the background, wearing a bow tie. *IAL*

TWENTY

The LNER: An Appreciation

William Whitelaw described the LNER as a system covering practically the whole of eastern Britain from the Thames to the Moray Firth, serving 80% of the urban population of the country; two-thirds of its business was in conveying freight and one third in passengers. Given that the purpose of the Railways Act was to produce a more efficient and economical railway system, how did the LNER measure up to the expectations of its creators? Hopes were high at the outset. 'There is no question that this new group will set out on its career with prospects of the most solid character', was a view heard in Scotland. But even in its first year the LNER began to experience the kind of hostile commercial environment which was to frustrate its efforts to achieve all round success, and which would require the greatest endeavours by all the men and women working for the Company to maintain and improve its services.

Whitelaw was careful to keep his options open, so far as the level of rates was concerned. Soon after amalgamation he expressed the hope that rates would be reduced and so stimulate trade and lead to more business for the LNER; at the same time he held the view that traffic revenue must, in the long run, be governed by the principle of what the traffic would bear. The architect of the Railways Act, Sir Eric Geddes, now a leading spokesman for industrial interests, claimed that the railways were not making the best use of the savings made possible by the Grouping, and pressed for further rate reductions, but it soon became clear that even if rate reductions did stimulate trade, any increase was insufficient to recompense the railways for the diminished revenue.

The LNER's response to the influences contributing to its worsening position was threefold: to press the Government to recognise the railways' difficulties, and to introduce means to relieve them; to set out to increase business; and an energetic attack on costs. Government aid turned out to be limited, and with strings attached, but nevertheless provided a welcome addition to spending power, whilst the road and rail traffic legislation introduced a certain amount of order into the unregulated road competition, although falling far short of the railways' wishes.

Obtaining new business was not easy in the absence of an upsurge in economic activity, and often the emphasis was defensive, to retain existing business in the face of predatory competition. Marketing, as it is nowadays understood, was in its infancy in 1923, but according to the practices of the day the LNER was not lacking in initiative.

Probably a centralised commercial policy-making office would have added to the Company's impact on the transport market by clarifying issues and identifying new opportunities, especially for all-line traffic, but apart from the innovations introduced by the Board and the chief General Manager, business-getting was delegated to the Passenger Managers and Goods Managers in the Areas, on the basis that this was where the traffic originated and it made good sense to be near your customers, and to know them.

Savings in costs were effected by methods far removed from the hatchet-wielding characteristic of recent times, and a ruthless management would have dealt more harshly with redundant staff. However, the saving in wages and salaries was substantial in some years, and the strict imposition of a brake on increases, whilst not perhaps significant in itself, helped by inducing the middle and lower strata of management to impose their own strictures on the resources which they in turn controlled. Also, there was a great deal of unwillingness to give up facilities, or to close branch lines, such actions only being authorised when it was clear these services were desparately unprofitable. A harder look at the more attenuated parts of the system, with a stricter cost/benefit discipline, would have declared much more mileage redundant than was the case.

In 1925, the Board set up a committee on expenditure charged with investigating certain aspects of costs, comparing them with those of other railways. Several questions centred on operational matters. Why, for example, were the LNER's costs of maintaining rolling stock higher than those of the LMS? And was it really necessary for light engine mileage to exceed four million miles a year? An appeal from the Chief General Manager to all enginemen brought home the way in which individual effort could help to save money. 'Coal costs £1 10s a ton, and we use $4\frac{1}{2}$ million tons a year. If every locomotive used 1lb of coal less per mile, we would save £80,000.'

An important decision was taken in 1930, when it was concluded that the Company was large enough to carry its own fire insurance. An allocation of £500,000 was made to a special fund to cover contingencies arising from fire damage, whilst substantial savings were made in premiums paid to insurance companies.

Criticism by shareholders was often heard at annual meetings, but was rarely helpful. In 1930 an LNER stockholders' association was formed, and a persistent critic, Ben Ivison, an insurance broker from Bradford, was formally proposed for membership of the Board; the motion was defeated. Attacks were made regularly on the level of salaries and wages, as were allegations of managerial inefficiency. Lord Monkswell, a well known 'enthusiast' of the period, let himself go on one occasion on the subject of 'the slack and inefficient management'. All such criticism, whether of the Board or of the staff, was dealt with robustly by the Chairman, as was the suggestion put forward from time to time that more work should be diverted from the Company's shops to the independent locomotive manufacturers.

The regionalised organisation of the LNER, with the free hand allowed to the Divisional General Managers, stood up well to the stresses on it, and no serious proposals were made for total centralisation, even after the war when the time might have been ripe for such a review. William Whitelaw clearly appreciated the benefits of devolution, and in his presidential address to the Institute of Transport in 1933 he not only justified it by results, but by reference to Jethro's advice to Moses in Chapter 18 of the Book of Exodus.

The formula of speed and comfort which began soon after Grouping with the Pullman trains, and which was carried through into the three all too short-lived streamline expresses, was the result of imaginative thinking and firm administration, and brought the LNER into the highest repute in the railway world. Under the Chief General Manager, successful collaboration between the civil and mechanical engineers and the operating departments in establishing the feasibility of fast travel at an average of 70mph, with service speeds of up to 100mph not uncommon, called for acceptance of responsibility of the highest order. Wholehearted support was given by the enginemen, who were prepared to run fast schedules to time, and by those whose duties involved preparing and attending the trains, and keeping a safe route open for them.

The story of the LNER's contribution to the war effort is, of course, a book in itself, being at the same time the operator's nightmare, and his success. Financial, commercial and even engineering matters were subordinated to the immense task of keeping the traffic moving. As the end of the war approached, thought was given to postwar plans, and it was clearly seen that if the LNER was to remain in private ownership a good deal more money would have to be found for modernisation than the Government was prepared to allow for rehabilitation as a result of wartime neglect. The postwar programmes were an important and purposeful contribution to the series of plans put forward by various other authorities, which were generally noted more for their impractibility than for their positive features.

With the conclusion of the war, and the election of a Labour Government in 1945 with a strong overall majority, some form of nationalisation was inevitable. All the symptoms which had been present during and immediately after World War 1 came to prominence once more, with the result that a complete amalgamation of all the four groups was seen as the only solution; consequently under the Transport Act of 1947 the LNER was vested in the British Transport Commission as from 1 January 1948. However, the Government terms were less than fair to the past owners of the railways, and had the LNER received its reasonable entitlement from the additional revenues accruing from wartime traffic, the position would have been a good deal brighter and the final results might have recompensed shareholders for part of what they had foregone over many years. Even so, despite allegations to the contrary, and notwithstanding working under severe operational stress during the war and under continual financial stress for virtually all its existence, the LNER was never within close sight of bankruptcy. A working profit was achieved every year, at least half the dividends were paid, and reserve funds remained high — including, for example, in 1947 £22 million in cash and Government securities. Moreover, although the Company was clearly over-capitalised in its later years, no scheme of capital reconstruction, to the disadvantage of any class of shareholder, was ever contemplated.

Despite the constant pressure on wages, and the inadequate and often adverse environments in which their tasks were performed, staff morale generally remained at a high level. Good personal relations plus the knowledge that by 1938 the LNER led the world in fast steam locomotive-hauled trains reacted throughout the system in terms incapable of measurement by normal methods; the result was an inherent sense of pride in the LNER. Further, reference has been made in the Introduction to the friendly spirit which was said to pervade the LNER. Richard Hardy, a premium apprentice who has recounted his earlier railway days in his book *Steam in the Blood*, said that he was told by his careers adviser at Marlborough to join the LNER because 'it is run by gentlemen'. Perhaps these comments are well illustrated when, with nationalisation imminent, and in a reversal of the usual order of things, 66 senior officers of the LNER signed a tribute to the Directors in the form of an illustrated booklet setting out the railway's principal achievements during the years 1923 to 1947.

Whitelaw, Wedgwood and Gresley steered the LNER through 15 years of peace, and Matthews and Newton saw it through the war. They, and the staff they led, certainly knew How to Run a Railway.

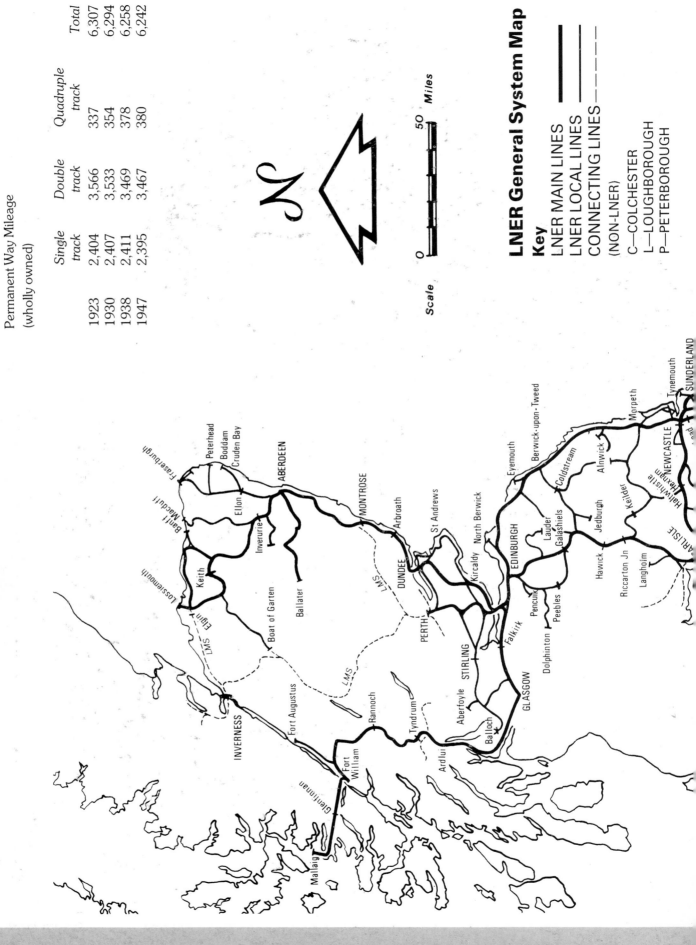

Permanent Way Mileage
(wholly owned)

	Single track	Double track	Quadruple track	Total
1923	2,404	3,566	337	6,307
1930	2,407	3,533	354	6,294
1938	2,411	3,469	378	6,258
1947	2,395	3,467	380	6,242

Scale

0   50   Miles

LNER General System Map
Key
LNER MAIN LINES
LNER LOCAL LINES
CONNECTING LINES -------
(NON-LNER)

C—COLCHESTER
L—LOUGHBOROUGH
P—PETERBOROUGH

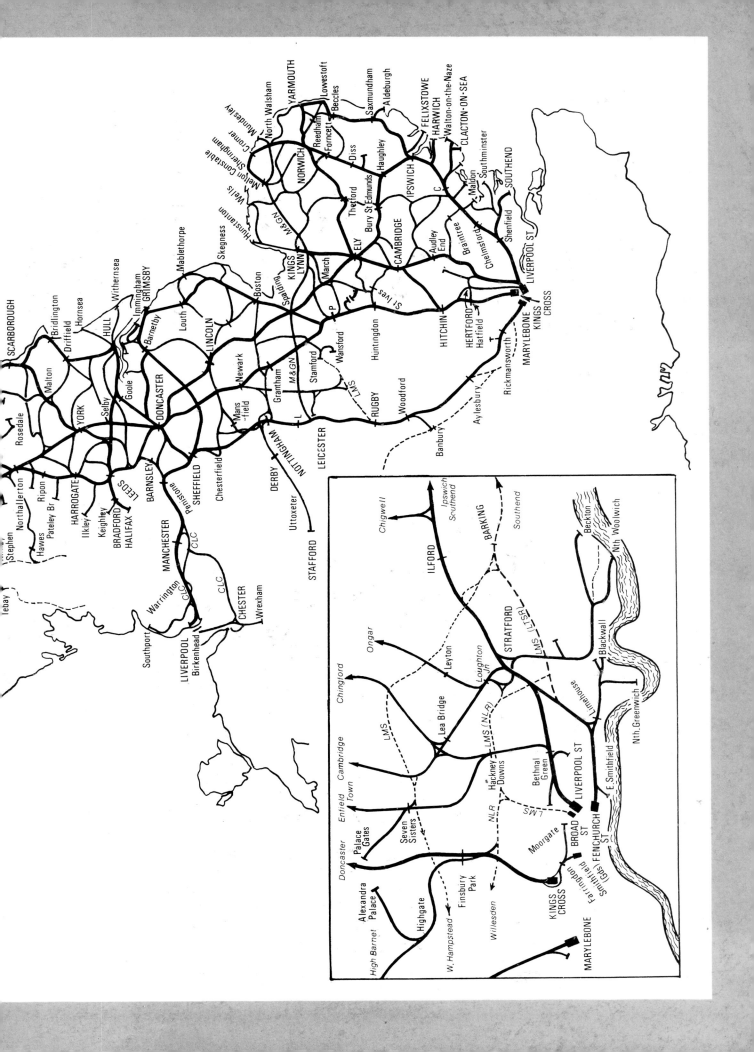

Appendices

In common with the other main line railways, the LNER published an annual report and set of accounts which were in a form prescribed by the Ministry of Transport. Returns of the staff employed were submitted separately to the Ministry of Labour. Changes in the detail of the reports took place from time to time, but in general it is possible to compare one year's figures with another. However, gaps appear in the war years, when material was either not collected, or certain information — such as volume of traffic — was regarded as secret, as it might have provided information helpful to the enemy.

A great deal of other interesting material is found elsewhere than in the annual reports, such as in minute books or in internal unpublished files, but these are often disappointing as whilst a sequence of events may be traced for a period of years, very few of the files present a complete year-by-year history of their subject for the entire 25 years of the LNER.

Much detailed information concerning locomotives and train operating is only available through the courtesy of the small team of LNER enthusiasts, who from their own notebook recordings have enabled much more to be known about locomotive practice and performance than can be discovered from official records.

1
Organisation and Staffing

1A
Board of Directors

Under the terms of the Railways Act, the maximum number of Directors was set at 28, but only 26 were appointed initially, representing each of the pre-Grouping companies. However, the total tended to diminish, as Directors left the Board, and moves were made to reduce the statutory numbers. At the Annual Meeting in 1931, for instance, William Whitelaw moved a Resolution which would have the effect of reducing the maximum number to 24, and subsequently 22. A group of shareholders thought that this was not going far enough, and Mr Walter Spyer proposed that the number in office should be reduced to the statutory minimum of 16, whilst Mr Ben Ivison, of Bradford, believed that statutory powers should be sought to set the minimum number at six. Neither of the last two resolutions was carried.

Taking the year 1930 as an example, the following is a list of members of the LNER Board at the end of the year, and their associations. Col Charles Trotter, who had been Chairman of the Hull & Barnsley, decided to retire at the end of the year, and Col W. J. Galloway, a member of the Great Eastern Board since 1903, died during the year.

William Whitelaw (Chairman, NBR): Chairman, LNER; Chairman, Organisation Committee. Director, Bank of Scotland.
Lord Faringdon (Chairman, GCR): Deputy Chairman, LNER; Chairman, Finance Committee. City of London interests.
Lord Ailwyn (LNER). Landowner, Norfolk; agricultural interests in East Anglia.
Hubert T. Bailey (GER). Berkshire.
Sir Charles Barrie (LNER). Interests in Dundee.
Hon Rupert Beckett (GNR). Leeds.
Sir Hugh Bell (NER). Chairman, Dorman Long, Horden Collieries.
A. Harold Bibby (LNER). Chairman, Bibby Line, Liverpool.
Oliver Bury (General Manager and later Director, GNR): Chairman Works Committee.
Hon Eric Butler-Henderson (GCR). Rugby.
William Henton Carver (LNER): Chairman, Property Committee. Interests in Hull.
Walter Burgh Gair (Deputy Chairman, GCR).
Alexander Reith Gray (NBR). Interests in Aberdeen.
Viscount Grey of Falloden (NER): Chairman, Traffic Committee. Landowner, Northumberland; Foreign Secretary 1905-16.
Marquess of Londonderry (LNER). Lord Lieutenant, Co Durham. Chairman, Londonderry Collieries, Co Durham.

Ronald W. Matthews (LNER). Chairman, Turton Brothers and Matthews, Sheffield.
Andrew K. McCosh (NBR): Chairman, Locomotive Committee. Mining Engineer.
Hon A. C. Murray (NBR). Elibank, Peebles-shire.
Sir Christopher Needham (LNER). Chairman, District Bank; cotton interests, Manchester.
Sir John Noble (NER). Argyllshire.
Clarence D. Smith (LNER). Chairman, Consett Iron Co.
F. L. Steel (Deputy Chairman, GNR): Chairman, Stores Committee.
Col Charles W. Trotter (NER): Chairman, Hull & Barnsley Railway.
Walter K. Whigham (NER). Banker; High Sheriff, City of London.
Sir Murrough Wilson (NER). Landowner, Co Durham.

1B
Staff Trees

Three charts of staff trees are shown: (1) General Management, (2) the Southern Area — the largest of the three Areas — and, (3) in view of the special interest generated by the company's rolling stock, the Chief Mechanical Engineers' Department. The year illustrated is 1930, by which time the organisation had settled down, but was in the throes of the drive for economies. No significant changes took place before 1947, except that, as described in Chapter Three, there were additions and alterations at Head Office. The three Areas differed in detail according to local needs and practice — the Southern Area was the only one to have a Mineral Manager, for example — whilst there was a gradual movement towards rationalising the District organisation as needs changed and officers retired. In some localities the posts of Goods Manager and Passenger Manager were combined.

The breadth of the span of management by the General Managers would be considered seriously excessive by today's standards, and it reflects both the pressing need for economy in salaries, as well as the company's deliberate policy to delegate authority wherever it was convenient and effective to do so. A frequent and regular reporting system was in being, to keep senior managers appraised of day-to-day happenings, and the hand of a General Manager was generally laid lightly on his subordinates unless things began to go seriously wrong. At the very top, the Chief General Manager kept the Board and its Committees well informed on their appropropriate subjects, and many management decisions were taken in the light of a Board Room discussion.

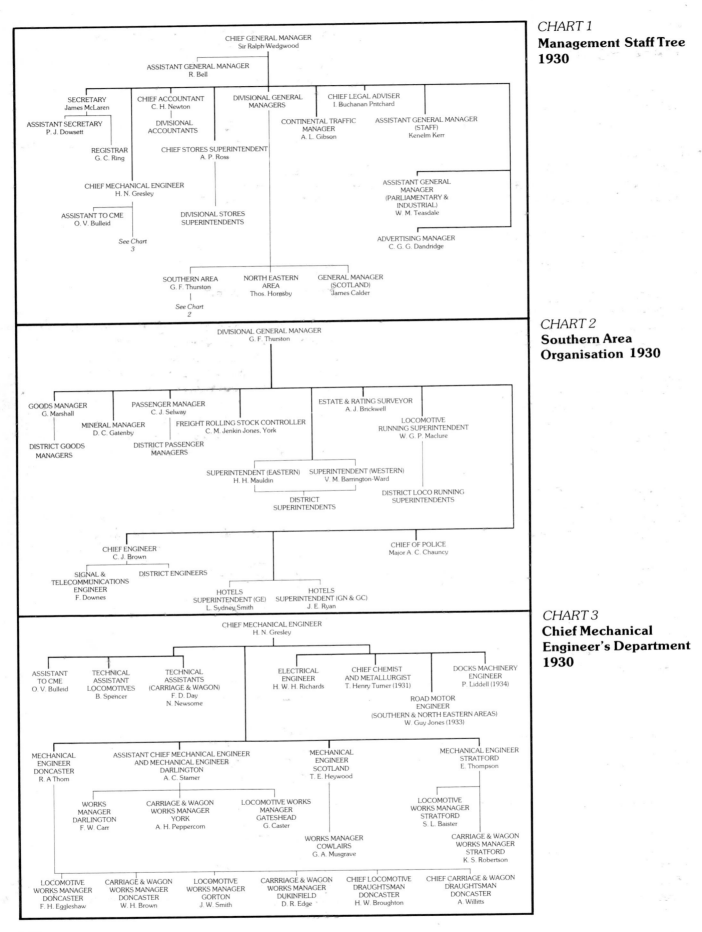

CHART 1
**Management Staff Tree
1930**

CHIEF GENERAL MANAGER
Sir Ralph Wedgwood

ASSISTANT GENERAL MANAGER
R. Bell

SECRETARY
James McLaren

CHIEF ACCOUNTANT
C. H. Newton

DIVISIONAL GENERAL
MANAGERS

CHIEF LEGAL ADVISER
I. Buchanan Pritchard

ASSISTANT SECRETARY
P. J. Dowsett

DIVISIONAL
ACCOUNTANTS

CONTINENTAL TRAFFIC
MANAGER
A. L. Gibson

ASSISTANT GENERAL MANAGER
(STAFF)
Kenelm Kerr

REGISTRAR
G. C. Ring

CHIEF STORES SUPERINTENDENT
A. P. Ross

CHIEF MECHANICAL ENGINEER
H. N. Gresley

ASSISTANT GENERAL
MANAGER
(PARLIAMENTARY &
INDUSTRIAL)
W. M. Teasdale

ASSISTANT TO CME
O. V. Bulleid

DIVISIONAL STORES
SUPERINTENDENTS

ADVERTISING MANAGER
C. G. G. Dandridge

*See Chart
3*

SOUTHERN AREA
G. F. Thurston

NORTH EASTERN
AREA
Thos. Hornsby

GENERAL MANAGER
(SCOTLAND)
James Calder

*See Chart
2*

CHART 2
**Southern Area
Organisation 1930**

DIVISIONAL GENERAL MANAGER
G. F. Thurston

GOODS MANAGER
G. Marshall

PASSENGER MANAGER
C. J. Selway

ESTATE & RATING SURVEYOR
A. J. Brickwell

MINERAL MANAGER
D. C. Gatenby

FREIGHT ROLLING STOCK CONTROLLER
C. M. Jenkin Jones, York

LOCOMOTIVE
RUNNING SUPERINTENDENT
W. G. P. Maclure

DISTRICT GOODS
MANAGERS

DISTRICT PASSENGER
MANAGERS

SUPERINTENDENT (EASTERN)
H. H. Mauldin

SUPERINTENDENT (WESTERN)
V. M. Barrington-Ward

DISTRICT LOCO RUNNING
SUPERINTENDENTS

DISTRICT
SUPERINTENDENTS

CHIEF ENGINEER
C. J. Brown

CHIEF OF POLICE
Major A. C. Chauncy

SIGNAL &
TELECOMMUNICATIONS
ENGINEER
F. Downes

DISTRICT ENGINEERS

HOTELS
SUPERINTENDENT (GE)
L. Sydney Smith

HOTELS
SUPERINTENDENT (GN & GC)
J. E. Ryan

CHART 3
**Chief Mechanical
Engineer's Department
1930**

CHIEF MECHANICAL ENGINEER
H. N. Gresley

ASSISTANT
TO CME
O. V. Bulleid

TECHNICAL
ASSISTANT
LOCOMOTIVES
B. Spencer

TECHNICAL
ASSISTANTS
(CARRIAGE & WAGON)
F. D. Day
N. Newsome

ELECTRICAL
ENGINEER
H. W. H. Richards

CHIEF CHEMIST
AND METALLURGIST
T. Henry Turner (1931)

DOCKS MACHINERY
ENGINEER
P. Liddell (1934)

ROAD MOTOR
ENGINEER
(SOUTHERN & NORTH EASTERN AREAS)
W. Guy Jones (1933)

MECHANICAL
ENGINEER
DONCASTER
R. A Thom

ASSISTANT CHIEF MECHANICAL ENGINEER
AND MECHANICAL ENGINEER
DARLINGTON
A. C. Stamer

MECHANICAL
ENGINEER
SCOTLAND
T. E. Heywood

MECHANICAL ENGINEER
STRATFORD
E. Thompson

WORKS
MANAGER
DARLINGTON
F. W. Carr

CARRIAGE & WAGON
WORKS MANAGER
YORK
A. H. Peppercorn

LOCOMOTIVE WORKS
MANAGER
GATESHEAD
G. Caster

LOCOMOTIVE
WORKS MANAGER
STRATFORD
S. L. Baister

WORKS MANAGER
COWLAIRS
G. A. Musgrave

CARRIAGE & WAGON
WORKS MANAGER
STRATFORD
K. S. Robertson

LOCOMOTIVE
WORKS MANAGER
DONCASTER
F. H. Eggleshaw

CARRIAGE & WAGON
WORKS MANAGER
DONCASTER
W. H. Brown

LOCOMOTIVE
WORKS MANAGER
GORTON
J. W. Smith

CARRRIAGE & WAGON
WORKS MANAGER
DUKINFIELD
D. R. Edge

CHIEF LOCOMOTIVE
DRAUGHTSMAN
DONCASTER
H. W. Broughton

CHIEF CARRIAGE & WAGON
DRAUGHTSMAN
DONCASTER
A. Willitts

1C
Top Management

Chairmen
William Whitelaw (1923-38)
Sir Ronald Matthews (1938-48)

Deputy Chairmen
Lord Faringdon (1923-34)
Sir Murrough Wilson (1934-46)
Walter K. Whigham (1946-48)

Chairmen of Locomotive Committee
B. A. Firth (1923-29)
Andrew K. McCosh (1929-47)

Chief General Managers
Sir Ralph Wedgwood (1923-39)
Sir Charles Newton (1939-47)
Miles Beevor (Acting) (1947)

Secretaries
James McLaren and G. F. Thurston
    (Joint Secretaries, 1923-25)
James McLaren (1925-38)
P. J. Dowsett (1938-42)
W. H. Johnson (1942-48)

Chief Mechanical Engineers
Sir Nigel Gresley (1923-41)
Edward Thompson (1941-46)
A. H. Peppercorn (1946-47)

Chief Engineer
J. C. L. Train (1942-47)

Chief Accountants
C. L. Edwards (1923-28)
C. H. Newton (1928-36)
G. Sutherland (1936-42)
L. C. Glenister (1942-47)

Chief Legal Advisers
Sir Francis Dunnell (1923-28)
I. Buchanan Pritchard (1928-43)
Miles Beevor (1943-47)

Divisional General Managers, Southern Area
S. A. Parnwell (1923-24)
Alexander Wilson (1924-29)
G. F. Thurston (1929-36)
C. H. Newton (1937-39)
H. H. Maudlin (1939-41)
George Mills (1941-45)
V. M. Barrington-Ward (1945-47)

Divisional General Managers, North Eastern Area
Alexander Wilson (1923-24)
George Davidson (1924-28)
Thos. Hornsby (1928-36)
C. M. Jenkin Jones (1936-47)

Divisional General Managers, Scotland
James Calder (1923-34, with the title of General Manager,
    Scotland)
George Mills (1934-41)
R. J. Inglis (1941-44)
T. F. Cameron (1944-47)

1D
Numbers of Staff

None of the major railways employed a fixed establishment of staff, and a census of those on the payroll was conducted in March each year. Every grade was counted separately, the results not only being used for management purposes, but also to provide information for detailed returns made each year to the Ministry of Labour. These were then published for each railway, except for the years affected by the war, when total figures only were made available. LNER figures for these years have been estimated.

1923	202,232	1942	180,000*
1924	207,528	1943	184,000*
1925	206,893	1944	185,000*
1926	201,695	1945	187,000*
1927	200,757	1946	193,853
1928	200,517	1947	195,100
1929	190,758		
1930	195,030		
1931	180,163		
1932	173,597		
1933	166,714		
1934	169,772		
1935	171,339		
1936	171,798		
1937	175,849		
1938	177,236		
1939	177,000*		
1940	175,000*		
1941	176,000*		

* Estimated.

The numbers employed during the war years and after reflect the employment of temporary staff, and the return of ex-servicemen.

Selected Categories of Staff

The following table gives numbers of staff in selected categories for the four years 1923, 1930, 1937 and 1947. In some cases the figures may not be strictly comparable due to changes in descriptions of the grades, and the figures for 1947 are estimated as a proportion of the totals employed by all the railways. However, they are sufficiently accurate for comparisons to be made and trends discerned. It is of particular interest to note the virtual cessation of recruitment of junior clerks during the 1920s, whilst by 1937, in an age in which married women were discouraged from working, one-fifth of the clerical staff were females.

In view of the reduction in numbers of locomotives, one might have expected a greater fall in the numbers of footplate staff, but the figures are probably reflective of more intensive use of motive power. The drop in engine cleaning standards is clearly shown by the dramatic reduction in the number of cleaners employed, with juniors taking an increased share of the work; by 1947 the pattern was of five lads to every adult. Closure of signalboxes was the main contributor to the lesser numbers of signalmen employed, whilst more use seems to have been made of signalbox lads.

Each category shows the effects of the war, not least in the number of police officers needed to combat the increased amount of pilfering.

Grade	Male Adult	Female Adult	Male Junior	Female Junior	Total
Officers and Clerical Workers					
1923	20,639	2,589	1,252	117	24,597
1930	20,721	1,778	163	86	22,748
1937	17,824	2,896	538	455	21,713
1947	13,198	7,658	1,100	880	22,836
Engine Cleaners					
1923	3,064	2	623	—	3,689
1930	2,341	—	679	—	3,020
1937	1,530	—	587	—	2,117
1947	272	—	1,294	—	1,566

Grade	Male Adult	Female Adult	Male Junior	Female Junior	Total
Engine Drivers and Motormen					
1923	11,152	—	2	—	11,154
1930	11,718	—	—	—	11,718
1937	10,699	—	—	—	10,699
1947	13,115	—	—	—	13,115
Firemen and Assistant Motormen					
1923	11,658	—	12	—	11,670
1930	11,590	—	—	—	11,590
1937	10,474	—	—	—	10,474
1947	11,791	—	4	—	11,795
Number Takers					
1923	469	1	266	—	736
1930	282	—	379	—	661
1937	236	—	296	—	532
1947	343	186	58	4	591
Permanent Way Staff					
1923	19,020	—	59	—	19,079
1930	17,775	—	24	—	17,799
1937	16,053	—	24	—	16,077
1947	16,337	16	155	—	16,608
Policemen					
1923	1,167	1	—	—	1,168
1930	974	57	—	—	1,031
1937	822	47	—	—	869
1947	1,248	1	49	—	1,298
Signalmen					
1923	8,792	2	227	—	9,021
1930	7,957	—	—	—	7,957
1937	6,716	—	—	—	6,716
1947	7,198	—	234	—	7,432
Signalbox Lads					
1923	—	512	—	—	512
1930	—	711	—	—	711
1937	—	564	—	—	564
1947	11	527	20	7	565

2
Commercial Results

2A
Traffic Volume and Receipts

(Excluding Joint Lines — see Miscellaneous Receipts)

	Passenger Journeys ordinary (mn)	season (mn)*	Passenger Receipts (£mn)	Mail and Parcels (£mn)	Merch- andise (mn tons)	Coal (mn tons)	Live- stock (mn)	Freight Receipts (£mn)	Misc Receipts (£mn)†	Total Receipts (£mn)
1923	240	0.24	17.5	4.5	27.4	102.4	7.5	36.1	3.2	61.3
1924	239	0.24	17.7	4.4	28.0	93.3	7.9	34.5	3.2	59.8
1925	233	0.23	17.1	4.4	27.5	86.8	8.3	33.5	3.2	58.2
1926	190	0.21	14.8	4.4	24.5	49.8	7.7	26.7	2.7	48.6
1927	202	0.20	15.3	4.7	27.6	85.1	8.5	36.2	3.2	59.4
1928	200	0.20	14.8	4.8	26.2	83.0	8.1	34.0	0.5	54.1
1929	214	0.19	14.3	4.8	26.7	94.4	7.7	36.0	0.5	55.6
1930	206	0.18	13.5	4.9	24.4	87.6	6.8	33.6	0.4	52.4
1931	189	0.17	12.2	4.7	21.5	78.5	5.6	29.9	0.4	47.2
1932	182	0.16	11.5	4.3	18.9	75.3	5.2	26.5	0.4	42.7
1933	187	0.15	11.4	4.3	18.9	75.3	4.7	26.6	0.4	42.7
1934	193	0.15	11.8	4.3	20.0	80.4	4.5	28.4	0.4	44.9
1935	201	0.15	12.1	4.3	20.0	80.0	4.2	28.3	0.4	45.1
1936	207	0.15	12.5	4.4	21.4	82.8	4.4	29.6	0.4	46.9
1937	214	0.16	13.1	4.5	22.3	86.6	3.9	31.1	0.4	49.1
1938	196	0.16	12.8	4.5	19.8	78.7	3.6	28.9	0.4	46.6
1945	213	0.10	—	—	21.4	59.2	2.6	—	—	—
1946	175	0.11	—	—	19.4	60.8	2.5	—	—	—
1947	147	0.11	—	—	17.9	62.7	1.7	—	—	—

* This is the number of season tickets issued, on an annual basis. Another series of figures gives total journeys on the basis of 600 per season ticket per year.

† Originally this figure included gross receipts from joint lines, but after 1927 the net revenue from these was included in the 'other sources' column in the revenue account.

During the war years, the Railway Executive Committee handled receipts and expenditure, the LNER receiving an agreed figure of net revenue, irrespective of the actual amount of traffic.

2B
Selected Freight Loads

	1923	1930	1938
		(million tons)	
Bricks	2.0	2.7	1.7
Grain	2.3	2.3	1.2
Iron Ore	4.9	4.9	4.8
Iron and Steel Products	5.7	5.7	6.6
Manure	1.5	1.0	0.7

	1923	1930	1938
		(million tons)	
Timber	3.1	2.3	1.6
Vegetables	1.6	2.5	1.0

Note particularly the fall in merchandise and livestock traffic, generally easily handled consignments which were lost to the roads — during a period in which, moreover, the total of such traffic was increasing. On the other hand, bulk loads, for which the railway was the more suitable carrier, held up reasonably well.

2C
Revenue and Expenditure

	(A) Traffic receipts (£mn)	(B) Traffic expenses (£mn)	(C) Net revenue (£mn) (A-B)	(D) Operating ratio % (B/A)	(E) Income from other sources (£mn)	(F) Total net income (£mn) (C+E)
1923	61.3	50.1	11.2	81.7	2.8	14.0
1924	59.8	50.5	9.3	84.4	2.4	11.7
1925	58.2	50.1	8.1	86.1	2.0	10.1
1926	48.6	45.6	3.0	93.8	1.6	4.6
1927	59.4	48.9	10.5	82.3	1.7	12.2
1928	54.1	43.3	10.8	80.0	0.5	11.3
1929	55.6	43.3	12.3	77.9	0.7	13.0
1930	52.4	41.9	10.5	80.0	0.7	11.2
1931	47.2	38.2	9.0	80.1	0.4	9.4
1932	42.7	35.7	7.0	83.6	0.2	7.2
1933	42.7	35.2	7.5	82.4	0.2	7.7
1934	44.9	36.9	8.0	82.2	0.3	8.3
1935	45.1	37.1	8.0	82.3	0.4	8.4
1936	46.9	38.2	8.7	81.4	0.4	9.1
1937	49.1	39.6	9.6	80.7	0.5	10.1
1938	46.6	40.5	6.1	86.9	0.6	6.7
1939	—	—	8.3	—	1.0	9.3
1940	—	—	9.5	—	0.9	10.4
1941	—	—	9.8	—	0.8	10.6
1942	—	—	9.8	—	0.9	10.7
1943	—	—	9.8	—	0.9	10.7
1944	—	—	9.9	—	0.9	10.8
1945	—	—	10.1	—	0.9	11.0
1946	—	—	9.9	—	1.2	11.1
1947	—	—	9.6	—	1.8	11.4

The 'other income' set out in column E includes the profits from steamship services, hotels, road services, net income from the joint lines, and income from interest and rents. From 1939 it only includes the profits from the road transport investments, plus the agreed net revenue from the joint lines, as the other aspects of the business were taken into account in reaching the officially agreed net revenue, shown from 1939 in Column C. By then the road companies were beginning to show increased profits.

The operating ratio in Column D was regarded by management as a useful yardstick of performance, a lower percentage generally reflecting greater efficiency. Sir Ralph Wedgwood must have looked with askance at figures in the 80s however; in his younger days on the North Eastern, the operating ratio was mostly in the lower 60s.

3
Passenger Services

3A
Main Passenger Departures from King's Cross 1938
(Mondays to Fridays, 4 July to 25 September)

1.05am	Edinburgh (9.36)
1.10	Leeds (5.14), Hull (5.17)
4.45	Leeds (9.20), York (9.18)
5.02	Stopping train to Doncaster (10.50)
7.25	Leeds (11.15), York (11.21), Edinburgh (3.50pm)
7.45	Stopping train to Doncaster (2.29pm)
8.45	Semifast train to Doncaster (12.23pm)
10.00	'Flying Scotsman': non-stop to Edinburgh (5.00pm), Aberdeen (8.15pm)
10.05	Edinburgh (5.25pm), Glasgow (6.45pm), Aberdeen (9.00pm)
10.10	(Mondays and some Fridays only) Newcastle (3.22pm)
10.15	Leeds (2.01pm), Bradford (2.21pm)
10.40	Stopping train to Doncaster (5.13pm)
11.00	'Scarborough Flier': York (2.00pm), Scarborough (2.55pm)
11.20	'Queen of Scots': Leeds (2.31pm), Edinburgh (7.05pm) and Glasgow (8.13pm)
11.30	Semifast train to York (4.30pm)
1.10pm	Newcastle (6.22)
1.20	Edinburgh (8.45), Glasgow (9.57)
1.30	Leeds (5.14), Hull (5.23)
1.40	Harrogate (6.10), York (5.46)
3.00	Peterborough (4.34), Cromer (Beach) (7.36)
4.00	'Coronation': Edinburgh (10.00)
4.00	Leeds (7.56), Bradford (8.18), Newcastle (10.07)
4.05	Grimsby (7.33), Cleethorpes (7.49)

4.15 Semifast train to Grantham (7.26)
4.45 'Yorkshire Pullman': Leeds (8.13), Harrogate (8.45), Hull (8.15)
5.00 Semifast train to Cambridge (6.24), Grantham (8.21)
5.00 'Silver Jubilee': Newcastle (9.30)
5.45 Newcastle (10.55)
5.50 (Fridays excepted) Leeds (9.43), Harrogate (10.17)
5.50 (Fridays only) Hull (9.45)
5.55 (Fridays only) Leeds (9.47), Harrogate (10.24)
6.15 Semifast train to Cambridge (6.24), Peterborough (8.22)
7.10 'West Riding Limited': Leeds (9.53), Bradford (10.15)
7.15 Leeds (11.06), Hull (11.15)
7.25 'Highlandman': Fort William (9.22am), Inverness (8.45am)
7.40 'Aberdonian': Aberdeen (7.30am), Lossiemouth (10.27am)
8.25 Edinburgh (6.06am)
10.25 'Night Scotsman': Dundee (9.15am)
10.35 Edinburgh (7.30am)
10.45 (Tuesdays and Wednesdays only) Newcastle (5.10am)

This summary omits stops made on the way, many at important stations, as well as the large number of connecting services. At the busiest times, such as before holiday weekends, many trains would be run in two or more parts, for which provision was made in the working timetable. The streamline trains did not run at weekends, and there were other alterations to the timetable on Saturdays. Fewer trains ran on Sundays although there were a number of late evening trains to Newcastle and Scotland. Excursion trains would also be run in midweek, and at the weekends, either as a special deal by the railway, at special low fares, or chartered on behalf of organisations such as travel agents, clubs or Sunday Schools.

Note that the summer only 'Scarborough Flier' interrupts what would otherwise be a lengthy period without any fast trains.

Stopping trains had lengthy periods of layover at important intermediate stations.

3B
Selected East Coast Passenger Schedules 1938

Station	Distance (miles)		Timing (mins)		Start to stop speed (mph)	
	(a)	(b)	(a)	(b)	(a)	(b)
King's Cross	—	—	—	—	—	—
Hatfield		17.7	24½	19	—	—

Station	Distance (miles)		Timing (mins)		Start to stop speed (mph)	
	(a)	(b)	(a)	(b)	(a)	(b)
Hitchin		31.9	38	30	—	—
Huntingdon		56.0	59	49	—	—
Peterborough		76.4	76	54	—	—
Grantham		105.5	109	88	—	—
Newark		120.1	121	99½	—	—
Retford		141.7	139	114½	—	—
Doncaster		156.0	156	128½	—	—
Selby		174.4	173½	143½	—	—
York		188.2	190	157	—	71.9
Thirsk	210.4	22.2	214	20	—	—
Northallerton	218.2	30.0	221½	26	—	—
Darlington	232.3	44.1	235½	38	—	—
Durham	254.3	66.1	262½	62	—	—
Newcastle	268.3	80.1	279	77	—	62.4
Edinburgh	392.7	124.4	420	120	56.1	62.2

(a) Non-stop 'Flying Scotsman' 10.00am down.
(b) 'Coronation' 4.00pm down.

The 'Coronation' stopped for three minutes at York and Newcastle, and was made up of nine coaches grossing some 325 tons. Taking six hours on its journey to Edinburgh, the overall speed was 65.4mph. The 'Flying Scotsman' took an hour longer on its non-stop run, but had a 12-coach formation of 450 tons or so.

Station	Distance (miles)		Timing (mins)		Start to stop speed (mph)	
	(c)	(d)	(c)	(d)	(c)	(d)
King's Cross	—	—	—	—	—	—
Hatfield	17.7	17.7	27	19½	—	—
Hitchin	31.9	31.9	41	30½	—	—
Huntingdon	56.0	56.0	63	49½	—	—
Peterborough	76.4	76.4	81	64½	—	—
Grantham	105.5	105.5	114	89	55.5	—
Newark	14.6	120.1	15	101	—	—
Retford	36.2	141.7	32½	116	—	—
Doncaster	50.5	156.0	50	130½	60.6	—
Selby	18.4	174.4	20	146	—	—
York	32.2	188.2	37	159	52.2	—
Thirsk	22.2	210.4	27	179	—	—
Northallerton	30.0	218.2	32½	185	—	—
Darlington	44.1	232.3	41	198	64.5	70.4
Durham	22.0	22.0	28	25	53.6	—
Newcastle	14.0	36.0	18	40	46.7	54.0

(c) 5.45pm down Newcastle.
(d) 5.30pm down 'Silver Jubilee'.

The 5.45pm down Newcastle was loaded to 13 or 14 coaches, one of the heaviest turns of the day, with a gross weight of perhaps 520 tons. The five intermediate stops occupied 16 minutes within a journey time of 5 hours 10 minutes and the overall speed was 51.9mph. In contrast, the 'Silver Jubilee' consisted of an eight-coach formation weighing no more than 260 tons, and with one stop at Darlington reached Newcastle in just four hours at an average speed of 67.0mph.

3C
Titled Trains

At the formation of the LNER, very few of the express trains running in Great Britain were officially titled, but of these the LNER possessed the longest established and most famous — the 'Flying Scotsman'. However, the benefit of recognising particular services by an easily remembered name was soon to be accepted, and as the years passed more and more trains were given titles. The first were the new Pullman trains, to be followed by selected day expresses and sleeping car services, whilst the streamline trains were naturally given names appropriate to their style.

In the following list, the timings are generally those when the title was first introduced, and although only one direction may be given, trains ran in both up and down directions. Most were withdrawn during World War 2, only the 'Flying Scotsman' and the 'Aberdonian' surviving throughout. Generally (but not always) the titles were *not* prefaced by 'The'.

'**Aberdonian**' (Named 1927) 7.30pm sleeping car express to Aberdeen and other destinations north of Edinburgh. An earlier proposal to name this train the 'Moray Firth Sleeper' was rejected.

'**Antwerp Continental**' Boat train connection with Antwerp Ferry, departing Liverpool Street at 8.40pm for Parkeston Quay.

'**Clacton Belle**' Summer Pullman excursion train to Clacton, in early years of Grouping.

'**Coronation**' (1937) Six-hour schedule between King's Cross and Edinburgh Waverley, departing King's Cross at 4pm and Waverley at 4.30pm.

'**East Anglian**' (1937) Liverpool Street (6.40pm), Ipswich and Norwich.

'**Eastern Belle**' Summer Pullman excursions to East Anglian coastal resorts.

'**Fife Coast Express**' (Previously 'Fifeshire Coast Express') Two trains, Glasgow and Edinburgh to Dundee and St Andrews.

'**Flushing Continental**' (1926) 10am from Liverpool Street to Parkeston Quay, connecting with the day sailing to Flushing.

'**Flying Scotsman**' Popularly known as such for many years before being officially recognised. 10am departures from King's Cross and Edinburgh Waverley.

'**Garden Cities and Cambridge Buffet Express**' (1932) Five trains in each direction between King's Cross and Cambridge.

'**Harrogate Pullman**' (1923 to 1928) 11.15am from King's Cross to Leeds and Harrogate.

'**Highlandman**' Summer relief for the 'Aberdonian', 7.25pm for King's Cross. (Original proposal, 'Highland Night Flier')

'**Hook Continental**' (1927) 8.30pm from Liverpool Street to connect with the Hook of Holland ferry at Parkeston Quay. The up train left at 6.55am.

'**Master Cutler**' (1947) 6.15pm from Marylebone to Sheffield. The only named train on the Great Central section.

'**Night Scotsman**' 10.25pm sleeper from King's Cross to Glasgow and Aberdeen.

'**Norseman**' Late 1930s, running on specified days only. King's Cross to Tyne Commission Quay.

'**Northern Belle**' (1933) Summer 'land cruise' to Northern England and Scotland.

'**Queen of Scots**' (1928) 11.15am Pullman train from King's Cross to Harrogate, Edinburgh and Glasgow.

'**Scandinavian**' Liverpool Street to Parkeston Quay, connecting with sailings to Esbjerg.

'**Scarborough Flier**' Summer only, 11am from King's Cross to York, Scarborough and Whitby.

'**Sheffield Pullman**' (1924/25) King's Cross, Nottingham and Sheffield.

'**Silver Jubilee**' (1935) Four-hour schedule, Newcastle (10am) to King's Cross and return at 5.30pm.

'**Thames-Forth Express**' The LNER hauled this LMS train between Carlisle and Waverley.

'**West Riding Limited**'. (1937) Bradford and Leeds (depart) 11.31am) to King's Cross, returning at 7.10pm.

'**West Riding Pullman**'. Leaving King's Cross at 4.45pm, it became the '**Yorkshire Pullman**' in 1935, when a Hull portion was included. Withdrawn with other luxury services in September 1939, it was reinstated in November 1946, leaving Harrogate at 10.20am and returning from King's Cross at 3.50pm.

4
Rolling Stock

4A
Annual Totals of Rolling Stock

Year	Locomotives	Carriages	Wagons
1923	7,399	21,218	281,748
1924	7,485	21,012	279,639
1925	7,469	20,906	281,987
1926	7,423	20,350	279,961
1927	7,438	21,128	278,554
1928	7,439	21,015	278,059
1929	7,393	20,723	273,028
1930	7,331	20,582	273,050
1931	7,209	20,170	268,998
1932	7,107	19,531	273,406
1933	6,916	19,241	254,825
1934	6,861	19,056	247,919
1935	6,802	18,811	244,981
1936	6,733	19,297	244,389
1937	6,591	19,225	253,912
1938	6,533	19,626	258,236
1939	6,491	18,889	256,159
1940	6,503	18,412	258,686
1941	6,533	18,030	258,212
1942	6,563	17,904	258,162
1943	6,425	—	—
1944	6,300	—	—
1945	6,356	17,459	254,638
1946	6,614	16,935	244,963
1947	6,545	16,451	241,565

These figures may differ in detail with other published data, as even within the LNER there were discrepancies. These mainly arose between the accountancy stock figures, which noted an alteration when an item was completed, or delivered from contractors, and figures used by the operating department, which rested on actual dates in or out of traffic.

Not all the variations in the totals of coaches and wagons were the result of withdrawal or new construction, but reclassification took place on a number of occasions. One such was in 1938, when over 400 vacuum-fitted fish vans were transferred from wagon to coaching stock.

The locomotive totals include all steam engines, other than those classed as service stock, plus electric locomotives and petrol and diesel-electric shunters.

4B
Summary of Coaching Stock

	1923	1930	1938	1946
Compartment and open	13,467	13,114	11,833	11,124
Restaurant	210	223	306	269
Sleeping	56	112	129	126
Fish vans and trucks	—	3,255	4,280	2,775
Post Office vans	41	34	28	26
Luggage brake vans	1,345	1,493	1,309	1,282
Carriage trucks	915	749	476	416
Horse boxes	1,767	1,557	1,194	828
Miscellaneous	3,417	45	71	89
Totals	21,218	20,582	19,626	16,935

The increase in restaurant cars by 1938 was largely due to the popularity of the newly introduced buffet cars.

The inclusion of certain fish vans and trucks from 1930 is due to reclassification, all vehicles of this kind fitted with automatic brakes having previously been included in the total of wagons.

4C
Summary of Wagon Stock

	1923	1930	1938	1946
Open				
Under 8 tons	201	74	21	3
8 tons to under 12 tons	125,395	62,005	27,779	10,748
12 tons		58,795	77,932	79,186 (1)
12 tons to under 20 tons	1,232 (3)	638	484	230 (2)
20 tons and over	82	332	407	382
Covered				
Under 8 tons	2,087	1,537	467	163
8 tons to under 12 tons	23,907	16,285	12,583	11,058
12 tons		14,960	27,702	39,393 (1)

	1923	1930	1938	1946
12 tons to under 20 tons	749 (3)	442	178	91 (2)
20 tons and over	101	127	101	94
Mineral				
Under 8 tons	89	20	1	—
8 tons to under 12 tons	64,697	27,790	14,232	2,550
12 tons		21,803	27,144	31,707 (1)
12 tons to under 20 tons	33,858 (3)	14,701	11,606	12,992 (2)
20 tons and over	399	24,512	25,642	25,332
Wagons for heavy or bulky loads	1,282	3,382	7,951	9,696
Cattle trucks	6,720	7,290	4,884	2,826
Rail and timber trucks	16,369	13,687	14,452	13,841
Miscellaneous	14	—	—	—
Brake Vans	4,566	4,670	4,670	4,671
Total	281,748	273,050	258,236	244,963

(1) 12 tons to under 14 tons in 1946.
(2) 14 tons to under 20 tons in 1946.
(3) Including 20 tons.

5
Locomotive Running

5A
Locomotive Coal and Oil Consumption 1937

Class	Average miles run per engine in year	Coal burned per mile (lb)	Oil used per 100 miles (pints)
A1 (GN Sec)	68,581	50.7	7.90
(NE Area)	82,680	49.2	6.94
(S Sc Area)	49,489	60.1	7.76
A3 (GN Sec)	67,748	52.9	7.76
(NE Area)	83,568	49.1	7.07
A4 (GN Sec)	82,895	46.1	10.76
(NE Area)	77,432	41.1	7.75
B7 (GC Sec)	38,259	61.8	7.83
B12 (GE Sec)	39,527	54.8	8.55
(N Sc Area)	43,774	61.4	7.32
B16 (NE Area)	29,826	63.8	8.23
B17 (GC Sec)	57,987	44.4	6.98
(GE Sec)	39,190	53.0	8.46
C1 (Gn Sec)	31,970	53.6	6.83
C2 (GN Sec)	26,353	57.8	6.53
C4 (GC Sec)	35,344	53.1	6.83
C7 (NE Area)	34,606	54.3	8.56
C11 (S Sc Area)	39,300	68.2	7.62
D2 (GN Sec)	25,864	50.9	5.84
D11 (GC Sec)	36,611	51.6	7.24
(S Sc Area)	39,057	63.0	6.38

Class	Average miles run per engine in year	Coal burned per mile (lb)	Oil used per 100 miles (pints)
D16 (GE Sec)	34,300	55.3	7.46
D20 (NE Area)	31,228	48.5	6.61
D49 (NE Area)	45,586	47.0	6.37
(S Sc Area)	34,000	60.7	6.66
J27 (NE Area)	19,660	62.8	6.05
J39 (NE Area)	32,427	52.7	6.41
K3 (GN Sec)	38,044	60.5	7.36
O2 (GN Sec)	25,470	94.0	8.35
O4 (GC Sec)	25,476	74.0	6.92
P1 (GN Sec)	17,123	93.4	13.27
V2 (GN Sec)	53,822	59.0	7.59
A5 (GC Sec)	43,834	48.0	6.97
J50 (GN Sec)	18,027	52.7	5.72
J52 (GN Sec)	19,159	44.9	5.37
N2 (GN Sec)	30,172	52.5	6.12
N7 (GE Sec)	33,367	61.5	6.66
U1 (GC Sec)	21,207	143.1	19.38
Sentinel Railcar			
(NE Area)	26,692	16.6	4.76
(S Sc Area)	23,932	18.1	1.76

Figures based on miles run do not have regard for the weight of the trains hauled, and the data would have been better had it been on the basis of *ton*-miles, ie taking note also of the weight of the trains hauled. However, it seems to have been difficult to collect this additional information.

Several contrasts are brought out in this table: the economy of Gresley's Pacifics, for example — particularly if their heavier loads are considered — and the expense of running slow goods trains subject to frequent stops for traffic purposes. Some perhaps are unexpected, such as the evident greater economy of the 'B17s' on the Great Central than on the Great Eastern. Heavy mixed traffic loco-motives, such as the 'B7', 'B16' and 'K3', are all comparatively heavy on coal, but again this ignores the weight factor, as their typical journey was one over a fair distance with a heavy load. However, there is little apparent justification for dubbing the 'B7s' 'Colliers Friends', as their performance was not significantly different from that of other similar classes.

One important aspect, which is rarely appreciated, is the effect of the generally lower calorific value of the coal used in Scotland. Together with a higher ash content than most locomotive coal produced south of the border, this had the effect of increasing the specific weight of coal burned by over 10%.

The fuel economy of the Sentinel Railcars is evident, but it seems strange that those in Scotland should have used only a third of the oil of those in Northeast England.

5B
Locomotive Failures in Service

	1924	1929	1938	1946	1947
Passenger	906	760	786	1,209	974
Freight	1,538	1,052	564	1,071	897
Total	2,444	1,812	1,350	2,280	1,871
% of stock maintained	32.71	24.56	20.71	34.58	28.67

Train miles per failure					
Passenger	66,885	88,972	89,378	47,395	54,998
Freight	31,205	46,759	82,593	44,527	47,700

These figures show the considerable improvement made in general locomotive reliability up to 1938, but even so the authorities must have been concerned that on average more than two passenger trains a day suffered delay from locomotive breakdown. Information is not available on which classes were most prone to failure. The figures for 1946 and 1947 provide a dramatic illustration of the effects of the lack of maintenance during the war years, but with a good effort made to improve matters during the company's last year.

6
Steamships

Name	Acquired		Gross tons	Indicated horsepower	Passengers/ cargo (C)	Fate
Lutterworth	MSL	1891	1,007	1,400	12+C	sold 1931
Nottingham (1)	MSL	1891	1,051	1,450	12+C	sold 1935
Staveley	MSL	1891	1,047	1,540	12+C	sold 1931
Amsterdam	GER	1894	1,777	5,800	320	sold 1928
Roulers (2)	GER	1894	1,753	5,800	320	sold 1930
Cromer	GER	1902	812	1,952	C	sold 1933
City of Bradford	GCR	1903	1,360	2,000	12+C (3)	sold 1936
City of Leeds	GCR	1903	1,361	2,000	12+C (3)	sold 1937
Frinton (4)	GER	1903	1,361	3,500	142	sold 1936
Marylebone	GCR	1906	2,082	2,000	425	sold 1932
St Denis (5)	GER	1908	2,410	9,396	696	lost 1940 Rotterdam
Accrington	GCR	1910	1,680	1,850	416	—
Archangel (6)	GER	1910	2,448	10,692	650	lost 1941 North Sea
Dewsbury	GCR	1910	1,686	1,850	422	—
Bury	GCR	1911	1,686	1,850	420	—
Stockport	GCR	1911	1,681	1,600	418	lost 1943 North Atlantic
Macclesfield	GCR	1914	1,018	1,600	12+C	—
Felixstowe (7)	GER	1919	892	1,895	C	—
St George (8)	GER	1920	2,676	12,420	700	sold 1929
Antwerp	GER	1920	2,957	12,204	758	—
Bruges	GER	1920	2,947	12,636	776	lost 1940 Le Havre
Malines	GER	1920	2,968	12,100	776	lost 1942 Alexandria
Sheringham	—	1926	1,088	2,300	C	—
Vienna	—	1929	4,227	13,000	716	retained by MoT
Amsterdam	—	1930	4,220	13,000	716	lost 1944 Cherbourg Peninsula
Prague	—	1930	4,220	13,000	716	—
Jeanie Deans	—	1931	635	2,200	Clyde paddle steamer	—
Train Ferry No 1 (9)	—	1933	2,683	2,928	C	—
Train Ferry No 2 (10)	—	1933	2,678	2,928	C	lost 1940 Le Havre
Train Ferry No 3 (11)	—	1933	2,672	2,928	C	lost 1945 English Channel
Tattershall Castle	—	1934	550	1,200	Humber paddle steamer	—
Wingfield Castle	—	1934	550	1,200	Humber paddle steamer	—
Lincoln Castle	—	1940	598	858	Humber paddle steamer	—
Arnhem	—	1947	4,891	12,000	422	—
Suffolk Ferry	—	1947	3,200	3,000	C	—
Waverley	—	1947	693	2,100	Clyde paddle steamer	—

In addition, in 1947 there were 41 miscellaneous vessels (eg tugs, dredgers, barges and small paddle steamers), plus the diesel electric *Talisman* and two Loch Lomond boats jointly owned with the LMS.

Figures of tonnage, horsepower and passenger accommodation differ between various authorities, and the dates on which they are quoted. Details of passenger accommodation will vary according to the allowance made for deck passengers.

(1) *Notts* between 1915 and 1919.

(2) Originally *Vienna*.

(3) Accommodation for 199 and 182 passengers in summer.

(4) Originally *Kilkenny*.

(5) Originally *Munich*.

(6) Originally *St Petersburg*.

(7) *Colchester* between 1941 and 1946.

(8) Bought from CPR; built 1905.

(9) Built 1916. Renamed *Princess Iris* whilst requisitioned and *Essex Ferry* after return to LNER.

(10) Built 1917.

(11) Renamed *Princess Daffodil* whilst requisitioned.

7
Hotels

Most of the hotels owned by the LNER were also managed by the company, but a number of small ones, mainly in the Southern Scottish Area, were leased out to tenants. The Great Eastern Hotel at Harwich was closed soon after Grouping, as the nearby hotel at Parkeston Quay provided better accommodation and was more convenient. Several hotels were requisitioned for use by the services in the war years, and were not returned to the company before nationalisation.

Owned and worked by the company

Aberdeen	Palace (destroyed by fire 1941)
Aberdeen	Station*
Bradford	Great Northern Victoria
Felixstowe	Felix
Edinburgh	North British Station
Glasgow	North British Station
Grimsby	Yarborough
Grimsby Docks	Royal*
Harwich	Great Eastern (closed 1923)
Hull	Royal Station
Hunstanton on Sea	Sandringham*
Leeds	Great Northern
London (King's Cross)	Great Northern
London (Liverpool Street)	Great Eastern
London (Marylebone)	Great Central* (purchased 1947)
Newcastle upon Tyne	Royal Station
New Holland	Yarborough*
Parkeston Quay	Great Eastern
Peterborough	Great Northern*
Cruden Bay	Cruden Bay*
Saltburn by the Sea	Zetland*
Sheffield	Royal Victoria Station
West Hartlepool	Grand
York	Royal Station
Perth	Station (jointly owned and managed with the LMS, the LNER having a third share)

Owned but not worked by the company

Burntisland	Royal
Dalkeith	Harrow Inn
Edinburgh	Crown (sold 1923)
Fort Augustus	Lovat Arms and Station (sold 1936)
Glasgow	Ivanhoe (sold 1936)
Lincoln	Great Northern Station
Linlithgow	Star and Garter
St Neots	Station

* Requisitioned during the war.

8
Road Operating Companies

As explained in Chapter 17, the LNER operated its road services in a number of different ways. As well as the internal merchandise collection and delivery fleet there was a wholly owned, but separately managed, road organisation, whilst substantial minority holdings were held in certain independent operating companies. This investment was mainly in the form of ordinary shares, but some preference shares were also held. In 1938 the following were the firms concerned, and the LNER investment in them:

W. Alexander & Sons Ltd	£225,000
Carter Paterson & Co Ltd	£335,749
Currie & Co (Newcastle) Ltd	£84,808
Eastern Counties Omnibus Co Ltd	£231,060
Eastern National Omnibus Co Ltd	£199,743
East Midland Motor Services Ltd	£120,411
East Yorkshire Motor Services Ltd	£41,606
Hay's Wharf Cartage Co Ltd	£209,991
Hebble Motor Services Ltd	£12,500
Lincolnshire Road Car Co Ltd	£68,357
Northern General Transport Co Ltd	£349,440
North Western Road Car Co Ltd	£123,078
J. W. Petrie Ltd	£17,000
Scottish Motor Traction Co Ltd	£241,209
Trent Motor Traction Co Ltd	£74,664
United Automobile Services Ltd	£514,054
West Yorkshire Road Car Co Ltd	£125,592
Yorkshire Traction Co Ltd	£65,070
Yorkshire Woollen District Transport Co Ltd	£44,428

Total: £3,083,760

9
Docks and Quays 1938

	Linear ft		Linear ft
Alloa (near Stirling)	2,800	Middlesbrough	8,941
Blyth (Northumberland)	4,833	Parkeston Quay	3,930
Bo'ness (Firth of Forth, south bank)	4,100	Percy Main (River Tyne)	714
Burntisland (Fife)	4,395	Pettycur (Fife)	370
Charlestown (Fife)	1,650	Silloth (Solway Firth)	3,615
Connah's Quay (River Dee, near Chester)	2,466	Winteringham (River Humber, south bank)	252
Craigendoran (River Clyde, near Helensburgh)	1,477		
Dunston (River Tyne)	4,116		Total: 196,193
Grimsby	23,554		
(plus leased)	5,989		
Hartlepools	24,429		
Harwich	3,044		
Hull	63,988		
Immingham (near Grimsby)	9,097		
Lowestoft	11,263		
Mallaig	930		
Methil (Fife)	10,240		

The larger ports handled coal exports, and the import and export of general goods. Blyth and Dunston loaded coal through staithes, and the docks in Fife handled traffic from the local coalfield. Fish was landed at Hull, Grimsby, Lowestoft and Mallaig. The main passenger sailings were from Parkeston Quay and Hull to the Continent, whilst Craigendoran dealt with the Clyde steamer traffic.

Above:
Shortly before the outbreak of war in 1939, Parkeston Quay was already in partial use by the Royal Navy. *Prague* is seen at the quayside, on which is one of the coaling plants known as 'elephant trunks'. *IAL*

Index

References in italics refer to portraits

On 1 May 1968, 40 years to the day after it had hauled the original non-stop 'Flying Scotsman' from London to Edinburgh, No 4472 *Flying Scotsman* worked the last steam hauled non-stop between the two capitals. This however was a special occasion, the engine being provided with a second tender to ensure adequacy of water supply. The normal 10 o'clock down was headed by a 'Deltic', No D9021 *Argyll and Sutherland Highlander*, and in this photo, taken at Belle Isle, the two trains are running side by side. *Patrick Russell*